The Macmillan Arabic Course

Book 2

Introduction to Peninsular Arabic

T. Francis M. Frost

M

First published 1981

Published by
THE MACMILLAN PRESS LIMITED
London and Basingstoke
Associated companies throughout the world

ISBN 0 333 23090 6

Printed in Hong Kong

Contents

The authors and publishers wish to thank the following who have kindly given permission for the use of copyright material:
Hodder & Stoughton Education for an extract from *Language Made Plain* by Anthony Burgess;
Oxford University Press for extracts from *The Spoken Arabic of Iraq* by John van Ess, 2nd edition 1938;
Penguin Books Limited for an extract from *Islam* by A. Guillaume.

The authors and publishers also wish to acknowledge, with thanks, the following illustration sources: Allied Arab Bank Ltd p 258; The Economist p 130; MEPHA, London pp 24, 33, 179, 187, 229, 252; Saudi International Bank Ltd p 258; The Nestle Company, Switzerland p 26.
All other photographs were taken by Timothy Francis.

Every effort has been made to trace all copyright holders but if any have been inadvertently overlooked, the publishers will be pleased to make the necessary arrangement at the first opportunity.

Preface

This is the second part of the Macmillan Arabic Course and follows directly from the first volume in the series by the same authors — *Write to Left, An introduction to Arabic script and pronunciation.*

Knowledge of Arabic among Westerners has until quite recently been limited to a small number of scholars who, with few exceptions, studied it as a 'dead' language on a par with Latin and Greek. Such an approach has shown scant regard for the primary function of the language as a living tool for oral and written communication in the contemporary Arab world. Those few foreigners who have in the past attained a level of competence in spoken Arabic belonged for the most part to a select elite — diplomats and government officials trained at public expense, and wealthy travellers and explorers with ample time and money for the pursuit of such an esoteric hobby.

The last decade has seen a phenomenal increase in the interest in spoken Arabic on the part of Europeans and Americans from a broad cross-section of professional and educational backgrounds living and working in the Middle East, particularly in Saudi Arabia and the Gulf countries. The diplomats and explorers have been joined by tens of thousands of businessmen, salesmen, teachers, doctors, nurses, and skilled and semi-skilled workers in many areas of industry and technology. All to a greater or lesser degree share the need to be able to speak some Arabic in their jobs and everyday lives, and it is for them that this book has primarily been designed.

Like Book 1 of the course, this book has developed out of materials used in the pre-service training of British and American volunteers and government personnel working on aid programmes in the Arab world. The material has been substantially re-organised to make the course suitable for 'teach yourself' purposes and we have included much supplementary information which was originally delivered orally in the classroom, notes on localised pronunciation and vocabulary variants, comments and advice on reading and writing the Arabic script, cross-cultural information, general encouragement and hints to the student, drills and exercises, plus a 1000 word English-Arabic glossary. We have also produced a set of tapes to accompany the book. We strongly recommend that the course be used in conjunction with the tapes, particularly by those studying without regular contact with a native Arabic-speaking teacher or friend.

The primary aim of this course book is to explain and illustrate the major features of elementary spoken Arabic through a variety of everyday situations and subjects within a range of approximately 500 high-frequency words. The form of spoken Arabic taught is not an exact reflection of any one of the dialects spoken within the Peninsula, but rather an amalgam of the features common to all – a kind of 'pan-Peninsular' dialect that should be generally understood by most native speakers within the area. Those important vocabulary and pronunciation variants whose use is on the whole characteristic of particular regions within the Peninsula are dealt with in comprehensive supplementary sections.

The Arabic in the book is presented in both type-set Arabic script and transliteration, a system whereby the sounds of Arabic are represented by letters of our own script. This system is fully explained in Macmillan Arabic Book 1. Though it is possible to follow this course entirely in transliteration, we firmly believe that a familiarity with the Arabic script is a prerequisite to a full appreciation of the language, as well as an invaluable aid in overcoming the feelings of extra disorientation people commonly experience when living in a country where advertisements, street signs, car number plates and public notices are written in an unfamiliar script. Transliteration is in any case only an approximate guide to pronunciation, and there are many problems associated with its exclusive use. We therefore urge prospective students to approach this course primarily through the medium of the Arabic script by first referring to Book 1, a self-study book (with accompanying tape) which is designed to teach an ability to write Arabic in a simple but clear hand, to read type-set Arabic, and to pronounce the sounds of the language in a manner clearly comprehensible to a native speaker of Arabic.

Introduction

In setting out to learn Arabic, you are tackling one of the world's major languages. With more than 100 million native speakers, Arabic is the official language of Mauritania, Morocco, Algeria, Tunisia, Libya, Egypt, Sudan, Syria, Lebanon, Jordan, Iraq, Saudi Arabia, the United Arab Emirates, Kuwait, Bahrain, Qatar, Oman and North and South Yemen. In addition, it is spoken in the south-western corner of Iran, some central republics of the Soviet Union, and in a number of countries bordering the southern Sahara. As the liturgical language of Islam, Arabic is also familiar to some 500 million Muslims far beyond the countries where it is used as the medium of day-to-day communication. For Muslims in Turkey, Iran, Afghanistan, Pakistan, India, Malaya, Indonesia, China, Russia and Africa, indeed wherever there are Muslim communities, Arabic is the language of prayer and ritual, no matter what the national language.

Arabic today is commonly classified in three categories; Classical Arabic, Modern Standard (or Modern Literary) Arabic, and colloquial Arabic. In the following pages we will give a brief account of the history and development of each of the three categories.

Classical Arabic

Arabic originated in the central and western areas of the Arabian Peninsula, in the Nejd and Hijaz regions of what is now Saudi Arabia. Its use as the spoken language of both the nomadic tribes of the desert and the city dwellers of long-established urban centres like Mecca and Medina predates by centuries the earliest known written examples of the 6th century AD. It is the language in which the Quran, the holy book of Islam, was orally revealed by God to Muhammad in the early part of the 7th century AD, and subsequently committed to writing in the course of the following hundred years.

The phenomenally rapid spread of Arabic beyond its

original home in the Peninsula can be attributed to the expansion of the Arab Empire in the 7th and 8th centuries AD. Within a hundred years of the early conquests, Arabic had developed into an imperial language used in the administration of a vast area, from the Indus River in the East to the Atlantic Ocean in the West, from the Arabian Sea in the South to Turkey and the Caucasus in the North. The use of Arabic by huge numbers of non-Arabs in the wake of the conquests was a source of great concern to Islamic scholars. They feared that the resultant evolution of the language, if allowed to proceed unhampered, would lead to a permanent adulteration of the Arabic of the Quran, a language which they held sacred as the medium of transmission of God's revelation. These fears prompted the codification of Arabic through pursuit of the sciences of grammar and lexicography beginning in the 8th century AD. The scholars attempted to establish a consistent grammatical and lexical code by setting standards of 'correct' usage based primarily on the written Arabic of the Quran. What we now know as 'Classical Arabic' dates from this period of codification, and is the language not only of the Quran but of all of the great poets and writers of early Islamic times.

Modern Standard Arabic

With the rise of the Ottoman Empire in the 15th century the ideals of the golden era of Arab civilisation fell into decline and Arabic culture and language entered a 400 year long period of stagnation. The middle of the 19th century witnessed the spread of Arab nationalist movements seeking to extricate their homelands from the effects of centuries of Ottoman colonial rule. Followers of these movements attempted to revive Arabic as a flexible instrument of thought, and at the same time make it a symbol of a cultural-political revival and a tool with which to forge Arab unity, drawing inspiration from the Classical Arabic of the Quran and the great writers of the golden age of Arabic literature. The efforts of these revivalist authors brought about the evolution of what is now known as Modern Standard (or Modern Literary) Arabic. It varies from the Classical language in idiom, vocabulary and structure, though the differences are very small when compared with the changes in European languages over a similar period, for example, the differences between the English of Geoffrey Chaucer and Charles Dickens.

Today Modern Standard Arabic is the main vehicle of

written communication throughout the Arab world — newspapers, magazines, novels and poetry, legal documents, official and commercial correspondence, advertising, etc. It is also the major spoken medium for radio and television broadcasts, plays, films and formal speeches. In fact Modern Standard Arabic is, together with Islam, one of the two chief pillars of pan-Arab unity, transcending cultural, political and linguistic differences within the wider Arabic speaking community.

Colloquial Arabic

Existing alongside the Classical Arabic of the Quran and early literature, and the Modern Standard Arabic of contemporary literature and broadcasting, are a wide range of colloquial Arabic dialects spoken by Arabs in their everyday communication with one another. While the Latin of the Roman Empire has developed into a number of distinct modern languages in Europe (French, Italian, Spanish, Portuguese, etc), Arabic, over roughly the same period and in an even wider geographical area, has not. This may in large measure be attributed to the restraining and uniting influences of the Quran. Consequently, the spoken Arabic of countries as mutually remote as Iraq and Morocco are related dialects rather than separate languages.

Each Arab country has its own more or less distinct form of spoken Arabic which exhibits certain major features common to the whole population, though within each country there may be considerable regional variations. In Saudi Arabia, for example, you will hear differences in pronunciation and vocabulary between Jedda in the West, Riyadh in the centre and Dammam in the East. These differences, though generally no bar to the mutual intelligibility of Saudis from all parts of the country, are sufficient to give a fairly accurate pointer to a speaker's geographical origins. Similarly, on a pan-Arab level, educated native speakers can generally guess the nationality of foreign Arabs simply from the way they speak, though they may experience a little difficulty in understanding one another. This is roughly analogous with the differences between the dialects of northern and southern England or, on the wider level, between British and American or British and Australian English.

It would however be very misleading to suggest that all spoken Arabic dialects are always mutually intelligible. The extent to which two native speakers of Arabic from different countries will understand each other depends on several factors, perhaps most importantly the level of education of the speakers, and the degree of geographical proximity between their areas of origin. In general, the further apart any two dialect areas, the more difficulty native speakers from those areas will experience in communicating with one another. Thus a little travelled inhabitant of a remote rural area of Oman or North Yemen, for example, would experience great difficulty in communicating with merchants in the markets of Fez or Marrakesh in Morocco. On the other hand, the various national and regional dialects do have enough in common that two native speakers educated to secondary or high school level will rarely encounter insuperable difficulties in communication, no matter what their countries of origin.

In the Arabian Peninsula the significant differences which do exist between the different dialects are gradually being eroded by the impact of 20th century communications on an area which has until very recently been outside the mainstream of world events and in which local dialects have for centuries remained unchanged in the desert splendour of their speakers' isolation. The effects of road and air travel, the telephone, and radio and television broadcasting, together with the spread of literacy and education, have all contributed to the breaking down of the isolation of the peoples of the Peninsula not only from one another, but from the rest of the Arab world and the wider international community.

The kind of Arabic people speak in any one given area of the Peninsula will vary according to a number of factors—age, sex, level of education and conversational context. There will be differences between the Arabic of the post World War Two generation, who have grown up with the dramatic development of their countries, and the language of their parents. Many of the younger generation do not speak the form of colloquial Arabic they learned as children. They favour instead a more sophisticated style of speech tempered by their study of Modern Standard Arabic at school, their exposure through modern communications to non-Peninsular dialects, and their personal contacts with the large numbers of expatriate Arabs (particularly Egyptians and Palestinians) teaching in the schools and universities of Saudi Arabia and the Gulf. There will also be differences between the Arabic spoken by men and women, even within the same family, because of the traditionally cloistered position of women in Islamic society and their consequent lack of exposure to outside influences.

Context is also an important determinant of the kind of Arabic people speak. Colloquial Arabic is used by everyone for all types of day-to-day communication on an informal level — with family, friends, colleagues at work, in shops and markets, and so on. In more formal situations, however, educated Arabs will tend towards a style of speech modelled more or less closely on Modern Standard Arabic—in formally constituted meetings, for example, in job interviews, in speeches, in interviews for radio or television and so on.

Learners of Arabic will have to accept the rather ambivalent attitude of many Arabs towards their own and other dialects of spoken Arabic. Arabs display pride and reverence for the Classical and Modern Standard forms of their language, which are considered immeasurably more expressive and elegant than the dialect forms, regardless of whether they themselves can read, write and understand them with ease. Educated Arabs will sometimes maintain that they never use colloquial Arabic at all, despite the fact that direct observation shows they constantly use it in conversation. Similarly, speakers of Arabic will say that someone 'doesn't know Arabic', which means that person is not proficient in reading and writing the Classical and Modern Standard forms, ignoring the fact that he or she is a fluent native speaker of a particular dialect of colloquial Arabic. One important consequence of this situation for foreign learners is that if they ask an educated Arab friend for help in learning the spoken language, their friend will often try to teach them the grammar and vocabulary of the Classical language, insisting against all evidence to the contrary that these are the forms he or she regularly uses in conversation. This attitude is not an attempt at deliberate deception, but simply reflects the common view that the colloquial dialects are a debased, degenerate form of the universally revered Classical Arabic.

It is important to realise that spoken forms of Arabic rarely appear in writing. Arabs learn to speak colloquial dialect Arabic as their native language in the same way that we learn English as children, with no explicit discussion of grammatical structure. Whereas English-speaking children then go on to learn at school how to read and write what is essentially the same language as they speak, Arab school children are actively discouraged from learning to write their own spoken language. Instead they study the grammatical rules of Classical and Modern Standard Arabic in much the same way as Latin and Greek are presented in our own schools, and they are taught that these are the only acceptable written forms of their language. Thus young children spend many anguished hours struggling to attain literacy in a language which is not their native tongue and live with the paradox of discussing in a language they rarely write or see written a language they read and write but will rarely have occasion to speak. It is hardly surprising therefore that most adult Arabs' passive understanding of Modern Standard Arabic is far superior to their active ability to read, write and speak it. In other words, the Arabic spoken in radio and television broadcasts and written in newspapers and magazines is widely understood by people who can only begin to approximate it in their own speech or writing. Despite the difficulties many Arabs encounter in manipulating the written forms of their language, there is still enormous resistance to writing the dialect forms with which they are so much more familiar. The only common occasions on which spoken Arabic is ever written are in letters between friends and relatives, in captions to newspaper cartoons, in some modern poetry, and to represent colloquial dialogue in novels and plays.

In keeping with these deeply-rooted attitudes, the authors of most course books dealing with spoken dialects have presented their materials entirely in transliteration. There are in existence many different systems of transliteration which attempt to overcome the problems of representing sounds unique to Arabic by letters of our own Latin alphabet. Such attempts involve the use of capital letters, underlinings, dots below or above letters, or combinations of two letters, devices which prove daunting to the majority of learners and serve to make transliterated Arabic look like some tongue-twisting hybrid of Swedish and Polish. Faced with the prospect of perpetuating the use of transliteration, we have decided to break with tradition and write spoken Arabic in the Arabic script, a somewhat radical departure when Arabs themselves do not. In our tcaching experience we have discovered that the great majority of our students (several hundred from a wide cross-section of age groups and educational backgrounds) have found it easier and more satisfying to learn to read, write and pronounce the Arabic script than to manipulate combinations and mutilations of letters of our own alphabet intended to represent unfamiliar Arabic sounds. Again we refer students of this course to Macmillan Arabic Book 1, *Write to Left, An introduction to Arabic script and pronunciation.* We have naturally been hesitant about encouraging students to write in Arabic script purely colloquial words which they will rarely again encounter in written form, but our doubts are vastly outweighed by the advantages in terms of accurate pronunciation, visual orientation in an unfamiliar environment, and provision of an essential key to making the eventual transition to a study of Classical or Modern Standard Arabic.

How to use the course

The book is divided into fifteen units. The first ten units exploit those structural peculiarities of Arabic which allow you to say a great deal without the use of verbs. Units One and Two in particular are primarily concerned with a selection of the wide range of commonly recurring Arabic greetings and general courtesy phrases, since a facility in the use of such ritual formulas is an important first step towards being accepted in Muslim society. Units Eleven to Fifteen concentrate on the manipulation of a limited number of common verbs in talking about present and future time.

Supplementary sections

Since it is important for you to realise from an early stage that there is rarely only one way of saying something in any language, we have included a limited number of the most common variants within the body of each unit. At the end of each unit you will find supplementary sections giving additional information on variants whose use is on the whole restricted to certain regions within the Peninsula. How you use these supplementary sections will depend largely on your particular learning circumstances. Familiarity with the supplementary sections is not assumed in subsequent units, so if you are studying out of general interest and not with the intention of familiarising yourself with the dialect of any particular country, you may decide to work only on the core material contained within the units themselves and then later return to the supplementary sections to broaden your knowledge of the language. If however you are already living in the Peninsula, or are about to do so, you should consult the supplementary sections as you progress through the book and familiarise yourself with those variants indicated for your particular location.

In later units, supplementary vocabulary sections are included on topics which may not be of immediate interest to all students. These sections are primarily intended for reference, though you may decide to use them for active vocabulary acquisition should you find you have the capacity to do so.

Drills

We have included a large number of drills to encourage you to practise new grammatical structures and vocabulary in a manner which will help you to manipulate the language in common everyday situations. The main types of drills are detailed here.

Translation drills

These exercises are designed to test your general retention of key structures and vocabulary. Don't hesitate to go back in the book and check anything you're not sure of. When you've finished the exercise check your answers with the key at the back of the book, then go back and re-write any sentences you may have got wrong. The translation drills are not on tape.

Substitution drills

The purpose of substitution drills is to practise an important grammatical point or a commonly recurring sentence pattern. You start with a model sentence and then make a series of new sentences by changing either one or two words in the model, but retaining the same basic sentence pattern throughout. The changes you are expected to make to form each new sentence are indicated on the page and will be heard as cues on the accompanying tape. Items on tape are identified by the symbol Ⓣ appearing in the margin.

a Listen to the model sentence and repeat in the gap provided
b Listen to each cue or pair of cues and make the new sentence incorporating them
c Listen to the correct version of the new sentence and repeat in the gap provided

Transformation drills

The principle of transformation drills is similar to that of substitution drills in that you are asked to make changes to a model sentence. In transformation drills, however, you are given a series of model sentences, all on the same pattern, each of which you are asked to change in the same way. The model sentences themselves serve as cues on the tape.

a Listen to the model sentence
b Make the indicated transformation
c Listen to the correctly transformed sentence and repeat in the gap provided

Dialogues

The dialogues take the form of short conversations between two people, identified as **A** and **B.** The dialogues illustrate exchanges which recur frequently in everyday conversation, so you should do your best to memorise them and then try them out as often as possible in your real conversations. Since Arabic makes distinctions between addressing a man and a woman, we generally present each dialogue in two forms, first for men or women talking to a man, and second for men or women talking to a woman.

a Listen to each line of the dialogue and repeat in the gap provided
b Listen to part **A** and supply part **B** in the gap provided
c Supply part **A** in the gap provided, listen to part **B**

Practice sentences

The purpose of the practice sentences is to provide you with model sentences incorporating key vocabulary and grammatical features for reading, pronunciation and writing practice.

a Listen to the practice sentence and repeat in the gap provided
b Listen and repeat again

New vocabulary

New words are introduced in blocks within each unit, and you should make a determined effort to learn each new word as it appears. At the end of Unit Four and all subsequent units you will find a complete list of new words introduced in each unit. With the aid of these lists you should make sure you have memorised the meanings of all words introduced in the core of a unit before proceeding to the next unit.

a Listen to each new word and repeat in the gap provided
b Listen and repeat again

Miscellaneous

In addition to the major categories of drills listed above, we have for the sake of variety included a number of drills on slightly different lines (picture drills, question and answer drills, structured conversations, etc). Instructions on how to use these drills are given when they occur.

Hints to learners

The individual units have not been designed with any particular study time in mind. Indeed the amount of information and drills contained in each unit varies considerably and the time it takes you to cover a unit will very much depend on your individual learning circumstances and rates of assimilation and retention. Above all, don't try to rush through the material; overlearning is very important in the early stages of learning a language, and the more automatic you can make your responses at this time, the more rapid will be your progress in the future.

The drills in the book represent the absolute minimum of practice you need to reinforce the vocabulary and structures you learn. Don't feel satisfied with having done each drill just once; as you make progress in the book, go back frequently and re-do selected drills to check your retention of vocabulary and structures you have already learned. Formulate additional drills along the lines of those in the book, incorporating any extra vocabulary and idioms you may learn elsewhere. If you are fortunate enough to have access to a native Arabic-speaking friend or teacher let them help you to construct new dialogues to practise extra vocabulary you may feel you need, and variants peculiar to your location. When working with an Arab teacher or friend bear in mind the warning given earlier in the Introduction: Arabs are very proud of their classical language and often unwilling to teach foreigners what they regard as debased dialect forms. You should make it absolutely clear to your teacher that the Arabic you are primarily interested in learning is the language which he or she uses for everyday communication with family and friends, bargaining in the markets, etc.

Don't forget that the purpose of this book is not only to teach you the basics of spoken Arabic, but also to improve your standard of literacy in that language. You may at first find it a daunting prospect to tackle this course through the medium of the Arabic script, but with perseverance and practice the task will become easier and you will gain great satisfaction from your developing skills. Once you have completed a drill for oral practice, go back and write it out in full, then read it back to yourself. Use the tapes for 'auto-dictation'; play each sentence or complete utterance in turn, then try to write it down without consulting the book, correcting any errors before you go on. Write out each new word you learn several times. You will find this serves to impress the visual shape of the word on your memory and thus improve your pronunciation and rate of retention. Keep a careful record in Arabic script of any new words or phrases you come across from other sources. Be alert to the many examples of Arabic script you will see around you, and whenever possible take time to decipher advertisements, shop signs, brand names, etc. The streets of an Arab city offer you endless opportunities to develop your reading skills on a wide variety of decorative script styles.

No amount of practice at home or in the classroom is a real substitute for going out and using the language in real conversations. At first you may feel frustrated or nervous. Learning a new language is somewhat like learning to play a musical instrument or a sport — you have to do the same things over and over again until you can perform them perfectly and at will. If you get impatient at your ability to manipulate newly-learned vocabulary or structures under actual conversational conditions, try to remember how long it took you to learn to swim, play a few simple chords on the guitar, or drive a car. And don't forget how long it took you to develop sufficient confidence to perform in public. When you speak a language you are giving a public performance of your skill, just like the musician or the sportsman.

If you are already living in the Arab world at the time of studying, you should wherever possible make every attempt to put yourself in situations where you have no alternative but to speak Arabic. Try to build up a circle of friends or acquaintances who will get used to your attempts at learning their language and will make allowances for the mistakes you are bound to make in the early stages. Initiate conversations with taxi drivers, shopkeepers and any other native speakers you come into contact with in the course of your day. Above all, never hesitate to speak because you are afraid of making a mistake. Your progress will be minimal if you constantly restrict yourself to the use of words and structures you are sure of, so experiment and try out new ways of saying things at every opportunity. So few westerners have any knowledge of spoken Arabic that Arabs you meet will be delighted at your efforts and only too willing to help you and correct your mistakes. At first the process may appear painfully slow, constantly discussing a limited range of topics within a very limited range of words and structures, but only by frequent exposure, constant application and careful and patient listening will you make real progress.

The Arabic alphabet

This course has been designed to follow on from The Macmillan Arabic Course Book 1, to which you should refer for a comprehensive introduction to reading, writing and pronunciation of the Arabic script.

Name of letter		Transliteration symbol	Final + Medial + Initial	Final form	Medial form	Initial form	Isolated form
'alif	أَلِف	Initial: a, i, or u Medial: a: Final: a	non-connector	ـــا	...ـا	ا	ا
ba:'	باء	b	ببب	ـــب	...ـبـ...	بـ...	ب
ta:'	تاء	t	تتت	ـــت	...ـتـ...	تـ...	ت
tha:'	ثاء	th	ثثث	...ـث	...ـثـ...	ثـ...	ث
ji:m	جيم	j	ججج	...ـج	...ـجـ...	جـ...	ج
h̲a:'	حاء	h̲	ححح	...ـح	...ـحـ...	حـ...	ح
kha:'	خاء	kh	خخخ	...ـخ	...ـخـ...	خـ...	خ
da:l	دال	d	non-connector	...ـد	...ـد	د	د
dha:l	ذال	dh	non-connector	...ـذ	...ـذ	ذ	ذ
ra:'	راء	r	non-connector	...ـر	...ـر	ر	ر
za: y	زاي	z	non-connector	...ـز	...ـز	ز	ز
si: n	سين	s	سسس	...ـس	...ـسـ...	سـ...	س
shi: n	شين	sh	ششش	...ـش	...ـشـ...	شـ...	ش
s̲a: d	صاد	s̲	صصص	...ـص	...ـصـ...	صـ...	ص
d̲a: d	ضاد	d̲	ضضض	...ـض	...ـضـ...	ضـ...	ض

Name of letter		Transliteration symbol	Final + Medial + Initial	Final form	Medial form	Initial form	Isolated form
ta:'	طاء	t	ططط	...ـط	...ـطـ...	طـ...	ظ
dha:'	ظاء	dh	ظظظ	...ـظ	...ـظـ...	ظـ...	ط
ᶜayn	عَيْن	ᶜ	ععع	...ـع	...ـعـ...	عـ...	ع
ghayn	غَيْن	gh	غغغ	...ـغ	...ـغـ...	غـ...	غ
fa:'	فاء	f	ففف	...ـف	...ـفـ...	فـ...	ف
qa:f	قاف	q	ققق	...ـق	...ـقـ...	قـ...	ق
ka:f	كاف	k	ككك	...ـك	...ـكـ...	كـ...	ك
la:m	لام	l	للل	...ـل	...ـلـ...	لـ...	ل
mi:m	ميم	m	مِمم	...ـم	...ـمـ...	مـ...	م
nu:n	نون	n	ننن	...ـن	...ـنـ...	نـ...	ن
ha:'	هاء	h	ههه	...ـه	...ـهـ...	هـ...	ه
wa:w	واو	Initial: w Medial: w or u Final: u	non-connector	...ـو	...ـو	و	و
ya:	ياء	Inital: y Medial: y or i: Final: i	ييي	...ـي	...ـيـ...	يـ...	ي
hamza	هَمْزَة		See *Write to left*, Unit 10				ء
ta:' marbu:ta	تاء مَرْبوطَة		See *Write to left*, Unit 3				ة

Unit 1

1 Common greetings

Arabic, not only in the Arabian Peninsula, but all over the Arabic speaking world, is characterised by the abundant use of set-piece greetings, courtesies and expressions of goodwill. An ability to use and understand these traditional expressions will earn you the respect of people you meet and ease your social contacts with Arab friends and colleagues.

Greetings in the Arab world tend to be lengthier and more ritualised than in the West. Be prepared to shake hands frequently, even with all present in a room or office. Hands are shaken for longer and are often held while talking after shaking hands. You may find the same or similar greetings repeated again and again in the first few minutes of meeting.

It is considered impolite to curtail these traditional greetings and westerners are sometimes considered abrupt in their tendency to come straight to the point after only brief greetings.

Ⓣ One of the most common ways of greeting either an individual or a group is:

Hello (greeting)

is-sala:mu ʿalay-kum إِلسَّلامُ عَلَيْكُم

Although this phrase conveys the equivalent of the English 'hello', its literal meaning is 'the peace on you'. The invariable reply is the original greeting turned round and preceded by:

and

wa

represented by the letter *wa:w* with a *fatha*. وَ

In this book initial *hamza* will not be indicated in transliteration. The 'glottal stop' it represents is a sound which native speakers of English naturally produce when pronouncing a word which begins with a vowel.

See Macmillan Arabic Book 1 Unit 3.

Ⓣ Hello (response)

wa ʿalay-kum is-sala:m عَلَيْكُم إِلسَّلام

Note that the *damma* of *is-sala:mu* in the greeting is omitted in the response.

The full greeting and its stock response is:

Ⓣ Hello (greeting)

is-sala:mu ᶜalay-kum — إِلسَّلامُ عَلَيْكُم

Hello (response)

wa ᶜalay-kum is-sala:m — وَعَلَيْكُم إِلسَّلام

a Listen and repeat.

b Listen to the greeting, give the response.

c Give the greeting, listen to the response.

Arabs greeting each other

Pronunciation points

a Pay attention to the pronunciation of the letter *ᶜayn*.

b Where you see words beginning with a sun letter preceded by *il* (the), the 'l' is silent and the sun letter is doubled in pronunciation, as indicated by the *shadda*. So, in this example from the above greeting:

the peace

is-sala:m — إِلسَّلام

the 'l', though written as part of the word, is not heard. Pay attention to the sun letters in the early stages of learning Arabic and make sure that you know which letters of the alphabet they are. Practice now will eliminate confusion later. (Refer to Macmillan Arabic Book 1, Unit 9.)

c It is rare for words in spoken Arabic to end in a short vowel as in *is-sala:mu* in the above greeting. This is, however, a regular feature of the classical language, and certain greetings and courtesy phrases which have been in everyday use in the spoken language for centuries retain it, showing the antiquity and continuity of the language.

When is it appropriate to greet someone?

In English it is considered courteous to greet someone as soon as they appear. Thus if you are sitting in your office and someone enters, it is quite proper for you to welcome the newcomer.

In Arabic, however, this would be considered hasty and improper, for it is always the new arrival who should make the first greeting.

'The rider first salaams the walker, the walker the stander, the stander the sitter. It is courteous to salaam one who makes way for you on the road. After the preliminary salutation (of *is-sala:mu ᶜalay-kum)* said by the visitor at the door, and replied to by the host, good morning or good evening must be said by the host when all are seated, which is also replied to.' (J van Ess *The Spoken Arabic of Iraq)*

Greetings related to particular times of the day

Good morning

Ⓣ a Listen and repeat after the model
b Listen to the greeting, give the response
c Give the greeting on cue, listen to the response

Good morning (greeting)
s̲aba:h̲ il-khayr

Good morning (response)
s̲aba:h̲ in-nu:r

Although this greeting and response convey the equivalent of the English 'good morning', their literal translations are 'morning of the goodness' and 'morning of the light' respectively. We have given the literal meaning of these greetings for your interest only. It is not necessary to remember them — the important thing is that you should recognise the different situations in which these greetings are appropriate.

'Good morning' in Arabic

Pronunciation points

a Pay particular attention to the pronunciation of the letters /s̲/, /h̲/ and /kh/. Listen to the tape and/or a native speaker of Arabic very carefully. Always try to make a special effort to pronounce these sounds whenever saying this greeting and its response.

b Note the doubling of the sun letter /n/ as indicated by the *shadda* above it when preceded by *il,* the.

in-nu:r — إلنّور

Compare with:

is-sala:m — إلسَّلام

Good evening

Ⓣ a Listen and repeat after the model
b Listen to the greeting, give the response
c Give the greeting on cue, listen to the response

Good evening (greeting) — مَساء إِلْخيْر

masa:' il-khayr

Good evening (response) — مَساء إِلنّور

masa:' in-nu:r

Although this greeting and its response convey the equivalent to the English 'good evening', their literal translations are 'evening of the goodness' and 'evening of the light' respectively.

Pronunciation points

a Pay attention to the pronunciation of the letter /kh/ and the sun letter /n/

b Note — the only difference between the two pairs of greetings above is the use of either:

morning — صَباح

saba:h̲

or

evening — مَساء

masa:'

It will at first be strange to an English speaker that there is no particular greeting for the afternoon as in our 'good afternoon'. Instead the greeting and response for 'Hello' that you learnt at the beginning of this Unit may be used between midday and late afternoon. The greeting 'Good evening' can be used from late afternoon (4.30 — 5.00).

Good afternoon (greeting) — إِلسَّلامُ عَلَيْكُم

is-sala:mu 'alaykum

Good afternoon (response) — وَعَلَيْكُم إِلسَّلام

wa 'alay-kum is-sala:m

Note that each greeting has its own response, so make sure that you learn them as pairs, it can be very embarrassing to be greeted and not know the appropriate response.

Learn these greetings by heart, use them as often as you can in your everyday contact with people — use them with other foreigners as well. Pay particular attention to the 'new' sounds which are unfamiliar to most native speakers of English.

If you are studying outside an Arabic speaking country, make extensive use of the tapes and try to find a native speaker of Arabic to help you and practise with. If you are studying in an Arab country use the tapes, but listen very carefully to people meeting and greeting whether at work, in the street, cafe, shop or market. The cardinal rule is — imitate what you hear used around you. Approach learning Arabic with a positive attitude and an open, receptive ear.

Continuing a conversation

Greetings are generally followed by mutual enquiries about health. In English we ask 'How are you?' or when meeting someone for the first time, 'How do you do?', making no distinction between addressing a man, a woman or groups of people.

One of the most striking features of Arabic to an English speaker is that slightly different forms of the same address are used when addressing a man, a woman or groups of people.

(T) Addressing a man

How are you?

kayf h̲a:l-ak? كَيْف حالَك ؟

Addressing a woman

How are you?

kayf h̲a:l-ik? كَيْف حالِك ؟

Addressing a group of men and mixed company

How are you?

kayf h̲a:l-kum? كَيْف حالكُم ؟

Although the above question has been idiomatically translated as 'How are you?', the Arabic is not a direct translation of the English. If we look at this question and how it is built up, you will appreciate some basic differences between Arabic and English. To highlight these features we give a literal translation as well.

Addressing a man	كَ *-ak* your	+	حال *ha:l* condition	+	كَيْف ؟ *kayf?* how?
Addressing a woman	كِ *-ik* your	+	حال *ha:l* condition	+	كَيْف ؟ *kayf?* how?
Addressing a group of men and mixed company	كُم *-kum* your	+	حال *ha:l* condition	+	كَيْف ؟ *kayf?* how?

Points to note

a The Arabic for 'your' is a suffix joined to the last letter of the word — in English the word 'your' stands independently and comes in front of the word. When one of these suffixes is joined to the last letter of a word it changes the final form of that letter to a medial form. In transliteration the suffixes are joined by a hyphen; in the Arabic they appear as an integral part of the word.

b There is no equivalent to 'am, is, are' in Arabic. Thus the

Arabic translated directly into English, in 'How condition your?'. At first the lack of 'am, is, are' may make it seem as if you are speaking a kind of pidgin or broken Arabic, but Arabic works without them. It is one less thing for you to learn.

How suffixes are joined

a The suffixed كَ is preceded by a *fat̲ha* — the short vowel /a/ when addressing a man.

How are you? — كَيْف حالَك ؟

kayf h̲a:l-ak?

b The suffixed كِ is preceded by a *kasra* — the short vowel /i/ when addressing a woman.

How are you? — كَيْف حالِك ؟

kayf h̲a:l-ik?

c The suffixed كُم for addressing a group of men or mixed company is joined directly without a short vowel.

How are you? — كَيْف حالكُم ؟

kayf h̲a:l-kum?

A stock response to any enquiry about your health is:

إلْحَمْدُ لِلّه

il-h̲amdu li-lla:h

This is an invariable response. It means literally 'the praise to God' (compare the English 'Praise be to God'), and is normally used regardless of the state of the person making the response. It reflects the Muslim view that whatever state of mind or body he or she is in is a result of God's will. There can be no cause for complaint because whatever God wills is to be accepted without question. It can also be said at the end of a meal, a journey or any ordeal.

You will often hear this response either preceded or followed by:

بِخَيْر

bi-khayr

This gives you the alternatives:

إلْحَمْدُ لِلّه بِخَيْر

il-hamdu li-lla:h bi-khayr

or

بِخَيْر إلْحَمْدُ لِلّه

bi-khayr il-h̲amdu li-lla:h

These are equivalent to the English responses 'very well', 'fine', 'not too bad', 'can't complain'. Arabic does not use any equivalent for 'thank you' or 'thanks' when replying to enquiries about health, so the above would also cover the English 'very well, thank you', 'fine thanks', etc.

Ⓣ Man or woman addressing a man

How are you?

kayf ḫa:l-ak? كَيْف حالَك ؟

Very well.

il-ḫamdu li-lla:h bi-khayr إِلْحَمْدُ لِلّه بِخَيْر

Ⓣ Man or woman addressing a woman

How are you?

kayf ḫa:l-ik? كَيْف حالِك ؟

Fine, thanks.

bi-khayr il-ḫamdu li-lla:h بخَيْر إِلْحَمْدُ لِلّٰه

Man or woman addressing a group of men or mixed company with one person answering on behalf of the group

How are you?

kayf ḫa:l-kum? كَيْف حالكُم ؟

Very well.

il-ḫamdu li-lla:h إِلْحَمْدُ لِلّٰه

Note that the three responses are totally interchangeable.

Pronunciation points

a Pay attention to the pronunciation of the letter /ḫ/ which occurs in two words in the above exchanges.

b Note the *ḏamma* — the short vowel /u/ on the last letter of

إِلْحَمْدُ

This is a feature of the classical language, and although it is rare for words in spoken Arabic to end in a short vowel, it is retained in certain words and phrases. This phrase is frequently used in the Qur'an, indicating that it is of considerable antiquity, and has a record of continuous use, unchanged, for nearly 1500 years.

c Notice the 'dagger *alif*' (Macmillan Arabic Book 1, Unit 15) in the word

اللّٰه

This is another feature of the 'classical' writing system which has survived in only a few commonly used words, and as mentioned above, illustrates the extreme antiquity of this phrase.

Remember, for pronunciation purposes the 'dagger *alif*' is identical to regular ا *alif*, but it is written as a shortened ' *alif* above the letter which precedes it in pronunciation. 'Dagger *alif*' is represented by /a:/ in the transliteration system.

The phrase إِلْحَمْدُ لِلّٰه

is often used in calligraphic designs, and can be seen framed on the walls of private and public buildings, in mosques, and even on stickers on cars and motor-bikes.

Repetition drill Revise everything you have seen and heard so far, a) the greetings for different times of day and b) how to address a man, a woman or a group when asking 'How are you?' Pay attention to the pronunciation of the 'new' sounds,

/ʿ/ ع /s̱/ ص /ẖ/ ح /kh/ خ

and the 'sun letters'

/n/ ن /s̱/ س

Ⓣ Man or woman addressing a man

Hello. إِلسَّلامُ عَلَيْكُم
is-sala:mu ʿalay-kum

Hello. وَعَلَيْكُم إِلسَّلام
wa ʿalay-kum is-sala:m

How are you? كَيْف حالَك؟
kayf ẖa:l-ak?

Fine, thanks. إِلْحَمْدُ لِلّه بِخَيْر
il-ẖamdu li-lla:h bi-khayr

Ⓣ Man or woman addressing a woman

Good morning. صَباح إِلْخَيْر
s̱aba:ẖ il-khayr

Good morning. صَباح إِلنّور
s̱aba:ẖ in-nu:r

How are you? كَيْف حالِك؟
kayf ẖa:l-ik?

Very well. بِخَيْر إِلْحَمْدُ لِلّه
bi-khayr il-ẖamdu li-lla:h

Ⓣ Man or woman addressing a group of men or mixed company with one person answering on behalf of the group

Good evening. مَساء إِلْخَيْر
masa: il-khayr

Good evening. مَساء إِلنّور
masa:' in-nu:r

How are you? كَيْف حالكُم؟
kayf ẖa:l-kum?

Very well, thanks. إِلْحَمْدُ لِلّه بِخَيْر
il-ẖamdu li-lla:h bi-khayr

After you have finished the tape drill aloud, use this exercise as writing practice. Make sure that you can recognise each word and phrase and what it corresponds to in English. Pay special attention to the letters representing the 'new' sounds.

Practise these greetings and replies until they come fluently and naturally. Make use of them at every opportunity. Force yourself to talk and even if you can't say very much, say what you can say confidently.

Structured conversation

Structured conversations are outlines of conversations to be acted out in Arabic with your teacher or an Arabic speaking friend. Take turns in acting roles **A** and **B.**
A and **B** are strangers meeting for the first time.
A greets **B**.
B gives the appropriate response and asks how **A** is.
A says he/she is fine and asks how **B** is.
B says he/she is fine.
For this exercise choose from the supplementary sections of the unit the dialect variants most typical of your particular area. If at this stage you are unable to isolate the variants for which you will have most use, concentrate on the core of the unit, leaving some or all of the supplementary variants for later practice.

Don't hesitate to come back to drills like this one even when you are relatively advanced in the book, substituting variants you may by then have come across.

3 The numbers 1 to 10

'The cipher, the so-called Arabic numerals, and the decimal system of notation were all invented by the Indians, but it was the Arabs who brought them into the service of world civilization and handed them on to Europe, thus making possible not only everyday arithmetic as we know it, but also far-reaching mathematical developments which the Greeks, for all their original genius and intellectual power, had not been able to embark upon without the cipher and the Arabic numerals.' (Edward Atiyah, *The Arabs*)

Pay particular attention to the 'new' sounds in the Arabic for zero, one, four, five, seven, nine and ten.

Ⓣ

			Arabic numerals
0	*s̲ifr*	صِفْر	٠
1	*wa:h̲id*	واحِد	١
2	*ithnayn*	إِثْنَيْن	٢

3	*thala:tha*	ثَلاثَة	٣
4	*arba^{c}a*	أَرْبَعَة	٤
5	*khamsa*	خَمْسَة	٥
6	*sitta*	سِتَّة	٦
7	*saba^{c}a*	سَبَعَة	٧
8	*thama:niya*	ثَمانِيَة	٨
9	*tisa^{c}a*	تِسَعَة	٩
10	*^{c}ashra*	عَشْرَة	١٠

Arabic car number plates

Points to note

a The Arabic and English symbols for 'one' are identical
b The Arabic symbol for 'five' is very similar to English 'zero', while Arabic 'zero' is simply a dot.
c The Arabic symbol for 'six' is very similar to English 'seven'.
d The Arabic and English symbols for 'nine' are virtually identical.
e Arabic numbers are written from left to right, just like ours; look at 'ten'.

Beware of the potentially confusing situations which can arise from the visual similarity between certain Arabic and English numbers

Arabic		English
١٩٦٥	=	1965
١٥	=	15
٦٩	=	69

4 Days of the week

The names of most of the days of the week are closely allied to the numbers.

Ⓣ Listen and repeat after the models

Sunday
yawm il-aḥad يَوْم إلأَحَد

Monday
yawm il-ithnayn يَوْم إلْاثْنَين

Tuesday
yawm ith-thala:tha يَوْم إلثَّلاثَة

Wednesday
yawm il-arbaᶜa يَوْم إلأَرْبَعَة

Thursday
yawm il-khami:s يَوْم إلْخَميس

Friday
yawm il-jumaᶜa يَوْم إلْجُمَعَة

Saturday
yawm is-sibt يَوْم إلسِّبْت

Note that the words for 'Monday', 'Tuesday' and 'Wednesday' are exactly like the numbers 2, 3 and 4.

'Sunday' and 'Thursday' are only slightly different from the numbers, 1 and 5.

'Friday' and 'Saturday' are new words, though there is in

fact a connection between 'Saturday' and the Arabic number '7'

Supplementary section 1.1 Pronunciation

In making a serious attempt to learn Arabic, you must come to terms with the fact that the dialects of different areas of the Arabian Peninsula have varying pronunciations independent of the alphabetic writing system. Thus, sounds that occur in certain dialects do not occur in others, and all dialects contain sounds not found in the traditional pronunciation of classical Arabic as represented by the letters and symbols of the writing system.

Variations from a commonly accepted standard pronunciation exist in all languages. Compare, for example, the pronunciation of a BBC newsreader with some English regional dialects or the varieties of American English. This kind of variation occurs in areas where Arabic is spoken, and do not forget that Arabic is one of the world's most widespread languages, spoken by 100 million people over a vast geographical area spreading from Morocco in the West to Iraq in the East.

The generally accepted pronunciation of classical and Modern Literary Arabic exists side by side with local variants for some letters. If you have learned to read and write Arabic by using *The Macmillan Arabic Course Book 1* and are living or going to live in an Arab country, start out using a standard pronunciation, and gradually modify it to fit in with any local variants you hear used around you. Since these variants are usually specific to certain areas they have not been included in the main text of the book, but we will point them out in these supplementary sections when they occur over a wide enough area to deserve your attention.

The first letter to require comment is the letter

ka:f ك

In the eastern part of the Arabian Peninsula — Kuwait, Bahrain, Oman, eastern Saudi Arabia, the UAE and southern Iraq — /k/ is often pronounced as /ch/, like the 'ch' in English 'chest'.

Thus the word

how

kayf كَيْف

will also be heard as

how

chayf كَيف

Although /ch/ is often substituted for /k/ in the *spoken* Arabic of the eastern parts of the Arabian Peninsula, the *written* Arabic never changes; there is no letter in the Arabic alphabet to represent the /ch/ sound. This sound is a very distinctive feature of the spoken Arabic in the Gulf, and if you live in or visit the area you should be aware of this pronunciation variant. Listen for it in the Arabic you hear used around you, and if it is used in the area where you are living, incorporate it into your own pronunciation.

If you are living in the Gulf, and have learned some Arabic elsewhere in the Arab world, pay attention to how this variant affects the pronunciation of words you know with /k/ in them.

A second feature of the Arabic spoken in the Gulf states and the eastern parts of Saudi Arabia, is the pronunciation of the suffix /-ik/ 'your' when addressing a woman, as /-ich/

Addressing a woman

How are you?

kayf ẖa:l-ik? كَيف حالِك ؟

in the above mentioned areas would *sound* like

How are you?

chayf ẖa:l-ich? كَيف حالِك ؟

Compare with addressing a man

How are you?

chayf ẖa:l-ak كَيف حالَك ؟

This is a very helpful substitution since it cancels out any possible confusion between addressing a man and a woman.

These two pronunciations exist side by side in these areas, and you will hear both used. Depending on where you are living and what you hear used around you, you must decide on whether or not to use the /ch/ alternative for /k/ in your own speech.

In the YAR you may hear the suffix /-ik/ 'your' when addressing a woman pronounced as /-ish/, with /sh/ substituted for /k/.

Addressing a woman

How are you?

kayf ẖa:l-ik? كَيف حالِك

will *sound* like

How are you?

kayf ḫa:l-ish?

This is a feature of *spoken* Arabic in the YAR. Written Arabic will always use the letter /k/.

Supplementary section 1.2
Greetings in the Gulf

There is a good deal of variation in the greetings and replies used in different parts of the Arab world, but common variants peculiar to one area are generally understood elsewhere, even if not actively used. The greetings and responses given in Unit One are standard, and using them you will be understood anywhere in the Arabian Peninsula. However, in certain areas, especially the Gulf States and the eastern part of Saudi Arabia, variant greetings are used which will be outlined in this and other supplementary sections.

The immediate intention is to give you common variants used in different parts of the Arabian Peninsula; later there will be included some of the more common Egyptian, Lebanese, and Palestinian variants that you might hear used around you. As a foreigner learning Arabic it is essential that you are aware from the outset of this range of greetings and other social niceties considered so important in the Arab world.

Good morning

Addressing a man

Good morning

ṣabbaḫ-ak alla:h bi-l-khayr صَبَّحكْ أَللهْ بِالْخَيْر

Addressing a woman

Good morning

ṣabbaḫ-ich alla:h bi-l-khayr صَبَّحِكْ أَللهْ بِالْخَيْر

Pronunciation points

a Pay attention to the pronunciation of the letters

/ṣ/ ص /ḫ/ ح /kh/ خ

b Note that in this version the /b/ is doubled in pronunciation, as indicated by the *shadda* above it.

c Note the pronunciation of the suffix /-ik/ as /-ich/ when addressing a woman.

Depending upon where you are in the Gulf, you will hear a variety of responses: either the same phrase is repeated, making allowances for talking to a man or a woman, or you might hear this:

Addressing a man

Good morning (response)

s̲abbah̲-ak alla:h bi-n-nu:r صَبَّحَك أَللّه بِالنّور

Addressing a woman

Good morning (response)

s̲abbah̲-ich alla:h bi-n-nu:r صَبَّحِك أَللّه بِالنّور

or the response you learnt earlier,

Good morning (response)

s̲aba:h̲ in-nu:r صَباح إِلنّور

Pay attention to the pronunciation of the letters

/s̲/ ص /h̲/ ح /kh/ خ

In learning greetings and responses, be guided by what you hear used around you if you are living in an Arab country. At first use what you hear used most, and then as you gain confidence, experiment with other greetings, but always remember to make allowances for talking to a man or a woman.

Good evening

Just as there are different ways of saying 'good morning' in the Gulf and eastern parts of the Arabian Peninsula, there are alternative ways of saying 'good evening'. The phrase you learned earlier is used all over the Peninsula and Arab world, but the following, which are merely modifications of what you have already seen, are commonly heard in the Gulf states and eastern Saudi Arabia.

Addressing a man

Good evening

massa:-k alla:h bi-l-khayr مَسّاك أَللّه بِالْخَيْر

Addressing a woman

Good evening

massa:-ch alla:h bi-l-khayr مَسّاك أَللّه بِالْخَيْر

Pronunciation points

a Note that the 's' of *massa:* مسّا is doubled in pronunciation as indicated by the *shadda* above it.

b Note the pronunciation of the suffix /-ik/ as /-ich/ when addressing a woman.

As with 'good morning' you may hear a variety of responses, depending on where you are in the Gulf.

a The greeting can be used as the response.

b Or, addressing a man

Good evening (response)
massa:-k alla:h bi-n-nu:r مَسّاك أَللّه بِالنّور

Addressing a woman
Good evening (response)
massa:-ch alla:h bi-n-nu:r مَسّاك أَللّه بِالنّور

Or the response you learned earlier.
Good evening
masa:' in-nu:r مَساء إِلنّور

In learning these greetings and responses be guided by what you hear used around you if you are living in an Arabic speaking country. Try to build up a passive understanding of variants you hear, and as you grow more familiar with them, gradually include them in your own active language.

Supplementary section 1.3
Variants for 'How?'

It can be very frustrating when making an attempt to learn the language of the country you are living in to find that people seem to pronounce the same word differently, or use a new word for some common item instead of the word you have just learned. The use of alternative dialect or regional words for common standard words is a feature of all languages, with the variants and standard words being used side by side. While it is necessary for you to be aware of and use some local variants, you should treat the acquisition of these specific dialect variants as a secondary goal in learning the language.

Arabic, like English, is rich in synonyms (different words with the same meaning). To speak the language it is only necessary to know one word; to understand the language you need to learn to recognise the other words meaning the same thing, even if you do not use them in your own speech.

In the early stages of learning Arabic do not attempt to learn all the variants pointed out in these supplementary sections. Use what you hear used most around you, note variants, listen for them in people's speech, and as you become more familiar with them, use them in your own language.

Initially, except for greetings and courtesy phrases, the few dialect variants given here are for the question words like 'how?', 'what?', 'where?', 'when?', 'why?', etc. Variations in words like these can take a while to get used to, especially since we are used to these being constant wherever English is spoken.

The first example to pay attention to is the word for 'how?'

how
kayf كَيْف

This word is the standard word for 'how?' in Arabic, and using it you will be understood anywhere in the Arabian Peninsula and the rest of the Arab world. However, as you saw earlier, in the eastern parts of the Peninsula, /ch/ is often substituted for the standard /k/:

how
chayf كَيْف

A common alternative in the eastern part of the Peninsula is:

how
shlawn شلَوْن

This word can be used in an alternative way of asking 'How are you?'

Addressing a man

How are you?
shlawn-ak? شلَوْنَك ؟

Addressing a woman

How are you?
shlawn-ik? شلَوْنِك
shlawn-ich?

Addressing a group of men or mixed company

How are you?
shlawn-kum? شلَوْنكُم

Note the possible pronunciation of the suffix /-ik/ as /-ich/ when addressing a woman.

This alternative word for 'how?' is a feature of spoken Arabic only. Except in this book, where you are given dialect words written in the Arabic script, you will never see it written down.

If you are living in the eastern part of the Arabian Peninsula you will hear these two words for 'how?'. Use one of them to begin with, but aim for a passive understanding of the other. As you gain more confidence in speaking the language, try to incorporate all the variations you hear used around you into your own active vocabulary.

Unit 2

1 How to ask and reply to the question 'What's your name?'

What's your name

Points to bear in mind:

a There is no equivalent to 'am, is, are' in Arabic.

b The Arabic equivalents for 'your' are suffixes added to the last letter of the word they describe.

Thus the question 'What's your name?' will translate into Arabic literally as 'What name your?'. With the following vocabulary you can make this question and give the reply.

Vocabulary A Ⓣ

what?	*aysh*	أَيْش
name	*ism*	إِسْم
your name (to a man)	*ism-ak*	إِسْمَك
your name (to a woman)	*ism-ik*	إِسْمِك
Muhammad (man's name)	*muḫammad*	مُحَمَّد
Khadija (woman's name)	*khadi:ja*	خَديجَة
my	*-i*	ي

Pronunciation points

a For variants of 'what?' see the supplementary section at the end of the unit.

b Remember, if you are in the eastern part of the Arabian Peninsula, that when addressing a woman the /-ik/ suffix is often pronounced as /-ich/.

c Note that the woman's name

خَديجَة

ends in a *ta:' marbu:ṯa*. Remember that this letter occurs only as the final letter of a word. In a word isolated from context (as this example is) *ta:' marbu:ṯa* is not pronounced. For pronunciation purposes such a word is considered as ending with the /a/ sound represented by *fatḫa* which usually precedes the *ta:' marbu:ṯa*. (Macmillan Arabic Book 1, Unit 10.)

d Take care over the pronunciation of the two names used here.

Mohammad
    muḫammad مُحَمَّد

Khadija
    khadi:ja خَدِيجَة

Distinguishing between

/ḫ/ ح /kh/ خ

often poses problems for learners. Say these names over to yourself until you can approximate to your own satisfaction the pronunciation you hear on the tape. If you are living in an Arab country, listen for these sounds in the speech of the people around you.

Muhammad, the name of the Prophet, is reckoned to be the most common personal name in the world. Khadija was the name of his wife. The name of Muhammad is frequently used as the theme for decorative calligraphy. You are as likely to see this familiar shape written up in the streets of London as in an Arab city.

'Muhammad' in Arabic

'My name's . . .'

To be able to give a reply to the question 'What's your name?' you need to know how to say 'My name's . . .'. The Arabic for 'my' is represented by the letter *ya:'* added to the last letter of the word it describes.

My name إِسْمي = ي + إِسْم

At the end of a word *ya:'* ي is the long vowel /i:/. In spoken Arabic long vowels at the end of words are generally pronounced as their short vowel equivalents. In this case the /i:/ will sound like its short vowel equivalent /i/.

In this book, although the written Arabic will show the long vowel, the transliteration and tapes will reflect the tendency in spoken Arabic to pronounce long vowels at the end of words as their short vowel equivalents.

My name
ism-i إِسْمي

Since Arabic distinguishes between addressing a man and a woman, we include drills for men and women talking to a man, and for men and women talking to a woman.

Ⓣ Listen to both and repeat the drill relevant to you.

a Listen and repeat after the models.

b Listen to the question, give the response.

c Ask the question on cue, listen to the response.

Addressing a man

What's your name? أَيْش إِسْمَك؟
aysh ism-ak?

My name's Muhammad. إِسْمي مُحَمَّد
ism-i muḫammad

Addressing a woman

What's your name? أَيْش إِسْمِك؟
aysh ism-ik?

My name's Khadija إِسْمي خَديجَة
ism-i khadi:ja

With a little extra vocabulary, and drawing on what you have already seen, it is possible to build up quite an extended conversation between two people.

Vocabulary B Ⓣ

and
wa وَ

you (to a man)
inta إنْتَ

you (to a woman)
inti إنْتِ

Ahmad (man's name)
aḫmad أَحْمَد

Fatima
fa:ṯima فاطِمَة

Pronunciation points

a The words for 'you' addressing a man and a woman are distinguished by:
to a man, a *fatḫa* on the last letter, though this is often not pronounced, giving you the two possibilities:
you (to a man)

inta إنْتَ

int إنْت

to a woman, a *kasra* on the last letter. This is always pronounced.

b Pay attention to the pronunciation of the 'new' sounds in the two names used here.

Dialogues Ⓣ

The first of the two dialogues below is for a man talking to a man, and the second for a woman talking to a woman. Listen to them both but take part only in the dialogue which is appropriate to you.

Talking to a man

A Good evening.
masa:' il-khayr مَساء إلْخَيْر

B Good evening.
masa:' in-nu:r مَساء إلنّور

A How are you?
kayf ḫa:l-ak? كَيْف حالَك ؟

B Very well.
il-ḫamdu li-lla:h إلْحَمْدُ لِلّه

And you?
wa inta? وَإنْتَ ؟

A Fine, thanks.
bi-khayr il-ḫamdu li-lla:h بخَيْر إلْحَمْدُ لِلّه

What's your name?
aysh ism-ak? أيْش إسْمَك ؟

B My name's Muhammad.
ism-i muh̲ammad — إسْمي مُحَمَّد

What's yours?
aysh ism-ak? — أَيْش إسْمَك ؟

A My name's Ahmad.
ism-i ah̲mad — إسْمي أَحْمَد

Ⓣ Talking to a woman

A Good morning.
s̲aba:h̲ il-khayr — صَباح إلْخيْر

B Good morning.
s̲aba:h̲ in-nu:r — صَباح إلْنّور

A How are you?
kayf h̲a:l-ik? — كَيْف حالِك ؟

B Very well, thank you.
il-h̲amdu li-lla:h bi-khayr. — إلْحَمْدُ لِلّه بِخَيْر

And you?
wa inti? — وَإنْتِ ؟

A Fine.
bi-khayr il-h̲amdu li-lla:h — بخَيْر إلْحَمْدُ لِلّه

What's your name?
aysh ism-ik? — أَيْش إسْمِك ؟

B My name's Khadija.
ism-i khadi:ja — إسْمي خَديجَة

What's yours?
aysh ism-ik? — أَيْش إسْمِك ؟

A My name's Fatima.
ism-i fa:t̲ima — إسْمي فاطِمَة

Pronunciation points

Pay attention to the pronunciation of the 'new' sounds

/kh/ خ   /h̲/ ح   /s̲/ ص   /t̲/ ط

and the 'sun letter':

/n/ ن

When you have finished the tape drill aloud, use these dialogues as writing practice. Make sure that you can recognise each word and phrase. Pay special attention to the letters representing the 'new' sounds.

Practise these dialogues until they come fluently and naturally. Make use of every opportunity to practise your Arabic. Force yourself to talk. Start the conversation in Arabic with Arab friends, people will take it as a great compliment, even if you do continue in English. Even though you cannot say very much, make sure that what you do say is well pronounced and confidently delivered.

2 Polite forms of address

Arabic has a wide selection of terms of address to strangers, and of affection between friends, which in translation strike the European ear as rather curious, but which within the context of Arab society are very important and widely used.

When addressing someone directly, or trying to attract their attention, it is very common to use the following before their name or title,

ya يا

Note The long vowel *alif* at the end of the word is pronounced like its short vowel equivalent /a/. Remember that in this book, although the written Arabic will show the long vowel, the transliteration and tapes will reflect the tendency in spoken Arabic to pronounce long vowels at the end of words as their short vowel equivalents.

There is no direct equivalent of this word in modern English, though in archaic English 'Oh' was used in a similar way, and lives on in 'Oh God' and 'Oh Lord' etc. Where we use it in dialogues we make no attempt to translate it.

(T) How are you, Ahmad?
kayf ẖa:l-ak ya aẖmad? كَيْف حالَك يا أَحْمَد؟
How are you, Fatima?
kayf ẖa:l-ik ya fa:ṯima? كَيْف حالِك يا فاطِمَة؟

Next, a very common title used among friends and to strangers, especially as a sign of respect to someone who it is assumed is educated; it means 'professor' or 'teacher'. You will hear this word used with *ya* when the speaker is trying to catch someone's attention, especially if he doesn't know that person's name. You may well hear yourself addressed in this way.

(T) *usta:dh* أُسْتاذ

ya usta:dh يا أُسْتاذ

An older man may be addressed as

Ⓣ *shaykh* شَيْخ

ya shaykh يا شَيْخ

The literal meaning of this word is 'tribal leader' or 'old man', but in this context it is used as a term of respect and endearment.

Another common expression used in a similar way among friends and for addressing strangers or trying to attract someone's attention is

Ⓣ *ya akh-i* يا أَخي

Literally 'Oh, my brother'. This is heard very frequently all over the Peninsula, especially in the YAR, and, due to the large number of expatriate Yemenis living and working in other parts of the Peninsula, it is fairly certain that you will hear it used around you.

Listen for these words, and other equivalents. You will hear them used in many different contexts. They are polite terms of address used with no reference to their true meanings, in much the same way as a London taxi driver might call his fare 'guv'ner', 'squire' or 'mate'.

When addressing someone whose name you don't know, you can use the Arabic words for 'Mr' and 'Mrs', together with the suffix for 'my'.

Ⓣ Addressing a man

ya sayyid-i: يا سَيِّدي

Addressing a woman

ya sayyidt-i يا سَيِّدْتي

These are polite expressions, somewhat akin to English 'Excuse me, sir/madam', which do not convey the abruptness of 'Hey Mr/Mrs'.

On radio and television broadcasts you will frequently hear the plurals of these two words used in the introductory formula:

Ⓣ Ladies and gentlemen

sayyida:ti sa:dati سَيِّداتي سادَتي

3 Arabic names

You may already be familiar with many of the Arabic names we shall use in this book. They are commonly mispronounced by English speakers, and this mispronunciation is reflected in the variety of spellings used in English.

English spellings	Pronunciation in transliteration	Arabic
Mohammad Mohammed Mohamed Mahomet Mehmet	*muḫammad*	مُحَمَّد
Ahmad Ahmed Ahmet Achmed	*aḫmad*	أَحْمَد

You should make a special effort to pronounce names as accurately as possible. Unlearn mispronunciations by paying attention to the spelling in Arabic. For example, none of the English versions above make any allowance for the distinctive /ḫ/.

If you are living in an Arab country, listen carefully to how people around you pronounce each other's names and look at the names written around you in the streets, in shop signs, street names and so on.

Here is a list of common men's and women's names.

Ⓣ

Women's names			Men's names		
Khadija	*khadi:ja*	خَدِيجَة	Muhammad	*muḫammad*	مُحَمَّد
Fatima	*fa:ṯima*	فاطِمَة	Ahmad	*aḫmad*	أَحْمَد
Samira	*sami:ra*	سَمِيرَة	Hasan	*ḫasan*	حَسَن
Shaykha	*shaykha*	شَيْخَة	Husain	*ḫusayn*	حُسَيْن
Salma	*salma*	سَلْمَة	Salim	*sali:m*	سَلِيم

Hafsa	*h̲afs̲a*	حَفْصَة	Hamid	*h̲ami:d*	حَميد
Jamila	*jami:la*	جَميلَة	Jasim	*ja:sim*	جاسِم
Nouria	*nu:riya*	نورِيَة	Salah	*s̲ala:h̲*	صَلاح
Adila	*^{c}a:dila*	عادِلَة	Adil	*^{c}a:dil*	عادِل
Aziza	*^{c}azi:za*	عَزيزَة	Aziz	*^{c}azi:z*	عَزيز

Pronunciation points

a Female names generally, and all those in our examples, end in a *ta:ʼ marbu:t̲a*. Remember, this letter occurs only as the final letter of a word. In a word isolated from context (as all these examples are) *ta:ʼ marbu:t̲a* is not pronounced. For pronunciation purposes such a word is considered as ending with the short vowel sound /a/ represented by *fath̲a* which usually precedes *ta:ʼ marbu:t̲a*. (Macmillan Arabic Book 1, Unit 10.)

b Pay particular attention to the ‘new’ sounds.

/t̲/ ط /h̲/ ح /kh/ خ /^{c}/ ع /s̲/ ص

c Always look to the Arabic spelling to give you guidance on pronunciation.

d Be careful to distinguish between the long and short vowels in names which share the same letters but have slightly different vowels.

حامِد	*h̲a:mid*	and	حَميد	*h̲ami:d*
صالِح	*s̲a:lih̲*	and	صَلاح	*s̲ala:h̲*
سالِم	*sa:lim*	and	سَليم	*sali:m*

It takes time to get used to the subtle differences in Arabic speech, but if you listen carefully you will soon pick them out. An ability to pronounce and recognise people's names correctly will give you a lot of confidence in your early efforts to learn Arabic, and will be much appreciated by those whom you address.

After you have finished the tape drill aloud, use these names as writing practice.

4 Courtesy phrases

Tafaḏḏal

There is one word in Arabic that can be used in a wide variety of situations to cover a multitude of English equivalents:

tafaḏḏal تَفَضَّل

This word is most commonly used as follows:

1 When offering someone something to eat or drink. In such situations it corresponds to:
'Here you are' — handing food or drink to a guest, etc.
'Have some' — accompanied by a hand gesture indicating food and drink.
'Come on, dig in' — urging someone to begin eating.
'Lunch/dinner is ready' — informing a guest that it is time to move to where the food is.

2 Whenever handing something to someone, for example, money to a shopkeeper, when in English you might say 'here you are', or nothing at all.

3 When offering someone a seat, corresponding to:
'Please, take a seat.'
'Sit down, please.'
'Would you like to have a seat?'
'Make yourself at home.'
The word is usually accompanied by a hand gesture indicating where to sit.

4 When welcoming someone to your home, place of work, office, etc, corresponding to:
'Please come in.'
'Come on in.'
and when answering a knock at the door, without actually going to the door and opening it yourself:
'Come in.'
'Enter.'

5 When urging someone to go first, e.g. through a door, getting into a car, or taking something before you:
'After you.'
'Go ahead.'
and if more than one person reaches for the same thing at the same time, this word can be used to mean:
'Go on, take it.'

Obviously you are not going to be able to assimilate all these uses at once. Use this word whenever you know it is appropriate, and, by listening to others talking, try to notice the many different contexts in which it occurs.

You must use a slightly different form of this word depending on whether you are talking to a man, a woman or a group.

Ⓣ Addressing a man

tafad̲d̲al تَفَضَّل

Addressing a woman

tafad̲d̲ali تَفَضَّلي

Addressing a group of men and mixed company

tafad̲d̲alu تَفَضَّلو

Pronunciation points

a Note that in Arabic the form for addressing a woman is distinguished from the form for addressing a man by the addition of a ي.

Remember that in spoken Arabic long vowels at the end of words are generally pronounced like their short vowel equivalents. In this case the ي (normally /i:/) will sound like its short vowel equivalent /i/.

b Note that in the written Arabic the form for addressing a group is distinguished from the form for addressing a man by the addition of a و . As mentioned above, long vowels at the end of words are generally pronounced in spoken Arabic as their short vowel equivalents. In this case the و (normally /u:/) will sound like its short vowel equivalent /u/.

Learn these forms according to your needs. A foreign male does not have many opportunities to talk to single Arab women, so this form does not need to be practised with the same intensity as those for addressing a single man or groups of men. However, you should be familiar with all the forms so that you can recognise them when you hear them or see them written down.

For European women, however, the situation is different. European women can mix just as easily in exclusively male or female company, and are often referred to by Arabs as the third sex. If you have contacts with Arab women, you should address them as women and not use the masculine forms.

'Thank you' and its response

Let us now look at the word for 'thank you' and its stock response.

Thank you — شُكْراً
shukran

You're welcome
Don't mention it
It's nothing — عَفْواً
ʿafwan

Pronunciation points

a Both these words end in اً. This is an *alif* with double *fatḫa* resting above it. The *alif* is not pronounced, it is merely the bearer for the double *fatḫa* which is pronounced /an/.
This is a feature of the classical language which has survived in only a few commonly used words in the spoken language.

b The response to 'thank you' is one of several used in the Arabian Peninsula: alternatives will be given in supplementary sections later. It has no exact equivalent in British English, but is comparable to American 'you're welcome', and to European languages where 'thank you' is followed by a standard response; German, 'bitte'; French, 'pas de quoi'; Spanish, 'de nada'; and Italian, 'prego'.

Ⓣ Addressing a man

A Here you are. — تَفَضَّل
tafaḏḏal

B Thank you. — شُكْراً
shukran

A Don't mention it. — عَفْواً
ʿafwan

Addressing a woman

A Here you are. — تَفَضَّلي
tafaḏḏali

B Thank you. — شُكْراً
shukran

A You're welcome. — عَفْواً
ʿafwan

Addressing a group of men or mixed company

A Here you are. — تَفَضَّلو
tafaḏḏalu

B Thank you. شُكْراً
shukran

A It's nothing. عَفْواً
ᶜafwan

Pay attention to the pronunciation of the letter *ᶜayn* ع

Use this exercise as writing practice when you have finished the tape drill.

Please

When saying 'please' you must distinguish between addressing a man or a woman.

Ⓣ Addressing a man

Please

min fadl-ak مِن فَضْلَك

Addressing a woman

Please

min fadl-ik مِن فَضْلِك

Remember that in the Gulf and Eastern Saudi Arabia you will often hear the suffix /-ik/ pronounced as /-ich/.

Yes

There are several ways of saying 'Yes' in Arabic, and wherever you are living you must get used to many, if not all, of the following alternatives.

A word heard all over the Peninsula and used by many other Arab nationalities is:

Ⓣ *aywa* أَيْوَه

or

iywa إِيوَه

Notice that the final /ha:'/ is rarely audible in pronunciation and is therefore not reflected in transliteration.

'Yes' is often abbreviated to

Ⓣ *i:* إِي

in the Gulf and eastern parts of the Peninsula, and to

ay أَي

in other areas of the Arab world. The classical written word for 'Yes' is

Ⓣ *naᶜam* نَعَم

and you will hear it used interchangeably with the above. In the Gulf and eastern parts of the Peninsula you will often hear this combination used as well,

Ⓣ *i: naᶜam* إي نَعَم

When uttered questioningly, thus

Ⓣ *na ᶜ am?* نَعَم ؟

it conveys the Arabic equivalent to the English 'Can I help you?'. Listen for it, you may be greeted by this query in shops and offices.

No

There is only one word for 'No':

Ⓣ *la* لا

(Sometimes 'No' is conveyed by a simple clicking sound made by the tip of the tongue and the back of the upper teeth, and often accompanied by an upward movement of the head and raising of the eyebrows.)

5 Ways of saying 'Goodbye'

The person leaving says:

Ⓣ Goodbye

maᶜa s-sala:ma مَعَ السَّلامَة

which literally means 'with the safety'. The response to this is the same phrase repeated by the person spoken to,

Goodbye

maᶜa s-sala:ma مَعَ السَّلامَة

There are two other frequently heard responses,

Goodbye (response)

fi ama:n alla:h في أَمان الله

which literally means 'in the safety of God'; and the following (when you use this you must distinguish between talking to men and women):

Ⓣ Addressing a man

Goodbye (response)

alla:h yusallim-ak — اللهْ يْسَلِّمَكْ

Addressing a woman

Goodbye (response)

alla:h yusallim-ik — اللهْ يْسَلِّمِكْ

One of the above responses is itself sometimes used as a greeting, together with a stock response,

Ⓣ Goodbye

fi ama:n alla:h — في أَمان الله

Goodbye (response)

fi ama:n il-kari:m — في أَمان إلكَريم

This literally means 'in the safety of the Generous'.

Pronunciation points

a Pay attention to the pronunciation of the letter /^{c}/ *^{c}ayn* ع ^{c}

b When a word, which ends in a short vowel, such as,

ma^{c}a — مَعَ

is immediately followed by a word beginning with *il,* 'the', as in

Goodbye

ma^{c}a s-sala:ma — مَعَ السَّلامَة

note that the short /i/ of *il* is not pronounced and consequently is not represented either in Arabic or in transliteration. In this example the written 'l' of *il* is not pronounced either, since the following word begins with the sun letter *si:n*.

c We have given the literal meanings of the above phrases for your interest only. Don't spend too long learning these meanings if you find them difficult to remember. The important thing is that you should recognise the phrases in their appropriate contexts.

If you are living in an Arab country, listen very carefully to what people around you are saying, and if you find one of the above alternatives used more frequently than the others, use it, but try to maintain a passive awareness and understanding of the others.

Reading and repetition drill

1 Goodbye
ma^{c}a s-sala:ma — مَعَ السَّلامَة

Goodbye (response)
ma^{c}a s-sala:ma — مَعَ السَّلامَة

2 Goodbye
ma^{c}a s-sala:ma — مَعَ السَّلامَة

Goodbye (response)
fi ama:n alla:h — في أَمان الله

3 Goodbye
ma^{c}a s-sala:ma — مع السلامة

Goodbye (replying to a man)
alla:h yusallim-ak — الله يُسَلِّمَك

4 Goodbye
ma^{c}a s-sala:ma — مَعَ السَّلامَة

Goodbye (replying to a woman)
alla:h yusallim-ik — الله يُسَلِّمِك

5 Goodbye
fi ama:n alla:h — في أَمان الله

Goodbye (response)
fi ama:n il-kari:m — في أَمان إِلْكَرِيم

Pay attention to the pronunciation of the letter

ع /^{c}/

As you can see, the influence of Islam on the language of Muslims is very strong. The word for God is often on people's lips as part of a greeting, response or salutation. The Arabic word for God is frequently used in calligraphic designs. If you look around, you will see this word written up in public far more than its equivalent in English-speaking countries.

'Allah' in Arabic

Supplementary section 2
Variants for 'What?'

It will come as a surprise to many learners to hear such a wide range of words for one which is invariable in English, wherever it is spoken. 'What?' in Arabic is slippery and variable. Below we have given a fairly exhaustive list of variants, all of which are current in the Gulf, Saudi Arabia, Oman and Yemen. Most of these variants would be understood not only in the Peninsula, but in most neighbouring Arab countries.

The common variants for 'what?' current in the Arabian Peninsula are:

what?

aysh?	أَيْش ؟
waysh?	وَيْش ؟
shu?	شو؟
shinu?	شِنو؟

All of these alternatives are based around the letter

shi:n ش

These words for 'what?' are found in spoken Arabic only. Except in this book, where we are giving you dialect words written in the Arabic script, you will never see these words written down.

Note also that the common variant for 'how' given in Unit One,

how? شلَوْن ؟

shlawn?

is a contraction of

What (is the) colour (of)? أَيْش لَوْن ؟

aysh lawn?

Hence:

How are you? شلَوْنَك ؟

shlawn-ak?

(literally 'What colour your?'
ie 'What is your colour?')

Other variants for 'what?' are:

In Oman		In Yemen (YAR)	
min?	مِن ؟	*ma?*	ما ؟
mu?	مو ؟	*mu?*	مو ؟

Do not let this diversity put you off, it is better to know that there are several possible words for 'what?', than to learn only one and not understand when someone uses a variant.

We emphasise that you must listen to what you hear around you in everyday speech, and then use what seems to be the most common word to you. Of all the variants we have given

aysh? أَيْش

is probably the most widely used in the Peninsula .

Remember, the kind of Arabic someone will use depends upon the context. When talking to foreign Arabs or other foreigners trying to talk Arabic, many Arabs will revert to more standard, literary vocabulary, and sometimes you may hear the classical word for 'what?' used.

What?

ma:dha ماذا؟

What's your name?

ma:dha ism-ak? ماذا إسْمَك ؟

Structured conversations

Remember that these structured conversations are simply suggested outlines for practice with your teacher or an Arabic speaking friend. Vary them as much as you like and incorporate any useful variants you have learned from the supplementary sections or elsewhere.

1 **A** and **B** are strangers meeting for the first time
A greets **B**
B responds appropriately
A asks how **B** is
B responds appropriately
A asks **B**'s name
B responds and asks **A**'s name
A responds

2 **A** and **B** are friends meeting by chance
A greets **B** by name (using *ya* يا)
B responds and asks how **A** is (using *ya* يا +**A**'s name)
A responds

3 **A** and **B** are aquaintances meeting by chance
A greets **B** (using *ya* يا + a polite form of address)

B responds and asks how **A** is
A responds

4 **A** is sitting at his/her desk. **B** knocks at the door
A asks **B** to come in
B enters and greets **A**
A rises, shakes hands, and responds to the greeting
A asks **B** to have a chair
B says thank you
A says **B** is welcome and asks how **B** is
B responds and asks how **A** is
A responds

5 **A** is drinking coffee at a pavement cafe when he/she sees **B** passing with a friend
B greets **A** by name
A responds and asks how **B** is
B responds and asks how **A** is
A responds and invites **B** to join him/her
B declines with thanks, indicating the friend who has continued along the street unaware of the meeting.
A and **B** exchange hurried farewells

Unit 3

1 'Where are you from?'

Having learned to greet people, ask how they are, what their name is, and answer similar questions about yourself, a question you are going to want to ask and reply to is 'Where are you from?'

Vocabulary A Ⓣ

from
min مِن

where
wayn وَيْن

I
'ana أَنا

Saudi Arabia
is-su^cu:diyya السُّعودِيَّة

Bahrain
il-bahrayn إِلْبَحْرَيْن

Britain
brita:niya بريطانيا

America
amri:ka أَمْريكا

For regional variants for 'where?' see the supplementary section at the end of the unit.

When asking the question 'Where are you from?', bear these points in mind:

a There is no equivalent to 'am, is, are' in Arabic.
b In Arabic the word for 'you' can come either at the beginning or end of the sentence.

Addressing a man
Where are you from?
'inta min wayn? إِنْتَ مِن وَيْن ؟

min wayn 'inta? مِن وَيْن إِنْتَ ؟

Addressing a woman
Where are you from?
'inti min wayn? إِنْتِ مِن وَيْن ؟

min wayn 'inti? مِن وَيْن إِنْتِ ؟

The answer 'I'm from . . .', will be rendered in Arabic simply as 'I from . . .' with no equivalent for the English 'am'.

I'm from Bahrain
'ana min il-bah̲rayn — أَنا مِن إِلْبَحْرَيْن

I'm from Britain
'ana min brit̲a:niya — أَنا مِن بريطانِيا

Dialogues (T) Since Arabic distinguishes between addressing men and women, we include drills for talking to a man and for talking to a woman. Listen to both of them, and repeat the drill which is appropriate to you.

Addressing a man

A Where are you from?
'inta min wayn? — إِنْتَ مِن وَيْن؟

B I'm from Saudi Arabia.
'ana min is-suᶜu:diyya — أَنا مِن إِلسُّعودِيَّة

Where are you from?
min wayn 'inta? — مِن وَيْن إِنْتَ؟

A I'm from America.
ana min 'amri:ka — أَنا مِن أَمْريكا

'Saudi Arabia' in Arabic

Ⓣ Addressing a woman

A Where are you from?
'inti min wayn? إِنْتِ مِن وَيْن ؟

B I'm from Bahrain.
'ana min il-baẖrayn أَنا مِن إِلْبَحْرَيْن

Where are you from?
min wayn 'inti? مِن وَيْن إِنْتِ؟

A I'm from Britain.
'ana min brita:niya أَنا مِن بريطانِيا

Pronunciation points

a Pay attention to the 'new' sounds

/h/ ح and /t/ ط

b Remember that the *fatha,* the short /a/ sound, on the last letter of 'you' when addressing a man is often not pronounced, so you may well hear,

Where are you from?

'int min wayn? إِنْت مِن وَيْن ؟

min wayn 'int? مِن وَيْن إِنْت؟

c The word for 'I' ends in the long vowel *alif*. Remember that in spoken Arabic long vowels at the end of words are generally pronounced as their short vowel equivalents. So, although the written Arabic will show the long vowel, the transliteration and tapes will reflect this tendency. In this case the *alif* will sound like its short vowel equivalent /a/.

Vocabulary B Ⓣ

in
fi في

Jedda
jadda جَدَّة

London
lundun لُنْدُن

Take note of the word for 'in'. Remember point c above.

Dialogues Ⓣ

In conversation with a man

A Hello.
is-sala:mu ᶜalay-kum إِلسَّلامُ عَلَيْكُم

B Hello. وَعلَيْكُم إِلسَّلام
wa ᶜalay-kum is-sala:m

A Where are you from? إنْتَ مِن وَيْن ؟
inta min wayn?

B I'm from Saudi Arabia. أنا مِن إِلسعودِيَّة
ana min is-suᶜu:diyya

A From where in Saudi Arabia? مِن وَيْن في السُّعودِيَّة ؟
min wayn fi s- suᶜu:diyya?

B From Jedda. مِن جَدَّة
min jadda

Ⓣ In conversation with a woman

A Good morning. صَباح إِلْخيْر
s̱aba:ẖ il-khayr

B Good morning. صَباح إِلنّور
s̱aba:h in-nu:r

A Where are you from? مِن وَيْن إنتِ ؟
min wayn 'inti?

B I'm from Britain. أَنا مِن بريطانيا
'ana min briṯa:niya

A From where in Britain? مِن وَيْن في بريطانيا ؟
min wayn fi briṯa:niya

A From London. مِن لُنْدُن
min lundun

Pronunciation points

a Pay attention to the pronunciation of the 'new sounds'

/ᶜ/ ع /s̱/ ص /kh/ خ /ṯ/ ط

and the sun letters

/s/ س and /n/ ن

b Use this drill for writing practice when you have finished doing the tape drill.

c We have already pointed out that when a word ending in a vowel is immediately followed by a word beginning with *il* 'the', the short /i/ of *il* is not pronounced and is therefore not represented.

with	*maᶜa*	مَعَ	the safety *is-sala:ma*	إِلسَّلامَة

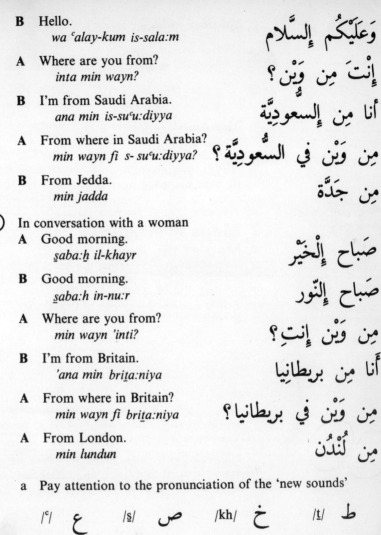

Goodbye ('with the safety')
ma^{c}a s-sala:ma مَعَ السَّلامَة

The same point is illustrated again in the first dialogue above.

in *fi*	فِي	Saudi Arabia *is-su^{c}u:diyya*	إِلسُّعودِيَّة

in Saudi Arabia
fi s-su^{c}u:diyya فِي السُّعودِيَّة

In both of these examples, the written /l/ of *il* is also silent because the following word begins with the sun letter *si:n*.

2 Maps in Arabic

A Map of the Arab world

The names of most of the countries, capitals and cities shown on this map will be familiar to you because our English names are mostly anglicised versions of the Arabic.

(T) **Key**

North *shima:l*	شِمال	East *sharg*	شَرْق
South *junu:b*	جُنوب	West *gharb*	غَرْب

(T)

Capitals		**Countries**	
Algiers *il-jaza:'ir*	إِلْجَزائِر	Algeria *il-jaza:'ir*	إِلْجَزائِر
Manama *mana:ma*	مَنامَة	Bahrain *il-bahrayn*	إِلْبَحْرَيْن
Cairo *il-qa:hira*	إِلْقاهِرَة	Egypt *masr*	مَصْر
Amman *^{c}amma:n*	عَمّان	Jordan *il-'urdun*	إِلْأُرْدُن
		Kuwait *il-kuwayt*	إِلْكُوَيْت
Beirut *bayru:t*	بَيْروت	Lebanon *lubna:n*	لُبْنان
Tripoli *tara:blus*	طَرابُلُس	Libya *li:biya*	لِيبِيا

Rabat		Morocco	
raba:ṭ	رَباط	il-maghrib	إلْمَغْرِب
		Palestine	
		filasṭi:n	فِلَسطين
Musqat		Oman	
masgaṭ	مَسْقَط	ʿuma:n	عُمان
Doha		Qatar	
du:ḥa	دوحَة	gaṭar	قَطَر
Riyadh		Saudi Arabia	
ir-riya:ḍ	إلرِّياض	is-suʿu:diyya	إلسُّعودِيَّة
Khartoum		Sudan	
il-kharṭu:m	إلخَرْطوم	su:da:n	سودان
Damascus		Syria	
dimashq	دِمَشْق	su:riya	سوريا
Tunis		Tunisia	
tu:nis	تونس	tu:nis	إلْتونِسي
		United Arab Emirates	
		il-ima:ra:t	إلإمارات
		il-ʿarabiyya	إلْعَرَبيَّة
		il-muttaḥida	إلْمُتَّحِدَة
		Abu Dhabi	
		ʾabu dhabi	أبو ظَبِي
		al-Ajman	
		il-ʿajma:n	إلْعَجْمان
		Dubai	
		dubay	دُبَي
		Sharja	
		sha:riga	شارِقة
		Umm al-Qaywan	
		umm il-gaywa:n	أم إلقَيْوان
		Yemen (YAR+PDRY)	
		il-yaman	إلْيَمَن
Sana'a			
ṣanʿa:'	صَنْعاءْ		
Aden			
ʿadan	عَدَن		

كورنيش ابوظبي
ABU DHABI CORNISH

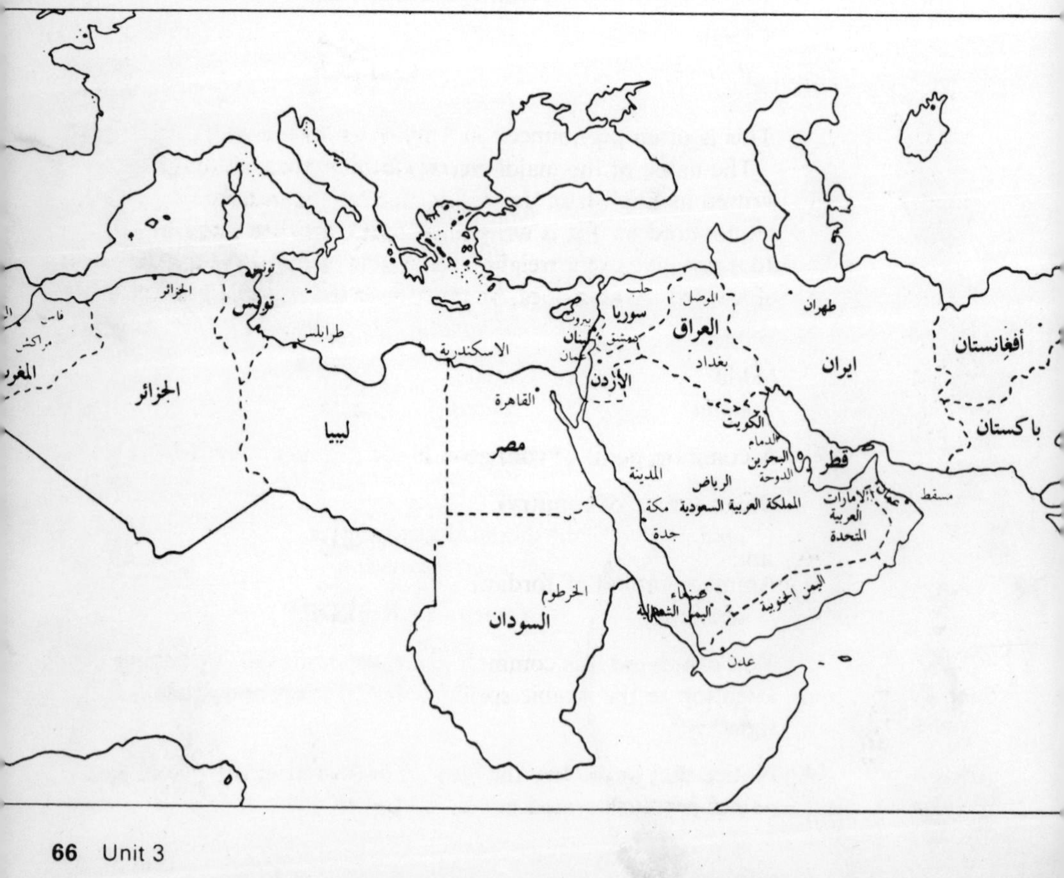

تونس
الجزائر
فاس
مراكش
تونس
طرابلس
الجزائر
ليبيا
الاسكندرية
القاهرة
مصر
السودان
الخرطوم
حلب
سوريا
بيروت
دمشق
عمان
الأردن
الموصل
العراق
بغداد
طهران
ايران
أفغانستان
باكستان
الكويت
الدمام
البحرين
الدوحة
قطر
المدينة
الرياض
المملكة العربية السعودية
مكة
جدة
مسقط
الإمارات
العربية
المتحدة
اليمن الجنوبية
عدن

1 Many Arabic names of Arab countries are preceded by *il* 'the', where in English we do not use 'the' in the name.

Saudi Arabia *is-su*^{c}*u:diyya*	إِلسُّعودِيَّة	Kuwait *il-kuwayt*	إِلْكُوَيْت
Bahrain *il-bah̲rayn*	إِلْبَحْرَيْن	Yemen *il-yaman*	إِلْيَمَن

2 Some names are not the same as our English versions.

Egypt *mas̲r*	مَصْر	Morocco *il-maghrib*	إِلْمَغْرِب

3 Try to avoid mispronouncing

Bahrain
il-bah̲rayn إِلْبَحْرَيْن

This is often mispronounced as 'bar-rain', with no attempt made to pronounce the /h̲/. Always look carefully at how a word is spelled in Arabic before attempting to say it.

Another common mispronunciation is of the name

Kuwait
il-kuwayt إِلْكُوَيْت

This is often pronounced in English as 'queue-wait'.

The name of the major Saudi Arabian port, although written in English as 'Jedda' or 'Jeddah', is usually pronounced as if it is written as 'Jeda', because English does not give extra weight to a double letter in the middle of a word. Arabic does, so try to give the /shadda/ its full value.

Jedda
jadda جَدَّة

A common point of confusion is the pronunciation of

Oman (name of country)
^{c}*uma:n* عُمان
and
Amman (capital of Jordan)
^{c}*amma:n* عَمّان

You can avoid this common source of confusion by paying attention to the Arabic spelling, short vowels and other signs.

4 Notice that in the key the *qa:f* ق in several of the place names is transliterated not as /q/ but as /g/.

In some areas of the Peninsula you will hear the *qa:f* given its 'standard' value /q/, particularly in the two Yemens south of the Samarra Pass in the YAR. Far more commonly though you will hear the /g/ variant, like the hard 'g' in English 'get'. Hence the modified transliteration of the two names:

Qatar
gaṯar قَطَر

and

Umm al-Qaywan
umm il-gaywa:n أُمّ إِلْقَيوان

Note that Arabs do generally make an attempt to approximate the 'standard' /q/ sound for *qa:f* in certain proper names no matter what their usual dialect pronunciation of this word would be. The two most notable examples are:

Cairo
il-qa:hira إِلْقاهِرَة

and
the Qu'ran
il-qur'a:n إِلْقُرْآن

In this book the letter *qa:f* will generally be transliterated as /g/, except in the very few instances, such as the two examples above, where the 'standard' /q/ is more common.

B Map of the world in Arabic

Having accustomed yourself to reading the familiar names of Arabic countries in Arabic, and seeing how we have changed the spelling and pronunciation of Arabic to fit English, it is interesting to see how the names of non-Arab countries are written in Arabic, and the changes and allowances made to fit non-Arabic sounds to the Arabic script. This makes very useful reading practice, for often the most stubborn things to read are familiar names lurking behind the unfamiliar lines of a new script.

This map of the world shows the names of the continents, some countries and major cities written in the Arabic script. This is how most of these names would appear in newspapers, magazines and advertisements.

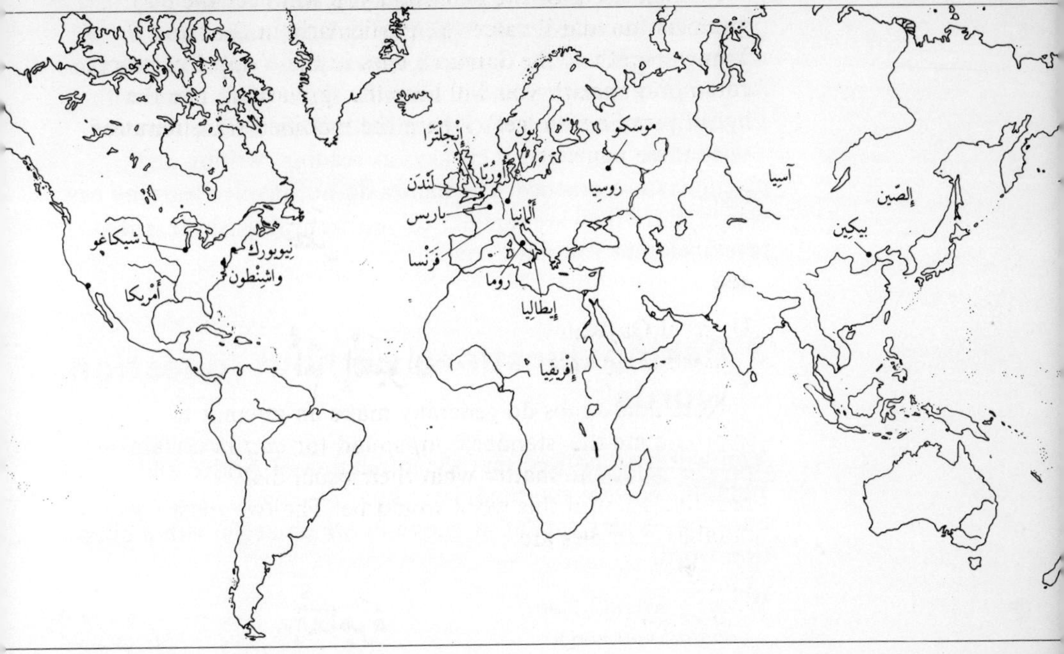

Key ②

Europe *'u:rubba*	أُورُبّا	
Asia *'a:siya*	آسيَا	
Africa *'ifri:qiya*	إِفْرِيقِيا	
America *'amri:ka*	أَمْرِيكا	
England *'ingiltarra*	إِنْجِلْتِرّا	
London *lundun*	لَنْدَن	
New York *ni:yu: yu:rk*	نيويورك	
Washington *wa:shint̲u:n*	واشِنْطون	
Los Angeles *lu:s anjili:s*	لوس أَنْجِليس	
Chicago *shika:ghu*	شيكاغو	
France *faransa*	فَرَنْسا	
Paris *ba:ri:s*	باريس	
Germany *'alma:ni:ya*	أَلْمانِيا	
Bonn *bu:n*	بون	
Italy *'it̲a:liya*	إيطاليا	
Rome *ru:ma*	روما	
Russia *ru:siya*	روسيا	
Moscow *mu:sku*	موسكو	
China *is-s̲i:n*	إِلصّين	
Peking *bi:kin*	بيكين	

Note how these names have been adapted to Arabic pronunciation and script. When using these names and those relating specifically to the Arab world, try to approximate the Arabic pronunciation and not merely slip a place name with English pronunciation into the middle of an Arabic sentence.

Use these maps and their keys as reading, writing and pronunciation practice. The names do not involve learning new words, since they are familiar to you from English. It is the pronunciation you must concentrate on.

3 Asking questions without 'question words'

You will have noticed that the intonation of Arabic and English, the way you modulate your voice when asking a question, is very similar in questions which begin with a question word.

Where's Ahmad from?
'aḫmad min wayn? أَحْمَد مِن وَيْن؟

What's your name?
'aysh 'ism-ik? أَيْش إِسْمِك؟

Now let's consider how you make questions where there is no need for a question word. Look at these two sentences:

1 Ahmad is from Yemen.
2 Jedda is in Saudi Arabia.

To make these statements into questions in English, you must do two things, change the order of the sentence and change your intonation.

1 Is Ahmad from Yemen?
2 Is Jedda in Saudi Arabia?

Say these examples aloud, and see if you can hear the change in intonation which occurs between each statement and its corresponding question. In fact no matter how you say the questions in English, it is apparent to a listener from the special word order that you are indeed asking about Ahmad and Jedda rather than making a statement about them. Only when expressing surprise in English do we generally pose questions whose word order is identical to that of corresponding statements.

Examples

'Jedda's in Saudi Arabia?' (i.e. 'I thought it was in Yemen')
'He's in America?' (i.e. 'I thought he was in Europe')

Now look at what happens with Arabic. Don't say anything

yet, just look at the statements and compare them with the questions made from them.

Ⓣ **Statement**

Jedda is in Saudi Arabia — جَدَّة في السُّعودِيَّة

jadda fi-s-suʿu:diya

Question

Is Jedda in Saudi Arabia? — جَدَّة في السُّعودِيَّة ؟

jadda fi-s-suʿu:diya?

Points to note

a There is absolutely no difference in the way both the statement and question are written, the word order is identical.

b In written Arabic, only the question mark at the end of the question indicates that a question is indeed being asked.

c Can you *hear* the difference? The pitch of your voice rises on the last part of the last word in the sentence. In future we will refer to this feature as 'rising intonation'.

Ⓣ

1 Hasan is from Qatar. — ١ حَسَن مِن قَطَر

ḫasan min gaṯar

Is Hasan from Qatar? — حَسَن مِن قَطَر؟

ḫasan min gaṯar?

2 Samira is from Bahrain — ٢ سَميرَة مِن إلْبَحْرَيْن

sami:ra min il-baḫrayn

Is Samira from Bahrain? — سَميرَة مِن إلْبَحْرَيْن ؟

sami:ra min il-bahrayn?

3 Dammam is in Saudi Arabia. — ٣ اِلدَّمام في السُّعودِيَّة

id-damma:m fi s-suʿu:diyya?

Is Dammam in Saudi Arabia? — اِلدَّمام في السُّعودِيَّة ؟

id-damma:m fi s-suʿu:diyya?

4 Khadija is in Jedda. — ٤ خَديجَة في جَدَّة

khadi:ja fi jadda

Is Khadija in Jedda? — خَديجَة في جَدَّة ؟

khadi:ja fi jadda?

5 Ahmad is from Kuwait. — ٥ أَحْمَد مِن إلْكُوَيْت

aḫmad min il-kuwayt

Is Ahmad from Kuwait? — أَحْمَد مِن إلْكُوَيْت ؟

aḫmad min il-kuwayt?

Try to imitate the intonation of the tape models as closely as possible.

Practice sentences

Ⓣ

Use the sentences in this drill for reading, writing and pronunciation practice. They use a selection of the vocabulary and structures introduced so far, names of countries and capitals from the map, and people's names. Pay attention to pronunciation of the 'new' sounds.

1 Where's Adila from?
ᶜa:dila min wayn?
١ عادِلَة مِن وَيْن ؟

2 Ahmad is in London.
'aẖmad fi lundun
٢ أَحْمَد في لَنْدَن

3 Where are you from? (to a woman)
'inti min wayn?
٣ إِنْتِ مِن وَيْن ؟

4 Manama is in Bahrain.
mana:ma fi l-baẖrayn
٤ مَنامَة في الْبَحْرَيْن

5 What's your name? (to a man)
'aysh 'ism-ak?
٥ أَيْش إِسْمك ؟

6 Is Salah from Oman?
ṣala:ẖ min ᶜuma:n?
٦ صَلاح مِن عُمان ؟

7 Is Qasim in America?
ga:sim fi amri:ka?
٧ قاسِم في أَمريكا ؟

8 Muhammad is from Abu Dhabi.
muẖammad min abu ḏhabi
٨ مُحَمَّد مِن أبو ظَبي

9 I'm from Britain.
ana min brita:niya
٩ أَنا مِن بَرِطانيا

10 Where's Matrah?
wayn maṯraẖ?
١٠ وَيْن مَطْرَح ؟

Pronunciation points

Pay attention when in

fi في

is immediately followed by a word beginning with *il* 'the'. For example,

in Bahrain
fi l-baẖrayn في الْبَحْرَيْن

note that the short /i/ of *il* is not heard in pronunciation, and consequently is not represented in the transliteration.

If the first letter of the word following *il* is a 'sun letter', for example,

in Saudi Arabia
fi s-suᶜu:diyya في السُّعودِيَّة

the /l/ is silent and the sun letter is doubled in pronunciation, as indicated by the *shadda*. This is indicated in the transliteration, though in the written Arabic, of course, the *la:m* is written.

Translation

Translate these sentences into Arabic. Take care over your spelling, check things you are not sure of. Compare your attempts with the key at the back of the book.

1 Jedda is in Saudi Arabia.
2 Where's Matrah?
3 Where's Aziza from?
4 Is Fatima in London?
5 Where are you from? (to a man)
6 Is Muhammad in Cairo?
7 Ahmad is in Washington.
8 How are you? (to a woman)
9 Where's Jasim?
10 What's your name? (to a man)

4 Talking about other people

Until now we have only dealt with situations where you are involved in direct conversation with another person. In the above sentences we talked about other people by using their personal names, i.e. 'Ahmad's in London', but you can't yet say 'He's in London'. You can ask 'What's your name?', but not 'What's her name?' To do this you need the Arabic equivalents for 'he' and 'she' and 'his' and 'her'.

Vocabulary B Ⓣ

he	*huwa*	هُوَ	his name	*'ism-a*	إِسمَهُ
she	*hiya*	هِيَ	her name	*'ism-ha*	إِسْمها

Pronunciation points

a The Arabic equivalent to 'his' is the letter

ha:' ه

added to the last letter of the word it describes. For example,

his name إِسمَهُ = ه + إِسْم

When this personal suffix is added to the last letter of a word the final form of that letter becomes a medial form, and the *ha:'* its final form. The 'his' suffix is joined to the preceding letter by either a *fatha* or a *damma,* and in pronunciation it is generally just the short vowel sound that is heard, the /h/ is lost. Thus you may hear either:

his name
ism-u   إِسْمُه

his name
ism-a   إِسْمَه

Find out what people say in the area where you are living, use what you hear used around you.

b The Arabic equivalent to 'her' is

ha   ها

added to the last letter of the word it describes. For example,

her name
ism-ha   إِسْم + ها = إِسْمها

When this personal suffix is added to the last letter of a word, the final form of that letter becomes a medial form, and the *ha:'* becomes its medial form.

Look carefully at the above examples to make sure that you are fully aware of the changes in the written forms of the words. Pay attention to the different forms of the letter *ha:'*. Of all the letters of the Arabic alphabet it is the least uniform in shape from form to form. Make sure that you can recognise and reproduce this letter in all its various guises.

Dialogues Ⓣ Talking about a man

A What's his name?
   'aysh ism-a?   أَيْش إِسْمَه

B His name's Jasim.
   'ism-a ja:sim   إِسْمَه جاسِم

   He's from Riyadh.
   huwa min ir-riya:d   هُوَ مِن إِلرِّياض

Talking about a woman
A What's her name?
   'aysh ism-ha?   أَيْش إِسْمها

B Her name's Nouria.
   'ism-ha nu:riya   إِسْمها نورِيَة

   She's from Egypt.
   hiya min masr   هِيَ مِن مَصْر

Review

1 Here is a complete list of the Arabic equivalents of 'I', 'you', 'he' and 'she'. Make sure you know them before continuing.

I *'ana*	أَنا	he *huwa*	هُو
you (to a man) *'inta*	إِنْتَ	she *hiya*	هِيَ
you (to a woman) *'inti*	إِنْتِ		

2 You have also seen all the singular suffixes used to indicate possession, 'my', 'your', 'his' and 'her'. So far you have used them with only two nouns, but, of course, they can be used with any relevant noun. In future we shall refer to them as 'personal suffixes'. Below is a list of all the singular personal suffixes together with the Arabic for 'name'. First the noun and the suffix are separate, then the suffix is joined to the last letter.

Ⓣ

my name *'ism-i*	إِسْم + ي = إِسْمي
your name (to a man) *'ism-ak*	إِسْم + كَ = إِسْمَك
you name (to a woman) *'ism-ik*	إِسْم + كِ = إِسْمِك
his name *'ism-a*	إِسْم + ه = إِسْمَه
her name *'ism-ha*	إِسْم + ها = إِسْمْها

Writing points

Note that all the suffixes except for *ha* 'her' are single letters of the alphabet. When such suffixes are added to the last letter of the preceding word, that last letter must be modified, changed to its medial form, while the suffixes are final forms. These suffixes never stand alone, unless the last letter of the word they describe is a non-connector, in which case, of course, they *must* stand alone.

Practice sentences

Ⓣ Use these sentences for reading, writing and pronunciation practice.

1 Where's he from?
huwa min wayn?

١ هُوَ مِن وَيْن ؟

2 What's her name?
'aysh 'ism-ha?

٢ أَيْش إِسْمْها ؟

3 His name's Ahmad.
'ism-a 'aẖmad — ٣ إِسْمَه أَحْمَد

4 Is he in London?
huwa fi lundun? — ٤ هُوَ في لَنْدَن ؟

5 Where's she from?
min wayn hiya? — ٥ مِن وَيْن هيَ ؟

6 She's from Qatar.
hiya min gaṯar — ٦ هيَ مِن قَطَر

7 Muhammad is in America.
muẖammad fi 'amri:ka — ٧ مُحَمَّد في أَمْريكا

8 Is she in Jedda?
hiya fi jadda? — ٨ هيَ في جَدَّة ؟

9 What's his name?
'aysh 'ism-a? — ٩ أَيْش إِسْمَه ؟

10 Is he from Kuwait?
huwa min il-kuwayt? — ١٠ هُوَ مِن إِلْكُوَيْت ؟

Pay attention to the pronunciation of any of the 'new' sounds used in words in this drill.

How is your 'rising intonation'?

Translation

Translate these sentences into Arabic. Look up anything you are not sure of. Take care over your spelling. If you must, write out words time and time again until you have memorised both their spelling and pronunciation. Check your answers with the key given at the end of the book.

1 What's her name?
2 Where's he from?
3 How are you? (to a man)
4 His name's Ahmad, and he's from Kuwait.
5 I'm from Dubai.
6 Where are you from? (to a woman)
7 What's his name?
8 She's from Iraq.
9 Is he from Yemen?
10 Where's she from?
11 He's from Qatar.
12 I'm from London.
13 Her name's Aziza, and she's from Abu Dhabi.
14 Where is Matrah?
15 How are you? (to a woman)

Structured conversation

For use with your teacher or an Arabic speaking friend.

A What's your name?
B My name's ———
A Where are you from?
B I'm from ———
A What's her name?
B Her name's ———
A Where's she from?
B She's from ———
A What's his name?
B His name's ———
A Where's he from?
B He's from ———

5 'We', 'you' and 'they'

Arabic has two forms of 'you' and 'they'. The masculine form is used for groups of men and mixed male-female groups, and the feminine form for groups made up *exclusively* of women.

To distinguish between the different forms of 'you' and 'they', these abbreviations are used:

mp — masculine plural, used in addressing, or talking about, groups of men and mixed male-female groups.

fp — feminine plural, used in addressing, or talking about, groups made up exclusively of women.

Both men and women will find that they will use the masculine forms most frequently since they cover mixed male and female groups, as well as groups made up exclusively of males.

Ⓣ

we
iḫna إِحْنا

you (mp)
intum إِنْتُم

you (fp)
intin إِنْتِن

they (mp)
hum هُم

they (fp)
hin هِن

Practice sentences Ⓣ

1 We are from London.
iḫna min lundun إِحْنا مِن لَنْدَن

2 They (m) are from Bahrain.
hum min il-baḫrayn هُم مِن اِلْبَحْرين

3 Where are you (mp) from?
intum min wayn? إِنْتُم مِن وَيْن ؟

4 They (f) are from Qatar.
hin min gaṯar هِن مِن قَطَر

5 Where are you (fp) from?
intin min wayn? إِنْتِن مِن وَيْن ؟

Substitution drill Ⓣ

Model sentence

hum min il-kuwayt — هُم مِن اِلْكُوَيْت

They are from Kuwait.

Example substitution

cue *iḥna* —— *briṭa:niya* — إِحْنا —— بِرطانِيا

response *ihna min briṭa:niya* — إِحْنا مِن بِرطانِيا

Cues

1	*iḥna* —— *briṭa:niya*	إِحْنا —— بِرطانِيا
2	*huwa* —— *il-baḥrayn*	هُوَ —— إِلْبَحْرَيْن
3	*hin* —— *amri:ka*	هِن —— أَمْرِيكا
4	*ana* —— *lundun*	أَنا —— لَنْدَن
5	*hiya* —— *maṣr*	هِيَ —— مَصْر
6	*hum* —— *is-suᶜu:diyya*	هُم —— إِلسُّعودِيَّة
7	*huwa* —— *filasṭi:n*	هُوَ —— فِلَسْطِين
8	*ana* —— *amri:ka*	أَنا —— أَمْرِيكا
9	*hiya* —— *faransa*	هِيَ —— فَرَنْسا
10	*iḥna* —— *amri:ka*	إِحْنَا —— أَمْرِيكا

6 Further greetings and courtesy phrases

Greetings and set courtesy phrases occur frequently in Arabic. People never tire of using them, and it is considered brusque and impolite to hurry over them. Phrases such as the following, and others you have learned, may be repeated within the first few minutes of meeting. They are very useful for filling a gap in a conversation.

One phrase you will hear frequently is,

Ⓣ Welcome

ahlan wa sahlan — أَهْلاً وَسَهْلاً

Note, both words end in *alif* with double *fatḫa* above it. The *alif* is not pronounced, it is merely the bearer for the double *fatḫa* which is pronounced /an/. This is a feature of the 'classical' language, which survives in only a few commonly used words in the spoken language. It is used to mean 'welcome' in the sense of a host greeting a guest, and in this case is said only by the host.

A polite response to this phrase in this context is:

Ⓣ *ahlan bi-kum* أَهْلاً بِكُم

In some parts of the Arab world it is used as a reply to 'thank you':

Ⓣ Thank you شُكْراً
shukran

(response) أَهْلاً وَسَهلاً
ahlan wa sahlan

You may also hear the following used as an informal way of saying 'hello':

Ⓣ hello أَهْلاً
ahlan

Hello (response literally 'welcome') مَرْحَبا
marḫaba

Sometimes the response *marḫaba* is itself used as a greeting:

Ⓣ Welcome مَرْحَبا
marḫaba

with the typical response, which means literally 'two welcomes',

marḫabt-ayn مَرْحَبْتَيْن

If you are living in an Arab country, listen to what people around you are saying and imitate what you hear. Remember that you may also be exposed to a very wide variety of greetings and courtesy phrases not commonly used in the Peninsula if you work with foreign Arabs. Make a note of anything new you hear and try to learn it.

Review chart of greetings and responses

When used	Greeting	Response
Any time	إِلسَّلامُ عَلَيْكُم *is -sala:mu ʿalay-kum*	وَعَلَيْكُم إِلسَّلام *wa ʿalay-kum is-sala:m*
Dawn to midday	صَباح إِلْخَيْر *s̲aba:h̲ il-khayr*	صَباح إِلنّور *s̲aba:h̲ in-nu:r*
5 pm onwards	مَساء إِلْخَيْر *masa:' il-khayr*	مَساء إِلنّور *masa:' in-nu:r*
Host to guest	أَهْلاً وَسَهْلاً *'ahlan wa sahlan*	أَهْلاً بِكُم *'ahlan bi:kum*
Any time	أَهْلاً *'ahlan*	مَرْحَبا *marh̲aba*
Any time	مَرْحَبا *marh̲aba*	مَرْحَبْتَيْن *marh̲abtayn*

In addition to the phrase you learned in Unit One for 'How are you?', there are a number of alternatives which, although they are more typical of areas outside the Peninsula, tend to crop up quite frequently as a result of the large numbers of expatriate Arabs living and working in Saudi Arabia and the Gulf. Among the most common are:

Ⓣ How (is) the health? كَيْف إِلصِّحَّة؟
kayf is̲-s̲ih̲h̲a?

How (is) the condition? كَيْف إِلْحال؟
kayf il-h̲a:l?

How (are) the conditions? كَيْف إِلْأَحْوال؟
kayf il-ah̲wa:l?

The stock response to all of these is:

The praise to God
il-ḫamdu li-lla:h

إِلْحَمْدُ لِله

or the alternative:

We thank God
nashkur alla:h

نَشْكُر أَلله

The Arab predilection for greetings, and the large number of alternative courtesy phrases available (those given in this and the first Unit are only a small selection, listen for others and note them as you hear them) means that the first few minutes of a conversation are often wholly given over to exchanges of greetings and mutual enquiries about health and well-being.

A typical conversation between two people meeting in the morning might go like this:

Dialogues Ⓣ

A Hello.
is-sala:mu ᶜalay-kum

إِلسَّلامُ عَلَيْكُم

B Hello, good morning.
wa alay-kum is-sal:m.
ṣaba:ḫ il-khayr

وَعَلَيْكُم إِلسَّلام . صَباح إِلْخَيْر

A Good morning, welcome.
ṣaba:ḫ in-nu:r marḫaba

صَباح إِلنّور. مَرْحَبا

B Welcome. How are you?
marḫabtayn. kayf ḫa:l:ak?|

مَرْحَبْتَيْن . كَيْف حالَك ؟

A Fine. How are things?
il-ḫamdu li-lla:h. kayf il-aḫwa:l?

إِلْحَمْدُ لله كَيْف إِلْأَحْوال ؟

B Fine. How's your health?
bi-khayr il-ḫamdu li-lla:h.
kayf is-siḫḫa?

بخَيْر إِلْحَمْدُ لِله . كَيْف إِلصِّحَّة ؟

A Can't complain, welcome.
nashkur alla:h. 'ahlan wa sahlan

نَشْكُر أَلله . أَهْلاً وَسَهْلاً

B Welcome to you.
'ahlan bi-kum

أَهْلاً بِكُم

Notice that we have given idiomatic English translations of the Arabic phrases so as to give you a better idea of the function of the Arabic. If you are interested in the literal meaning of the Arabic, check back in the book.

Structured conversations

1 **A** Enquiry about health. (How are you? etc.)
B Appropriate response. Return enquiry.
A Appropriate response.

2 **A** Greeting. (Hello/Good morning/Good evening/Welcome etc.)
B Appropriate response.
A Enquiry about health.
B Appropriate response.

3 **A** Where are you from? (Substitute 'he', 'she'.)
B Response. (Name of country only.)
A From where in . . .?
B Response. (Name of city/area.)
A Welcome.

4 **A** What's your name? (Substitute 'his', 'her'.)
B Response. Return enquiry.
A Response.

Supplementary section 3.1 Variants for 'Where?'

Although

where?
wayn? وَيْن ؟

is common throughout the Arabian Peninsula, you will hear other words used with exactly the same meaning.

In Oman you may hear

where?
hayn? هَيْن ؟

and in YAR you will hear the two following words:

where?
fayn? فَيْن ؟

ayna? أَيْنَ

As always, the cardinal rule is, listen carefully and imitate what you hear used around you most. *fayn* is generally associated with Egyptian Arabic, but is commonly heard all over the Arab world.

Note Sometimes when asking the question 'where from?' or 'from where?' the two words become run together in pronunciation:

from where?
minayn? مِنْ أَيْنْ ؟

Listen for this and if you hear it commonly used around you, incorporate it into your own pronunciation.

Supplementary section 3.2 Variants for 'we' and 'you'

You will hear some variation in how the word for 'we' is pronounced. In the Gulf and eastern parts of Saudi Arabia you will hear,

we
niḫin نِحِن

and in other areas you will hear,

we
niḫna نِحْنَ

Though you should find out what is used where you are living and use it in your speech, any of the three variations would be understood all over the Peninsula.

In YAR and perhaps other areas you will hear these variants for 'you' (mp) and 'you' (fp):

you (mp)
intu إِنْتو

you (fp)
intayn إِنْتَيْن

Unit 4

Note on short vowels and other signs

As you will be aware if you are familiar with *Write to Left, An introduction to Arabic script and pronunciation,* the short vowels in Arabic, though always pronounced, are rarely indicated in books, newspapers, magazines, advertisements or any handwritten material, and nor are the other writing signs such as *shadda* and *suku:n*. Thus far we have marked all vowels and other signs in order to encourage you in your early attempts to read Arabic in its own script. However, we don't want you to become over-dependent on short vowels since you will rarely come across them elsewhere. From now on, therefore, we will mark the short vowels only on new words when they appear for the first time, and also in the end-of-unit vocabulary lists. At first you will undoubtedly have some difficulty in reading unvowelled Arabic. Some common words will be easily recognised and pronounced without the aid of short vowels, while others, newly introduced or with which you are less familiar, may initially prove more of a problem. If you persevere, however, you will be surprised how quickly you begin to associate the visual shape of a word with its correct pronunciation, even in the absence of short vowels. You may find it helpful to pencil in the short vowels on those words which you repeatedly have difficulty in pronouncing — refer to the transliteration and/or the end-of-unit word lists to determine the correct vowelling.

1 Filler words

Vocabulary A

er . . . um . . ., I mean . . .
*ya*ᶜ*ni* يَعْنِي

This is a very common phrase used where in English we would probably say 'er . . .', 'um . . .' or 'I mean . . .' at the beginning, or in the middle of a sentence while thinking of what we want to say, or looking for the appropriate word.

'First let us not subscribe to the notion that although we cannot always think of the right word in our own language, we must nevertheless, never fumble in a foreign one. We use 'er', 'what's it', 'thingummy' to fill in our gaps; one of our first tasks must be to find out the equivalents in the language we are learning. Fumbling for a word is everybody's linguistic birthright'. (Anthony Burgess *Language Made Plain)*

Dialogues

Ⓣ 1 Talking to a man

A Good morning.
s̲aba:h̲ il-khayr — صباح الخير

B Good morning.
s̲aba:h̲ in-nu:r — صباح النور

How are you?
kayf h̲a:l-ak ya usta:dh? — كيف حالك يا استاذ؟

A Very well.
il-h̲amdu li-lla:h — الحمدُ لله

And you?
wa int? — وانت؟

B Fine, thanks.
bi-khayr — بخير

Where are you from?
min wayn int? — من وين انت؟

A From Saudi Arabia.
min is-su^{c}u:diyya — من السعودية

B Er ... from Riyadh?
ya^{c}ni . . . min ir-riya:d̲? — يعني من الرياض؟

A No, from Jedda.
la min jadda — لا من جدة

Ⓣ 2 Talking to a woman

A Hello.
ahlan — اهلاً

B Hello.
marh̲aba — مرحبا

What's your name?
aysh ism-ik? — ايش اسمك؟

A My name's Mary.
ism-i ma:ri — اسمي ماري

B Where are you from?
min wayn inti? — من وين انتِ؟

A From Britain.
min brit̲a:niya — من بريطانيا

B Er . . . from London?
yaᶜni . . . min lundun? يعني من لندن

A Yes.
naᶜam نعم

B Welcome.
ahlan wa sahlan اهلاً وسهلاً

2 Getting about

Initially one of the problems you are going to have, assuming that you have recently arrived in an Arab country, is finding your way around in what, at first, may seem an alien environment. Being able to read Arabic script will help you overcome the feeling of extra strangeness people commonly experience when living in countries where advertisements, street signs, car number plates and public notices are written in an unfamiliar script. When you are in the streets look around you and try to read what you see. It will help you to get accustomed to the wide variety of Arabic script styles, and it can be reassuring to see a word you have just learned in use. It takes time and patience to learn a new language through the medium of a new script, so use every opportunity to practise your reading skill. It is surprising how quickly a fifteen minute wait can pass while trying to make out a notice on a wall or the headline of a newspaper you find lying on a table.

Many Europeans suffer from severe disorientation in Arab cities. Accustomed as we are to fixed street names and postal codes that everybody knows and uses, and taxi drivers who know the cities where they work like the backs of their hands, it can be very disconcerting to discover that even a taxi driver does not recognise the name of what you were assured was one of the main streets in a town. You must get used to the fact that there is often more than one name for a certain street. The best way to get around is by using landmarks like a well-known hotel, the Post Office, a cinema, an embassy, etc. People generally know where these are. Using a taxi, you may have to reach your destination by giving the name of the general area you want, and once you arrive, direct the driver personally.

Vocabulary B Ⓣ Here are some words to help you get around, to ask where places are and to help you understand simple directions.

street
sha:riᶜ شارِع

shop
dukka:n دُكّان

office	*maktab*	مَكْتَب
restaurant	*mat̲ᶜam*	مَطْعَم
hotel	*uti:l*	أُتيل
house	*bayt*	بَيْت
building	*bina:ya*	بِنايَة
bank	*bank*	بَنْك
embassy	*sifa:ra*	سِفارَة
post office	*maktab il-bari:d*	مَكْتَب إِلْبَريد
market	*su:g*	سوق
hospital	*mustashfa*	مُسْتَشْفى
cinema	*si:nama*	سينَما

ministry	*wiza:ra*	وِزارَة
square	*mayda:n*	مَيْدان
car	*sayya:ra*	سَيّارَة
taxi	*taksi*	تَكْسي
address	*ᶜanwa:n*	عَنْوان
company	*sharika*	شَرِكَة
city	*madi:na*	مَدينَة
flat, apartment	*shigga*	شِقَّة
garden	*h̲adi:ga*	حَديقَة
here	*hina*	هِنا
there	*hina:k*	هِناك

Pronunciation points

Nouns in Arabic are either masculine or feminine. Words ending in *ta:' marbu:ṯa* are feminine. Words without *ta:' marbu:ṯa* are masculine.

Check the new vocabulary and work out which are the feminine nouns.

a Pay attention to the pronunciation of any of the 'new' sounds in these words.

b Note that the Arabic words for 'street', 'shop', 'market', 'cinema', 'car' and 'taxi' all begin with 'sun letters'. Remember that in words beginning with a 'sun letter' and preceded by *il* 'the', the /l/ is silent, and the 'sun letter' is doubled in pronunciation, as indicated by the *shadda*. For example,

the street
*ish-sha:ri*ᶜ الشّارع

the market
is-su:g السّوق

c Note the pronunciation of the words for 'building', 'embassy', 'ministry', 'car', 'company' and 'agency', all of which end in a *ta:' marbu:ṯa*. Remember, for pronunciation purposes, words ending in *ta:' marbu:ṯa* are considered as ending with the short vowel sound /a/ as represented by the *fatḫa* which precedes the *ta:' marbu:ṯa*.

d You will notice that there are a couple of words in the list, which in pronunciation end in /a/, but when written do not end in a *ta:' marbu:ta*. For example,

hospital
mustashfa مستشفى

which ends in an *alif maqṣu:ra*. In some words a final *alif* is represented by a *ya:'* without dots. This feature occurs only at the end of words. It is pronounced and transliterated exactly like a regular *alif* at the end of a word, i.e. /a/. This is a relatively rare feature of written Arabic; for the moment note it in the writing and pronunciation of this word, and when it occurs again we will point it out.

You will see other words written with an ordinary final *alif*. For example,
cinema
si:nama سينما

Note In spoken Arabic long vowels /a:/, /i:/ and /u:/, at the end of words are pronounced as their short vowel equivalents

/a/, /i/ and /u/. Therefore in the two words above, the *alif* sounds like and is transliterated as /a/.

e The Arabic for 'hotel', 'bank', 'cinema' and 'taxi' are words of European origin transliterated into Arabic script.
There is an alternative Arabic word for hotel which you may hear and see written,

hotel
fundug فُنْدُق

3 Position words

Vocabulary C

Learn the following. In combination with the words you have just seen, you will be able to extend what you are able to say considerably.

Ⓣ

in, at
fi في

to
ila إلى

from
min مِن

in front of, facing, opposite
gudda:m قُدّام

behind
wara وَراء

near to
gari:b min قَريب مِن

far from
ba^c*i:d min* بَعيد مِن

beside
bi-ja:nib بِجانِب

between
bayn بَيْن

Points to note

a The primary meaning of *fi* is 'in', but it is frequently used in situations where English can use either 'in' or 'at' with little or no effect on the meaning.

For example,
Ahmad's in the house
Ahmad's at home
ahmad fi l-bayt احمد في البيت

She's in/at the office
hiya fi l-maktab هي في المكتب

Remember that since *fi* ends in a vowel, the /i/ of *il* is dropped in pronunciation and the two are run together in speech. This is a pronunciation change only, and is not reflected in the way the Arabic is written. We attempt to represent this feature in the transliteration, but you must take the tape model, and/or a native speaker of Arabic as your guide in pronunciation.

b There are quite a few alternatives to these position words, and you may hear more than one word used wherever you are living, so instead of including variants in a supplementary section, we outline the most common alternatives here. As always, use what you hear used around you.

In the eastern part of the Peninsula, you will hear these alternatives:

1 The word for 'in front of' is sometimes pronounced *judda:m,* though it will always be written as it is above.

2 'Beside' is often
beside
yamm يَمّ

3 You will hear these alternatives for 'behind'.

'behind':
khalf خَلْف

ᶜugb عُقْب

Look at this map and work out the relationship of the places marked to one another.

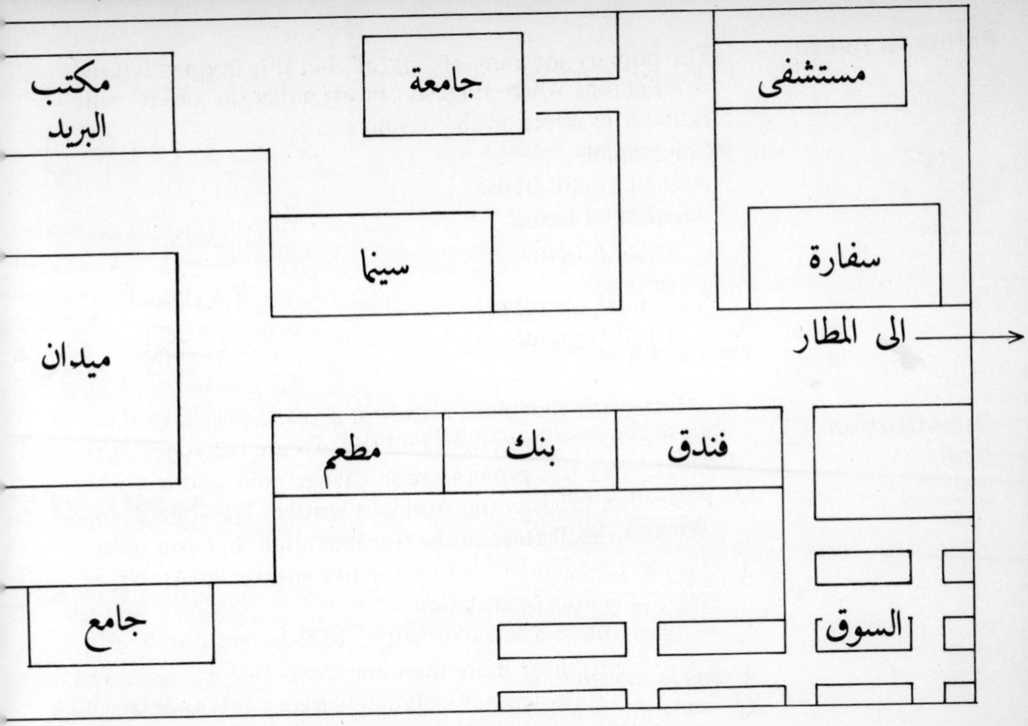

Question and answer drill

Listen to the question and give the answer on cue.

Example

Q *wayn il-bank?* وين البنك ؟
Where's the bank?

cue *bi-ja:nib il-maṯ^c^am* بجانب المطعم
Beside the restaurant.

response *il-bank bi-ja:nib il-maṯ^c^am* البنك بجانب المطعم
The bank's beside the restaurant.

1 *wayn il-bank?* وين البنك ؟

cue *bi-ja:nib il-maṯ^c^am* بجانب المطعم

2 *wayn il-mustashfa?* وين المستشفى ؟

cue *wara is-sifa:ra* وراء السفارة

3 *wayn maktab il-bari:d?* وين مكتب البريد؟

cue *fi l-mayda:n* في الميدان

4 *wayn is-si:nama?* وين السينما ؟

cue *fi l-mayda:n gari:b min* في الميدان قريب من

maktab il-bari:d مكتب البريد

5 *wayn is-sifa:ra?* وين السفارة ؟

cue *gudda:m il-uti:l* قدام الاتيل

Substitution drill Ⓣ Listen to the question, and answer on cue.

Model

Q *wayn fa:t̲ima?* وين فاطمة ؟
Where's Fatima?

A *hiya fi l-bayt* هي في البيت
She's in the house/at home.

Example substitution

Q *wayn fa:t̲ima?* وين فاطمة ؟

cue *il-maktab* المكتب

A *hiya fi l-maktab* هي في المكتب

Cues

1	*il-maktab*	المكتب	6	*is-sifa:ra*	السفارة
2	*il-mat̲ʿam*	المطعم	7	*il-wiza:ra*	الوزارة
3	*il-uti:l*	الاتيل	8	*maktab il-bari:d*	مكتب البريد
4	*is-su:g*	السوق	9	*il-bank*	البنك
5	*il-bayt*	البيت	10	*il-h̲adi:ga*	الحديقة

Substitution drill Ⓣ Repeat the drill above, this time replying to the question 'Where's Ahmad?'

Model

Q *wayn ah̲mad?* وين احمد؟
Where's Ahmad?

A *huwa fi l-bayt* هو في البيت
He's in the house/at home.

Reading and repetition drill Ⓣ

1 My house is near the hospital. ١ بيتي قريب من المستشفى
bayt-i gari:b min il-mustashfa.

2 Is Muhammad at home? ٢ محمد في البيت؟
*mu**h**ammad fi l-bayt?*

3 The restaurant is opposite the cinema. ٣ المطعم قدّام السينما
*il-ma**t**ʿam gudda:m is-si:nama*

4 My house is a long way (far) from the market. ٤ بيتي بعيد من السوق
bayti-i baʿi:d min is-su:g.

5 The bank is between the hotel and the restaurant. ٥ البنك بين الاتيل والمطعم
*il-bank bayn il-uti:l wa l-ma**t**ʿam.*

4 'There is' and 'Is there?'

You have seen that Arabic does not need an equivalent for 'am, is, are' in sentences where they are obligatory in English. Thus sentences like the following are rendered:

I'm from Kuwait. (literally, 'I from Kuwait') انا من الكويت
ana min il-kuwayt

Where are you from? (literally, 'You from where?') انت من وين؟
int min wayn?

He is in London. (literally, 'He in London') هو في لندن
huwa fi lundun

These Arabic sentences are complete as they stand, and on these and other models a large number of simple but very useful sentences can be made. The literal English translations might give you the impression that you are speaking 'broken' Arabic, but this is the way Arabic works.

There is, however, one use of 'is/are' which requires a means of expression in Arabic when making statements like, '*There is* a restaurant beside the bank', '*There are* a lot of people in Jedda', or when enquiring about the existence of something; '*Is there* a restaurant here?','*Are there* a lot of people in Jedda?' This use of 'there is/is there?' and 'there are/are there?' is covered in Arabic by one word:

fi: في

which you have already seen used with another meaning 'in/at'. Although the written form is the same, there is a difference in pronunciation. When it is used to mean 'in/at' the long vowel is pronounced like its short vowel equivalent /i/, as we have shown in the transliteration. When it is used to mean 'there is/is there?' and 'there are/are there?', the long vowel is given its full pronunciation as we indicate in the transliteration. In writing, however, there is no difference. When used in both senses it will appear the same; the pronunciation indicates the meaning.

In the following examples and exercises *fi:* will only be used in the sense of 'there is/is there?'. You have not seen any plurals yet so we cannot use it in its plural sense. For local variants of *fi:* see the supplementary section at the end of this unit.

Ⓣ

Statements

1 There's a cinema near the square.
fi: si:nama gari:b min il-mayda:n — ١ في سينما قريب من الميدان

2 There's a car outside the embassy.
fi: sayya:ra gudda:m is-sifa:ra. — ٢ في سيّارة قدام السفّارة

3 There's a restaurant between the hotel and the bank.
fi: maṯ^cam bayn il-uti:l wa l-bank. — ٣ في مطعم بين الاتيل والبنك

Questions

Ⓣ

Remember that you indicate you are asking a question in Arabic by using 'rising intonation', by raising the pitch of your voice at the end of the question.

1 Is there a restaurant near here?
fi: maṯ^cam gari:b min hina? — ١ في مطعم قريب من هنا؟

2 Is there a bank near the hotel?
fi: bank gari:b min il-uti:l? — ٢ في بنك قريب من الاتيل؟

3 Is there a taxi? ٣ في تكسي؟
fi: taksi?

4 Is there a cinema there? ٤ في سينما هناك؟
fi: si:nama hina:k?

Negative

The negative of *fi:* is made by putting *ma* in front of it in both statements and questions.

there isn't *ma fi:*	ما في	isn't there? *ma fi:?*	ما في؟

Ⓣ

1 There isn't a restaurant near the hotel. ١ ما في مطعم قريب من الاتيل
ma fi: maṯʿam gari:b min il-uti:l

2 Isn't there a cinema there? ٢ ما في سينما هناك
ma fi: si:nama hina:k?

3 No, there isn't (in reply to question 'is there . . .?') ٣ لا ما في
la ma fi:

5 Possession

The singular personal suffixes

The personal suffixes indicating 'my', 'your', 'his' and 'her' can be attached to any noun.
When a word ending in *ta:' marbu:ṯa* is followed by a personal suffix, the *ta:' marbu:ṯa* is 'opened', that is, it is both written and pronounced like a regular *ta:'*.

For example,
my car
sayya:rat-i سيارة + ي = سيارتي

her flat
shiggat-ha شقة + ها = شقتها

With all other words, the personal suffixes join directly to the last letter.
For example,
my house
bayt-i بيت + ي = بيتي

your address
ʿanwa:n-ak عنوان + ك = عنوانك

Go back and check that you are familiar with the following vocabulary: 'city', 'flat', 'room', 'garden', 'shop', 'house', 'embassy', 'car', 'company'.
Of the nouns you have seen so far you may find that these are the ones that you will most frequently use with the personal suffixes. This drill practises them in various combinations.

Ⓣ

1 your (m) city
madi:nat-ak مدينتك

2 his town
bila:d-u بلاده

3 my flat
shiggat-i شقّتي

4 her room
ghurfat-ha غرفتها

5 my garden
hadi:gat-i حديقتي

6 his shop
dukka:n-u دكانه

7 your (f) house
bayt-ik بيتك

8 my address
ᶜanwa:n-i عنواني

9 his company
sharikat-u شركته

10 my car
sayya:rat-i سيّارتي

Practise using the personal suffixes and these nouns in different combinations. Say them aloud to yourself, pay attention to the opening of the *ta:' marbu:ṯa*.
Note the change in the appearance of a word when you add a personal suffix to it. The final form of the last letter of the word becomes a medial form and changes the familiar appearance of a word just learnt.

Substitution drill Ⓣ

Model question
wayn bayt-ak? وين بيتك ؟
Where's your house?

Example substitution

cue *sayya:rat-ak* سيّارتك

response *wayn sayya:rat-ak?* وين سيارتك ؟

Cues

1 *sayya:rat:ak* سيّارتك

2 *dukka:n-u* دكّانه

3 *shiggat-ha* شقّتها

4 *bayt-ik* بيتك

5 *shiggat-ak* شقّتك

6 *sayya:rat-i* سيّارتي

7 *bayt-u* . بيته

8 *sayya:rat-ik* سيارتك

9 *shiggat-u* شقته

10 *bayt-ha* بيتها

The plural personal suffixes

These are the plural personal suffixes corresponding to 'our', 'your' and 'their'.
Note Arabic has two forms of 'your' and 'their', one masculine, the other feminine. The masculine form is used for groups of men and mixed male-female groups. The feminine form is used for groups made up exclusively of women.

Ⓣ our house
bayt-na بيتنا

your (mp) house
bayt-kum بيتكم

your (fp) house
bayt-kin بيتكن

their (m) house
bayt-hum بيتهم

their (f) house
bayt-hin بيتهن

These plural personal suffixes join directly to the last letter of the word they describe; if that letter happens to be a non-connector, of course, the personal suffixes stand alone.
For example,

Ⓣ our town
bila:d-na بلادنا

When these personal suffixes are joined to a word ending in a *ta:' marbu:ṯa* it is 'opened', both pronounced and written like a regular *ta:'*. For example,

Ⓣ our car
sayya:rat-na سيّارتنا

your (mp) room
ghurfat-kum غرفتكم

their (m) flat
shiggat-hum شقتهم

You have now seen all the singular and plural personal suffixes. Make sure you know them all and can use and recognise them in written Arabic. Check the different forms of 'you'. Remember that in Arabic you must distinguish between addressing a man and a woman, and groups of men and women.

Write out a full list of all the personal suffixes attached to sample nouns. Here is a model.

Ⓣ my address
ʿanwa:n-i عنوان + ي = عنواني

your (ms) address
ʿanwa:n-ak عنوان + ك = عنوانك

your (fs) address
ʿanwa:n-ik عنوان + ك = عنوانك

his address
ʿanwa:n-u عنوان + ه = عنوانه

her address
ʿanwa:n-ha عنوان + ها = عنوانها

our address
ʿanwa:n-na عنوان + نا = عنوانّا

your (mp) address
anwa:n-kum عنوان + كم = عنوانكم

your (fp) address
ʿanwa:n-kin عنوان + كن = عنوانكن

their (m) address
ʿanwa:n-hum عنوان + هم = عنوانهم

their (f) address
ʿanwa:n-hin عنوان + هن = عنوانهن

'Where' and the personal suffixes

You have now seen all the personal suffixes, both singular and plural, used to indicate personal possession with nouns. For example,

his house
bayt-u بيته

their book
kita:b-hum كتابهم

her car
sayya:rat-ha سيّارتها

The same suffixes are also commonly used in spoken Arabic to form questions such as 'Where is he?', 'Where is she?', 'Where are they?', etc.

1 Where is he?
wayn-u? وينه ؟

2 Where is she?
wayn-ha? وينها ؟

3 Where are they?
wayn-hum? وينهم ؟

In reply to such questions, you use the independent personal pronouns.

1 He's in Saudi Arabia
huwa fi s-suʿu:diyya هو في السعودية

2 She's in New York
hiya fi ni:yu yu:rk — هي في نيويورك

3 They're in the office
hum fi l-maktab — هم في المكتب

Substitution drill Ⓣ Listen to the questions and answer on cue

Model

Q *wayn-ha?* وينها ؟
Where is she?

A *hiya fi jadda* هي في جدة

Example substitution

Q *wayn-u?* وينه ؟

cue *amri:ka* امريكا

A *huwa fi amri:ka* هو في امريكا

Questions		Cues	
1 *wayn-u?*	وينه ؟	*amri:ka*	امريكا
2 *wayn-ha?*	وينها ؟	*jadda*	جدة
3 *wayn-ak?*	وينك ؟	*il-bayt*	البيت
4 *wayn-hum?*	وينهم ؟	*il-baḫrayn*	البحرين
5 *wayn-ik?*	وينك ؟	*il-maktab*	المكتب
6 *wayn-ha?*	وينها ؟	*bayru:t*	بيروت
7 *wayn-u?*	وينه ؟	*gaṯar*	قطر
8 *wayn-hum?*	وينهم ؟	*u:rubba*	اوربا
9 *wayn-ha?*	وينها ؟	*is-sayya:ra*	السيارة
10 *wayn-u?*	وينه ؟	*il-maktab*	المكتب

6 Plural nouns

Before looking at plurals and how they are formed in Arabic, consider briefly the two major groupings of plurals in English.

A Nouns whose plurals are formed by the addition of *-s, -es* or *-ies* to the singular word.

For example,

name	name*s*
box	box*es*
city	cit*ies*

We can call these plurals 'strong' as the root of the singular noun is retained intact and is made plural by the addition of a suffix. The vast majority of plurals are formed in this way in English.

B Plurals which are made by an internal vowel change in the singular form of the noun.

For example,

foot	f*ee*t
tooth	t*ee*th
man	m*e*n

In nouns of this kind, the singular is 'broken' and modified to make the plural form. Only a handful of plurals are formed in this way in English. Arabic, too, has strong and broken plurals which work on roughly the same lines.

Broken plurals

Unlike English, where strong plurals pre-dominate, the majority of Arabic plurals are broken. Here is a list of those nouns introduced in vocabulary B which take broken plurals.

Ⓣ	**Singular**		**Plural**	
street	*sha:ri^c*	شارع	*shawa:ri^c*	شَوارِع
shop	*dukka:n*	دكان	*daka:ki:n*	دَكاكين
office	*maktab*	مكتب	*maka:tib*	مَكاتِب
restaurant	*maṯ^cam*	مطعم	*maṯa:^cim*	مَطاعِم

hotel	*fundug*	فندق	*fana:dig*	فَنادِق
house	*bayt*	بيت	*buyu:t*	بُيوت
bank	*bank*	بنك	*bunu:k*	بُنوك
market	*su:g*	سوق	*aswa:g*	أَسْواق

Points to note

a The written appearance of a word undergoes quite a considerable change from singular to plural.

b The plural sounds different due to changes in the short vowels and the addition of a long vowel /a:/, /i:/ or /u:/ between letters of the singular.

These changes are not random, there are patterns. You should be able both to see and hear that the plurals of 'restaurant' and 'office' are formed in the same way.

offices		restaurants	
maka:tib	مكاتب	*maṯa:ᶜim*	مطاعم

The short vowels are the same and the *alif* is in the same place in both words, between the second and third letters of the singular form, which gives the words an internal rhyme. Go back and listen to these two words on the tape. Repeat them to yourself; can you hear the similarity?

There are rules to help in deciding which singular words follow which broken plural pattern, but they are not of much use until you have a considerably wider vocabulary. For the moment try to learn by heart the broken plurals of words you need.

Make an effort to learn the singular and plural of new words, but at first learn only those plurals you find you have a regular use for, and learn others that you have only occasional use for as and when you need them.

A full list of nouns and their respective plurals will be included in the vocabulary review at the end of each unit and in the general glossary at the end of the book.

Strong plurals

Perhaps you noticed that none of the nouns used as examples above were feminine nouns, i.e. ending in a *ta:' marbu:ṯa.* Most nouns ending in *ta:' marbu:ṯa* have strong plurals, that is the plural is formed by adding a suffix. The *ta' marbu:ṯa* is dropped and replaced by *alif* and *ta:'* pronounced /a:t/.

Ⓣ

	Singular		Plural	
car	*sayya:ra*	سيّارة	*sayya:ra:t*	سيّارات
building	*bina:ya*	بناية	*bina:ya:t*	بنايات
ministry	*wiza:ra*	وزارة	*wiza:ra:t*	وزارات
embassy	*sifa:ra*	سفارة	*sifa:ra:t*	سفارات

There are a few exceptions to this rule, where feminine words have broken plurals. They do not include many common words, and will be commented on when they occur.

'Loan' plurals

Many 'loan' words, European words like 'cinema', 'taxi', 'hotel', which are used in Arabic, make their plurals by the addition of *alif* and *ta:'* even though they are not feminine and do not end in *ta:' marbu:ṯa*.

	Singular		Plural	
hotel	*uti:l*	اتيل	*uti:la:t*	اتيلات
cinema	*si:nama*	سينما	*si:nama:t*	سينمات

On the other hand many loan words form broken plurals, as in the example we saw above.

bank	*bank*	بنك	*bunu:k*	بنوك

For the plural of 'taxi' you may hear both a broken and a sound plural,

taxi	*taksi*	تكسي	*taka:si*	تكاسي
			taksia:t	تكسيات

Pay attention to plurals. They are not as formidable as they at first appear. You will find many that stick first time, but others will need a little time to become familiar. Have patience.

As from the end of this unit, a full list will be given of all new vocabulary introduced in each unit, except for the vocabulary introduced in the supplementary sections.

7 Numbers 11 to 100

				Arabic numerals
(T)	11	*ẖida^{c}sh*	حِدَعْش	١١
	12	*ithna^{c}sh*	إِثْنَعْش	١٢
	13	*thala:ta^{c}sh*	ثَلاتَعْش	١٣
	14	*arba^{c}ta^{c}sh*	أَرْبَعْتَعْش	١٤
	15	*khamsta^{c}sh*	خَمْسْتَعْش	١٥
	16	*sitta^{c}sh*	سِتَّعْش	١٦
	17	*saba^{c}ta^{c}sh*	سَبَعْتَعْش	١٧
	18	*thamanta^{c}sh*	ثَمَنْتَعْش	١٨
	19	*tisa^{c}ta^{c}sh*	تِسَعْتَعْش	١٩

20	*^{c}ashri:n*	عَشْرين	٢٠
30	*thala:thi:n*	ثَلاثين	٣٠
40	*arba^{c}i:n*	أَربَعين	٤٠
50	*khamsi:n*	خَمْسين	٥٠
60	*sitti:n*	سِتّين	٦٠
70	*sab^{c}i:n*	سَبعين	٧٠
80	*thama:ni:n*	ثَمانين	٨٠
90	*tis^{c}i:n*	تِسْعين	٩٠
100	*miya*	مِيَّة	١٠٠

To make combinations of the units 1 to 9 and the multiples of ten, ie, 21, 22, 23, the unit comes first, followed by the multiple of ten joined by the Arabic for 'and' *wa,* which is sometimes heard as /u:/.

Arabic numerals

(T)

21	*wa:h̲id wa ^{c}ashri:n*	واحد وعشرين	٢١
22	*ithnayn wa ^{c}ashri:n*	اثنين وعشرين	٢٢
23	*thala:tha wa ^{c}ashri:n*	ثلاثة وعشرين	٢٣
24	*arba^{c}a wa ^{c}ashri:n*	اربعة وعشرين	٢٤
25	*khamsa wa ^{c}ashri:n*	خمسة وعشرين	٢٥
26	*sitta wa ^{c}ashri:n*	ستّة وعشرين	٢٦
27	*saba^{c}a wa ^{c}ashri:n*	سبعة وعشرين	٢٧
28	*thama:niya wa ^{c}ashri:n*	ثمانية وعشرين	٢٨
29	*tisa^{c}a wa ^{c}ashri:n*	تسعة وعشرين	٢٩

Saturday		6	13	20	27
Sunday		7	14	21	28
Monday	1	8	15	22	29
Tuesday	2	9	16	23	30
Wednesday	3	10	17	24	31
Thursday	4	11	18	25	
Friday	5	12	19	26	

ديسمبر

December

السبت		٦	١٣	٢٠	٢٧
الأحد		٧	١٤	٢١	٢٨
الاثنين	١	٨	١٥	٢٢	٢٩
الثلاثاء	٢	٩	١٦	٢٣	٣٠
الأربعاء	٣	١٠	١٧	٢٤	٣١
الخميس	٤	١١	١٨	٢٥	
الجمعة	٥	١٢	١٩	٢٦	

Part of an English – Arabic calendar

Supplementary section 4.1
More nouns

Ⓣ Here is some extra vocabulary that you may find useful in getting around and identifying places. Look around you, you will see some of these words written up in the streets. Learn what you find you need most, any items from this list which we use subsequently as an integral part of a drill or exercise will be introduced again.

'Airport' in Arabic

town
bila:d بِلاد

airport
mata:r مَطار

harbour
mi:na ميناء

University
ja:mi^c^a جامِعَة

school
madrasa مَدْرَسَة

mosque
masjid مَسْجِد

*ja:mi^c^* جامِع

museum
mathaf مَتْحَف

room
ghurfa غُرْفَة

hijra حِجْرَة

bath, bathroom
hamma:m حَمّام

garden
busta:n بُسْتان

desert
sahra صَحْراء

sea, beach
bahr بَحْر

garage
kara:j كَراج

roundabout, rotary
dawwa:r دَوّار

agency
wika:la وِكالَة

establishment
mu'assasa مُؤَسَّسَة

showroom
ma ^c^rad مَعْرَض

right
yami:n يَمين

left
shima:l شِمال

yasa:r يَسار

on the right
^c^ala l-yami:n عَلى الْيَمين

on the left
^c^ala sh-shima:l عَلى الشِّمال

^c^ala l-yasa:r عَلى الْيَسار

straight on, straight ahead
si:da سيدَة

Supplementary section 4.2
Variants for 'here' and 'there'

Earlier in this unit we introduced two common variants for 'here' and 'there',

here
hina هِنا

there
hina:k هِناك

Throughout the Peninsula you will hear various alternatives, all based around the two sounds /h/ and /n/ with a variety of vowels. In the Gulf and eastern Saudi Arabia you will hear these variants for 'here':

here
ihni إِهْني

hini هِني

Sometimes you will come across the standard Arabic pronunciation, which would be understood throughout the Arab world:

here
huna هُنا

For 'there' you may hear:

there
ihna:k إهْناك

or the standard Arabic:

there
huna:k هُناك

Supplementary section 4.3 Variants of *fi:*

The most commonly used word for 'there is/is there?' 'there are/are there?' in spoken Arabic, not only in the Peninsula but all over the Arabic-speaking world is:

fi: في

You will, however, hear some variants for this in the Gulf states and eastern areas of the Peninsula.

In Iraq, Kuwait and other areas of the Gulf the most common alternative to *fi:* is:

aku أكو

In UAE and Oman you will hear:

shay شَي
and
shi: شي

In Bahrain and Qatar:

hast هَسْت

In Yemen Arab Republic:

bu بو

If you are living in any of these areas listen for these alternatives, try to recognise them in other people's speech, and as you become more familiar with the language and gain more confidence in speaking it, try to use them in your own.

Negative

The negative of these variants is made with *ma:*

ma:ku	ما اكو	*ma hast*	ما هست
ma shayy	ما شَيّ	*ma bu*	ما بو
ma shi:	ما شي		

Note that the *alif* of *ma* and the initial /a/ of *aku* are run together in pronunciation. Remember that all of these alternatives can be used in exactly the same way as *fi:*.

New vocabulary in Unit 4

The plural forms follow the Arabic script and transliteration in brackets.

street
sha:ri^c (shawa:ri^c) — شارِع (شَوارِع)

shop
dukka:n (daka:ki:n) — دُكّان (دَكاكين)

office
maktab (maka:tib) — مَكْتَب (مَكاتِب)

restaurant
maṯ^{c}am (maṯa:^{c}im) — مَطْعَم (مَطاعِم)

hotel
uti:l (uti:la:t) — أُتيل (أُتيلات)

funduq (fana:diq) — فُنْدُق (فَنادِق)

house
bayt (buyu:t) — بَيْت (بُيوت)

building
bina:ya (bina:ya:t) — بناية (بنايات)

bank
bank (bunu:k) — بَنْك (بُنوك)

embassy
sifa:ra (sifa:ra:t) — سِفارَة (سِفارات)

post office
maktab il-bari:d (maka:tib il-bari:d) — مَكْتَب إِلْبَرِيد

market
su:g (aswa:g) — سوق (أَسْواق)

hospital
mustashfa (mustashfaya:t) — مُسْتَشْفى (مُسْتَشْفيات)

cinema
si:nama (si:nama:t) — سينما (سينمات)

ministry
wiza:ra (wiza:ra:t) — وزارة (وِزارات)

square
mayda:n (maya:di:n) — مَيْدان

car
sayya:ra (sayya:ra:t) — سيّارَة (سيّارات)

taxi
taksi (taksia:t) — تَكْسي (تَكْسِيات)

address
ᶜanwa:n (ᶜana:wi:n) — عَنْوان (عَناوين)

company
sharika (sharika:t) — شَرِكَة (شَرِكات)

city
madi:na (mudun) — مَدينَة (مُدُن)

flat, apartment
shigga (shigag) — شِقَّة (شِقَق)

garden
ẖadi:ga (ẖada:'ig) — حَديقَة (حَدائِق)

here
hina — هِنا

there
hina:k — هِناك

to
ila — إلى

opposite, in front of
gudda:m — قُدّام

behind
wara — وراء

near (to)	*gari:b (min)*	قَريب (مِن)
far (from)	*ba^{c}i:d (min)*	بَعيد مِن
beside	*bi-ja:nib*	بِجانِب
between	*bayn*	بَيْن
our	——*na*	نا
your (mp)	——*kum*	كُم
your (fp)	——*kin*	كِن
their (m)	——*hum*	هُم
their (f)	——*hin*	هِن
eleven	*h̲ida^{c}sh*	حِدَعْش
twelve	*ithna^{c}sh*	إِثْنَعْش
thirteen	*thala:ta^{c}sh*	ثلاتَعْش
fourteen	*arba^{c}ta^{c}sh*	أَرْبَعْتَعْش
fifteen	*khamsta^{c}sh*	خَمْسْتَعْش
sixteen	*sitta^{c}sh*	سِتَّعْش
seventeen	*saba^{c}ta^{c}sh*	سَبَعْتَعْش
eighteen	*thama:nta^{c}sh*	ثَمانْتَعْش
nineteen	*tisa^{c}ta^{c}sh*	تِسَعْتَعْش
twenty	*^{c}ashri:n*	عَشْرين
thirty	*thala:thi:n*	ثلاثين
forty	*arba^{c}i:n*	أَرْبعين
fifty	*khamsi:n*	خَمْسين
sixty	*sitti:n*	سِتّين
seventy	*saba^{c}i:n*	سَبعين
eighty	*thama:ni:n*	ثَمانين
ninety	*tis^{c}i:n*	تِسْعين
hundred	*miya*	مِيَة

Unit 5

Masculinity and femininity

As you have seen, Arabic makes a distinction between addressing a man and a woman.
For example,

Where are you from? (to a man)
inta min wayn? انتَ من وين ؟

Where are you from? (to a woman)
inti min wayn? انتِ من وين ؟

Many women's names are the same as men's names, but with the addition of a *ta:' marbu:ṯa*.
For example,

Adil (man's name)
ᶜa:dil عادل

Adila (woman's name)
ᶜa:dila عادلة

Aziz (man's name)
ᶜazi:z عزيز

Aziza (woman's name)
ᶜa:zi:za عزيزة

In Unit Four we saw that words ending in *ta:' marbu:ṯa* are considered feminine.
For example,

car
sayya:ra سيّارة

garden
ḫadi:ga حديقة

city
madi:na مدينة

In written Arabic the *ta:' marbu:ṯa* is the visual sign of a feminine word, though don't forget that for pronunciation purposes such a word ends with the short /a/ represented by the *fatha* which must always precede the *ta:' marbu:ta,* as shown in the transliteration.

1 Jobs and occupations

Vocabulary A Ⓣ

official, employee *muwadhdhaf*	مُوَظَّف	doctor *duktu:r*	دُكْتور
businessman, merchant *ta:jir*	تاجِر	secretary *sikriti:r*	سِكْرِتير
engineer *muhandis*	مُهَنْدِس	manager *mudi:r*	مُدير
teacher *mudarris*	مُدَرِّس	translator, interpreter *mutarjim*	مُتَرْجِم
clerk *ka:tib*	كاتِب	student, pupil *ta:lib*	طالِب

Masculine nouns describing jobs and occupations are made feminine by the addition of a *ta:' marbu:ta.*

teacher *mudarrisa*	مُدَرِّسَة	clerk *ka:tiba*	كاتِبَة
employee *muwadhdhafa*	مُوَظَّفَة		

Since the *ta: marbu:ta* is essentially a feature of the writing system and is not normally pronounced in spoken Arabic, the only audible difference between a masculine noun describing a job or occupation and its feminine equivalent is the short /a/ represented by the *fatha* which precedes the *ta:' marbu:ta.*

2 Talking about jobs

I'm an employee in the ministry (man talking)
ana muwadhdhaf fi l-wiza:ra — انا موظّف في الوزارة

I'm an employee in the bank (woman talking)
ana muwadhdhafa fi l-bank — انا موظّفة في البنك

Note Since there is no equivalent in Arabic for 'am', 'is', 'are' or 'a' and 'an', the sentences above translate literally as, '1 employee in the ministry' and '1 employee in the bank'.

To ask someone 'What's your job?' or 'What do you do?' you make the question in the same way as 'What's your name?' but substituting 'job' for 'name'.

Ⓣ

job *shughl*	شُغْل	your job (to a woman) *shughl-ik*	شُغلِك
my job *shughl-i*	شُغْلي	his job *shughl-a*	شُغْلَه
your job (to a man) *shughl-ak*	شُغْلَك	her job *shughl-ha*	شُغْلها

Remember that you are going to hear variations on the suffix /-ik/ when addressing a woman. In the eastern part of the Peninsula you will often hear /-ich/ and the suffix /-a/, 'his', may also be heard as /-u/.

Reading and repetition drill Ⓣ

Talking to a man

١ **Q** What do you do?
aysh shughl-ak?
ايش شغلَك ؟

A I'm an engineer.
ana muhandis
انا مهندس

Talking to a woman

٢ **Q** What's your job?
aysh shughl-ik?
ايش شغلِك ؟

A I'm a teacher.
ana mudarrisa
انا مدرّسة

Talking about a man

٣ **Q** What does he do?
aysh shughl-a?
ايش شغله ؟

A He's a merchant.
huwa ta:jir
هو تاجر

Talking about a woman

٤ **Q** What's her job?
aysh shughl-ha?
ايش شغلها

A She's a doctor.
hiya duktu:ra.
هي دكتورة

Pay attention to the pronunciation of this question.
The word for 'what' ends in /sh/ and the word for 'work' begins with /sh/.

Practice sentences (T)

1 **Q** What does he do?
aysh shughl-a? — ايش شغله؟ ١

A He's an official in the ministry.
huwa muwadhdhaf fi l-wiza:ra — هو موظّف في الوزارة

2 **Q** What's your job? (to a man)
aysh shughl-ak? — ايش شغلك؟ ٢

I'm a clerk in the bank.
ana ka:tib fi l-bank — انا كاتب في البنك

3 **Q** What's her job?
aysh shughl-ha? — ايش شغلها؟ ٣

A She's a doctor in the hospital.
hiya duktu:ra fi l-mustashfa — هي دكتورة في المستشفى

4 **Q** What do you do? (to a woman)
aysh shughl-ik? — ايش شغلك؟ ٤

A I'm a teacher at the university.
ana mudarrisa fi l-ja:mi^{c}a — انا مدرّسة في الجامعة

5 **Q** What does he do?
aysh shughl-a? — ايش شغله؟ ٥

A He's a merchant in the market.
huwa ta:jir fi s-su:g — هو تاجر في السّوق

Use these sentences for reading, writing and comprehension practice. Once you are happy with pronunciation and meaning, copy each of the pairs of sentences out in your own hand. Then use the tape drill for auto-dictation: play each sentence in turn, then try to write it down without consulting the book. Check your efforts, correct any errors and make sure you understand why the correct version is what it is before going on. Dictation is a very useful exercise, it helps attune the ear to the 'new' sounds, and is of general value in helping you develop your powers of comprehension. You may find dictation difficult at first; you will find it gets easier as you become more familiar with the language.

Translation

1 He's an engineer.
2 She's a student at the university.
3 He's in the office.
4 Is there an interpreter (m) in the office?
5 He's a doctor at the hospital in Abu Dhabi.

6 I'm a secretary (f).
7 Where's the manager (m)?
8 Is there a doctor in the building?
9 I'm an employee (f) at the airport.
10 I'm a teacher (f) at the school near here.

Points to note

a teacher
mudarris مدرّس *muᶜallim* معلّم

These words are synonymous and usually interchangeable within any one area. It may be that one of the two is used where you are living, in which case, learn that one and try to maintain at least a passive understanding of the other.

b employee, official
muwadhdhaf موظّف

This word has a wide application in Arabic. Used alone it is equivalent to English '(government) official' or 'civil servant', or employee; a person who works in an administrative or clerical capacity in an office, organization or company.

c manager
mudi:r مدير

This word is used to signify anyone who is in charge of anything, roughly equivalent to English 'manager', 'director', 'boss' or 'person in charge'.

d engineer
muhandis مهندس

This word tends to be used rather loosely in Arabic to describe anyone with any degree of practical technical skill. Thus in appropriate contexts it will translate as 'garage mechanic', 'plumber', 'electrician' or 'maintenance man',.as well as the more formal western classifications such as 'civil engineer', 'mechanical engineer', 'electrical engineer' etc.

e doctor
duktu:r دُكْتور *ṯabi:b* طَبيب

dakhtar دَخْتَر

You may hear all these versions of 'doctor'. The first two are clearly adopted from European languages, the third is the Arabic word. Use whichever you hear used most around you.

When they are used as titles, like English 'Dr Strangelove', they are preceded by *il,* 'the'. For example,

Dr Jekyll
id-duktu:r ji:kil — الدكتور جيكل

3 Some common adjectives

Adjectives in Arabic, like nouns, have different masculine and feminine forms. Here are three adjectives in their masculine form, as used when talking to or about a man.

Vocabulary B (T)

present
mawju:d — مَوْجود

busy
mashghu:l — مَشْغول

married
mitzawwij — مِتْزَوِّج

I'm busy. (man talking)
ana mashghu:l — انا مشغول

Is Ahmad married?
aḥmad mitzawwij? — احمد متزوّج ؟

He's present.
huwa mawju:d — هو موجود

Points to note

The Arabic word for 'present' is used in place of a wide range of English expressions signifying that someone is present or available. Thus in context this word can be variously translated as, 'he's here', 'he's around', 'he's in', 'he's present' or 'he's available'.

Feminine forms

The femine form of adjectives is made simply by the addition of *fatḥa* and *ta:' marbu:ṯa.*

I'm busy. (woman talking)
ana mashghu:la — انا مشغولة

Is Khadija married?
khadi:ja mitzawwija? — خديجة متزوجة ؟

She's present.
hiya mawju:da — هي موجودة

Negative

There are several versions of 'not' when making a noun or adjective negative.

All over the Peninsula, but especially in central and western Saudi Arabia, Riyadh and Jedda:

mu مو

In the Gulf States, Bahrain, Kuwait, Qatar, UAE and eastern Saudi Arabia, you will also hear:

mu:b موب

In Oman, Yemen and western parts of the Peninsula you will also hear:

mush مُش

mu:b is associated especially with the Gulf, the other two would be understood anywhere in the Peninsula. As always the cardinal rule is, listen and use what you hear used around you most frequently.

The examples below show all of the alternatives in use, and in future drills we will use them as interchangeable items.

(T) I'm not busy. (man talking)
ana mu mashghu:l انا مو مشغول

She isn't around.
hiya mush mawju:da هي مش موجودة

I'm not married. (woman talking)
ana mu:b mitzawwija انا موب متزوجة

He's not present.
huwa mu mawju:d هو مو موجود

Questions

In English, statements on the pattern of 'Ahmad's busy', 'she's married' are made into questions thus:

She's married. ——▷ Is she married?

In Arabic, the word order stays the same for both statements and questions of this kind. You show that you are asking a question simply by using rising intonation at the end of the sentence.

Is he around?
huwa mawju:d? هو موجود

Is Muhammad busy?
muḥammad mashghu:l?

محمد مشغول؟

Are you married? (to a woman)
inti mitzawwija?

انت متزوجة؟

Is she here?
hiya mawju:da?

هي موجودة

Are you busy? (to a woman)
inti mashghu:la?

انتِ مشغولة

Are you busy? (to a man)
inta mashghu:l?

انت مشغول؟

Answers

Q Is Hamid here?
ḥami:d mawju:d?

حامد موجود؟

A No, he isn't
la

لا

Q Is Adila married?
ʿa:dila mitzawwija?

عادلة متزوجة؟

A No
la

لا

In English it would usually be considered a little blunt to give
the bare reply 'yes' or 'no' to a question of this kind. We tend
to give 'short form' responses, ie, 'Yes, he is' or 'No, he isn't'.
In Arabic, the words for 'yes' and 'no' cover the full range of
English short form answers.

Substitution drill Ⓣ **Model question**
ḥami:d mawju:d?
Is Hamid here?

حميد موجود؟

Example substitution

cue *ʿa:dila*

عادلة

response *ʿa:dila mawju:da?*

عادلة موجودة؟

Cues

1	*muḥammad*	محمد	6	*khadi:ja*	خديجة
2	*jami:la*	جميلة	7	*sali:m*	سليم
3	*fa:ṭima*	فاطمة	8	*nu:riya*	نورية
4	*aḥmad*	احمد	9	*ḥusayn*	حسين
5	*ḥasan*	حسن	10	*sami:ra*	سميرة

Substitution drill Ⓣ

Model sentence
muhammad mush mawju:d. huwa fi l-maktab محمّد مش موجود. هو في المكتب
Muhammad's not here. He's in the office.

Example substitution

cue *jami:la —— jadda* جميلة—— جدّة

response *jami:la mush mawju:da.* جميلة مش موجودة .

hiya fi jadda هي في جدّة

cues

1 *muhammad —— mana:ma* محمّد —— منامة

2 *fa:tima —— il-bayt* فاطمة —— البيت

3 *ahmad —— is-si:nama* احمد —— السينما

4 *khadi:ja —— is-su:g* خديجة —— السوق

5 *husayn —— damma:m* حسين —— دمام

6 *sami:ra —— u:rubba* سميرة —— اوربّا

7 *hasan —— il-maktab* حسن —— المكتب

8 *jami:la —— amri:ka* جميلة —— امريكا

4 More about plurals

We saw in Unit Four both strong and broken plurals used to make the plurals of objects. In this unit we want to look at how to make the plurals of nouns and adjectives describing people.

The strong plural for words denoting males only is the suffix /-i:n/ added to the last letter of the singular word.

	Singular		Plural	
official	*muwadhdhaf*	موظّف	*muwadhdhafi:n*	موظّفين
teacher	*mudarris*	مدرّس	*mudarrisi:n*	مدرّسين

Although most nouns denoting males have strong plurals, some have broken plurals. Of those examples given earlier in this unit, two have broken plurals.

student, pupil	*ṯa:lib*	طالب	*ṯulla:b*	طُلّاب
doctor	*duktu:r*	دكتور	*daka:tira*	دَكاتِرَة

Since in the early stages of learning Arabic you cannot predict what the plural of a word is going to be, learn both the singular and plural of each noun as you encounter it. (A complete list of jobs and occupations, both singular and plural, is included in the vocabulary review at the end of this unit.)

The same strong plural suffix is added to adjectives describing males and mixed male-female groups. For example,

We are busy. (talking on behalf of a group)
iḫna mashgu:li:n احنا مشغولين

Are you married? (addressing a couple)
intum mitzawwiji:n? انتم متزّوجين؟

They are present.
hum mawju:di:n هم موجودين

As you have seen, all nouns describing jobs and occupations, and adjectives referring to women, are made feminine by the addition of a *ta:' marbu:ṯa* to the masculine form. The strong plural of feminine nouns and adjectives is formed by dropping the *ta:' marbu:ṯa* and replacing it by an *alif* and a *ta:'*, pronounced /-a:t/, as you saw in Unit Four. Thus the plurals of jobs and occupations when applied to women are formed as follows:

	Singular		**Plural**	
official	*muwadhdhafa*	موظّفة	*muwadhdhafa:t*	موظّفات
teacher	*mudarrisa*	مدرّسة	*mudarrisa:t*	مدرّسات
student	*ṯa:liba*	طالبة	*ṯa:liba:t*	طالبات
doctor	*duktu:ra*	دكتورة	*duktu.ra:t*	دكتورات

The same strong plural suffix is added to adjectives describing exclusively female groups. Thus,

We are busy. (speaking on behalf of a group of women)

iḫna mashghu:la:t احنا مشغولات

They are present. (talking about an all female group)

hin mawju:da:t هم موجودات

Note Unlike the strong masculine plural which is used only with nouns and adjectives relating to male persons, the strong feminine plural is used with things as well as people.

Make sure that you understand the principles behind plurals in Arabic. Study the section on broken plurals in Unit Four again.

Drills and exercises on these points will be included later in this unit and in following units. Learn only those plurals that you find you need most, never try to learn too much vocabulary at one time.

The 'dual'

Nouns in English are either singular or plural; in Arabic, nouns may be either singular (one), 'dual' (two) or plural (more than two). When talking about two of anything it is not usual to use *ithnayn* اثنين. Instead, the dual suffix *-ayn* ين is added to the end of the singular noun.

a book	*kita:b*	كتاب	two books	*kita:b-ayn*	كتابين
an office	*maktab*	مكتب	two offices	*maktab-ayn*	مكتبين
an employee	*muwaḏhḏhaf*	موظّف	two employees	*muwaḏhḏhaf-ayn*	موظّفين

If the singular noun ends in *ta:' marbu:ṯa* (as in the case of most feminine nouns), the *ta:' marbu:ṯa* is 'untied' and both pronounced and written as a regular *ta:* when the dual suffix is added.

a car *sayya:ra*	سيّارة	two cars *sayya:rat-ayn*	سيّارتين
a company *sharika*	شركة	two companies *sharikat-ayn*	شركتين

Transformation drill

office *maktab*	مكتب	two offices *maktab-ayn*	مكتبين
car *sayya:ra*	سيّارة	two cars *sayyarat-ayn*	سيّارتين
book *kita:b*	كتاب	two books *kita:b-ayn*	كتابين
company *sharika*	شركة	two companies *sharikat-ayn*	شركتين
building *bina:ya*	بناية	two buildings *bina:yat-ayn*	بنايتين
doctor *t̲abi:b*	طبيب	two doctors *t̲abi:b-ayn*	طبيبين
embassy *sifa:ra*	سفارة	two embassies *sifa:rat-ayn*	سفارتين
house *bayt*	بيت	two houses *bayt-ayn*	بيتين

Supplementary section 5.1 Greetings

Common alternatives you might hear in reply to 'How are you?' are,

zayn	زَيْن	*kwayyis*	كوَيِّس
t̲ayyib	طَيِّب	*murta:h̲*	مُرْتاح
mabsu:t̲	مبْسوط	*tama:m*	تَمام

These can be used instead of

bi-khayr بخير

either on their own, or in combination with

il-h̲amdu li-lla:h الحمدُ لله

When the above are used, they must be made feminine if a woman is answering or being talked about, by the addition of a *fatha* and *ta:' marbu:ta* to the last letter. In pronunciation, of course, you will only hear the short /a/ represented by the *fatha*.

Addressing a man

A How are you? كيف حالَك؟
kayf ha:l-ak?

B Very well. زين الحمدُ لله
zayn il-hamdu li-lla:h

How are you? كيف حالَك؟
kayf ha:l-ak?

A Fine, thanks. كويّس
kwayyis

Addressing a woman

A How are you? كيف حالِك؟
kayf ha:l-ik?

B Very well, thanks. مبسوطة
mabsu:ta

How are you? كيف حالِك؟
kayf ha:l-ik?

A Very well. زينة الحمدُ لله
zayna il-hamdu li-lla:h

Of these alternatives *zayn* is more specific to the Gulf region and eastern Saudi Arabia. *kwayyis,* although commonly used in Egyptian Arabic, has very common currency all over the Arab world. The others are used and understood all over the Peninsula.

Supplementary section 5.2
Jobs

Here is an extensive list of jobs and occupations you are likely to encounter among both western and Arab expatriates and local workers. At present, learn only those words which are relevant to your present needs, ie your own occupation, those of your family, friends and regular contacts. You can always come back to this list for reference later.

All the following words are given in their masculine singular form. In each case you arrive at the feminine singular by adding *fatḫa* and *ta:' marbu:ta* to the masculine.

Words which share certain common features have been grouped together. You may find this useful as an aid to learning and also as an insight into how Arabic works.

A

official, employee
muwadhdhaf — مُوَظَّف

teacher
mudarris — مُدَرِّس

muᶜallim — مُعَلِّم

manager, director
mudi:r — مُدير

delegate, representative
mandu:b — مَنْدوب

attaché
mulḫag — مُلْحَق

person responsible, in charge
masu:'l — مَسْؤول

engineer
muhandis — مُهَنْدِس

lawyer
muḫa:mi — مُحامي

accountant
muḫa:sib — مُحاسِب

translator, interpreter
mutarjim — مُتَرجِم

assistant
musa:ᶜid — مُساعد

nurse
mumarriḏ — مُمَرِّض

'Hairdresser' in Arabic

'Tailor' in Arabic

B

tailor		carpenter	
khayya:ṯ	خَيّاط	*najja:r*	نَجّار
barber		doorman, concierge	
ḥalla:g	حَلاّق	*bawwa:b*	بَوّاب
cook		driver	
ṯabba:kh	طَبّاخ	*suwwa:g*	سُوّاق
baker			
khabba:z	خَبّاز	*draywil*	دَرَيْوِل

fisherman
s̱ayya:d صَيّاد

sailor
baẖha:r بَحّار

pilot
ṯayya:r طَيّار

welder
laẖha:m لَحّام

porter
ẖamma:l حَمّال

C

minister
wazi:r وَزير

ambassador
safi:r سَفير

expert
khabi:r خَبير

prince
ami:r أَمير

doctor
ṯabi:b طَبيب

D

officer
ḏa:biṯ ضابِط

guard, watchman
ẖa:ris حارِس

clerk
ka:tib كاتِب

student
ṯa:lib طالِب

merchant, businessman
ta:jir تاجِر

E

These are miscellaneous items not sharing any common pattern.

secretary
sikriti:r سِكْرِتير

policeman
shurṯi شُرْطي

soldier
jundi جُنْدي

journalist
s̱aẖa:fi صَحافي

politician, diplomat
siya:si سِياسي

vet, veterinarian
ṯabi:b bayṯari طَبيب بَيْطَري

king
malik مَلِك

doctor
duktu:r دُكْتور

Supplementary section 5.3
Hospitality

The Arabs are a prodigiously hospitable people, a fact you will have ample opportunity to verify for yourself if you spend any length of time in the Middle East.

'A guest, whether rich or poor, city dweller or desert bedouin, is treated with the same courtesy and respect . . .. Though the actual standards of hospitality are set by custom, the Arab applies them with a spontaneity and warmth that reflects his sincere enjoyment in entertaining his guest. The most common gesture of hospitality among all Arabs is the serving of coffee. In the cities, especially in the summer, the visitor to a shop may well be offered a choice between coffee, tea or a cold soft drink. Coffee cups are generally small and without handles, like Oriental teacups. The server procedes around the circle of guests in order of their rank, pouring as many drinks as each desires. The guest indicates that he has had enough by shaking the cup and handing it back to the server. Although some say that it is good form to accept one cup or three, but never two or more than three, there is no firm rule. Small glasses of hot tea are frequently served to guests after coffee. The tea is always sweetened, and milk is sometimes added. When coffee is followed by tea, it is customary to offer guests yet another round or two of coffee.' (Dr J L Curtis *Bahrain: language, customs and people)*

It will be very well received by your Arab friends and social and business contacts if you make an effort to reciprocate in like manner the hospitality you are bound to encounter. You can use the following items and short dialogue in welcoming someone to your home or place of work.

Make yourself at home
bayt-i bayt-kum بيْتي بيْتكُم

tea
sha:i شاي

coffee
gahwa قَهْوَة

In the Gulf and eastern part of the Peninsula, this is pronounced
cha:i

Dialogue

A Hello.
ahlan اهلاً

B Welcome.
ahlan wa sahlan اهلاً وسهلاً

bayt-i bayt-kum بيتي بيتكم

A How are you (m)?
kayf ḥa:l-ak? كيف حالك؟

B Very well, thank you.
bi-khayr il-ḥamdu li-lla:h بخير الحمدُ لله

Here you are, have some coffee.
tfaḏḏal gahwa تَفَضّل قهوة

A Thank you.
shukran شكراً

'Coffee should not be received with the left hand . . .. The empty cup should never be placed on the floor nor turned over.' (J van Ess *Spoken Arabic of Iraq)*

Etiquette pertaining to the offering and receiving of hospitality in the Arab world is highly formalised. In particular, you should use only the right hand for drinking and eating, especially when taking food from a communal dish, since the left hand is considered unclean.

At meal times guests often sit on the floor, taking their food from a flat tray or mat. On such occasions you should avoid sitting in such a way that the sole of your foot is presented to another person — like the left hand, the sole of the foot is unclean, and its exposure carries the connotation of a deliberate insult.

New vocabulary in Unit 5

The plural forms follow the Arabic script and transliteration in brackets.

official/employee
muwadhdhaf (-i:n) مُوَظَّف (ين)

businessman, merchant
ta:jir (tujja:r) تاجر (تُجّار)

engineer
muhandis(-i:n) مُهَنْدِس (ين)

teacher
mudarris (-i:n) مُدَرِّس (ين)

clerk
ka:tib (kutta:b) كاتِب (كُتّاب)

doctor
ṯabi:b (aṯṯibba:') طَبيب (أَطِبّاء)

duktu:r (daka:tira) دُكْتور (دكاتِرَة)

dakhtar (dakha:tir) دَخْتَر (دَخاتِر)

secretary
sikriti:r (-i:n) سِكْرِتير (ين)

translator, interpreter
mutarjim (-i:n) مُتَرْجِم (ين)

student, pupil
ṯa:lib (ṯulla:b) طالِب (طُلّاب)

manager
mudi:r (mudara:') مُدير (مُدَراء)

work
shughl شُغْل

present
mawju:d مَوْجود

busy
mashghu:l مَشْغول

married
mitzawwij مِتْزَوِّج

not
mu مو

mu:b موب

mush مُش

Unit 6

1 More about adjectives

Position of adjectives

This advertisement, taken from an English magazine, showing the same sentence in a variety of European languages and Arabic clearly illustrates that there is no 'a' or 'an' in Arabic. It also highlights another feature of the language.

A new name in Luxembourg
Un nouveau nom à Luxembourg
Ein neuer Name in Luxemburg
Um novo nome em Luxemburgo
Un nuevo nombre en Luxemburgo
Un nuovo nome in Lussemburgo
Een neien Numm zu Letzeburg
En neue Name in Luxeburg
Новое имя в Люксембурге
اسم حديد في لوكسنبورغ
ルクセンブルグに新しい名前誕生！

You will see that in all the European languages represented (except Russian), the adjective corresponding to 'new' comes before the noun 'name'. As you know the words for 'name' and 'in', and as the last word is 'Luxembourg' transliterated into Arabic script, you can guess that

jadi:d جَديد

is the Arabic for 'new', and at the same time see that in Arabic *adjectives follow nouns.*

Vocabulary A

new
jadi:d جَديد

old
gadi:m قَديم

large, big, old
kabi:r كَبير

small, little, young
s̲aghi:r صَغير

cheap
rakhi:s̲ رَخيص

expensive
gha:li غالي

hot
h̲a:rr حارّ

cold
ba:rid بارِد

near, nearby
gari:b قَريب

far, far away
ba^{c}i:d بَعيد

(There is a more comprehensive list of adjectives in supplementary section 2 at the end of this unit.)

Note

a The Arabic for 'old' when talking about people is:

kabi:r كَبير

The other word for 'old':

gadi:m قَديم

is used only when talking about *things,* never people.

b In the Gulf States and eastern Saudi Arabia, you will hear the word for 'large' or 'big' pronounced thus:

big, large
chabi:r كَبير

Adjectives with nouns

The following examples show these new words in use with vocabulary you have seen earlier.

Ⓣ a hot day
yawm h̲a:rr يوم حارّ

an expensive restaurant
mat̲^{c}am gha:li مطعم غالي

a large hotel
fundug kabi:r فندق كبير

a small house
bayt ṣaghi:r بيت صغير

If the noun is feminine, that is ending in *ta:' marbu:ṭa,* the following adjective must also end in *ta:' marbu:ṭa*. Remember that since this letter is essentially a feature of the writing system and is not normally pronounced in spoken Arabic, the only audible effect is the short /a/ represented by the *fatḥa* which precedes it.

Ⓣ a new city
madi:na jadi:da مدينة جديدة

a big building
bina:ya kabi:ra بناية كبيرة

a small car
sayya:ra ṣaghi:ra سيّارة صغيرة

a cheap apartment
shigga rakhi:ṣa شقة رخيصة

Look at the map of the Arabian Peninsula and the Gulf below with some familiar geographical names written in Arabic.

Map of the Arabian Peninsula and the Gulf

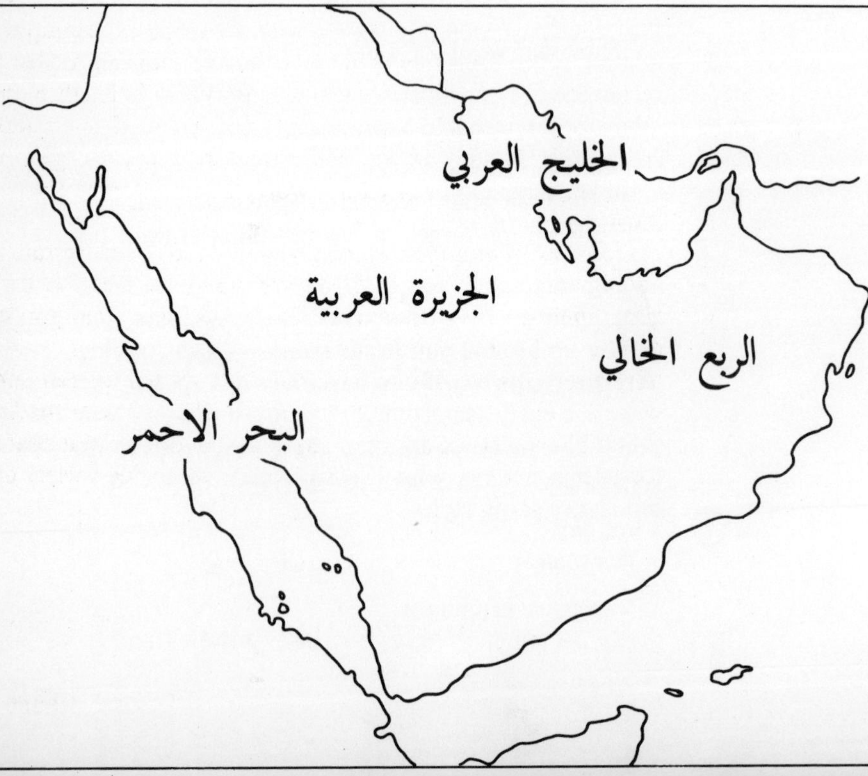

Adjectives with the definite article

Note the title of the map,

Ⓣ The Middle East
ish-sharg il-awsaṯ إِلشَّرْق إِلأَوْسَط

This literally means 'the east the middle'.

In Arabic, when a noun is definite, ie, prefixed by *il,* 'the', the following adjective describing it must also be made definite; it too must be prefixed by *il.* The literal translation sounds rather curious to our ears, but it is a feature of the language you must learn to use and get used to hearing.

The other names on the map also illustrate this feature.

Ⓣ The Arabian Gulf
il-khali:j il-ᶜarabi إِلْخَلِيج إِلْعَرَبِي

The Red Sea
il-baẖr il-aẖmar إِلْبَحْر إِلأَحْمَر

The Empty Quarter
ir-rubᶜ il-kha:li إِلرُّبْع إِلْخَالِي

If the noun is feminine, ie, ending in *ta:'marbuṯa,* the adjective must also end in *ta:'marbu:ṯa:*

Ⓣ The Arabian Peninsula
il-jazi:ra il-ᶜarabiyya إِلْجَزِيرَة إِلْعَرَبِيَّة

We have illustrated this feature with geographical examples related to the Peninsula to familiarise you with the Arabic for certain names and titles we assume you know in English and might be interested in learning. It is not intended as essential vocabulary. So long as you understand the principle operating in these examples you need not worry about learning the words involved.

However, if you look around you at shop, hotel, restaurant and cinema names you will discover the above mentioned geographical names often used. Try to decipher what you see written up around you in the streets — signs, notices, advertisements etc. If you have only just started to read and write use every opportunity you can to improve your reading skills. The streets of an Arab city provide an excellent chance for you to practice your reading ability on a wide variety of decorative script styles.

'Pharmacy' in Arabic

(T) the big house
il-bayt il-kabi:r — البيت الكبير

the cheap shop
id-dukka:n ir-rakhi:s̲ — الدكان الرخيص

the expensive restaurant
il-mat̲^{c}*am il-gha:li* — المطعم الغالي

the small car
is-sayya:ra is̲-s̲aghi:ra — السيّارة الصغيرة

the old city
il-madi:na il-gadi:ma — المدينة القديمة

the new building
il-bina:ya il-jadi:da — البناية الجديدة

Adjectives used without the definite article

Since there is no equivalent for 'is' or 'are' in Arabic, sentences like 'The house is big' can be made out of a noun and an adjective like this:

the house is big
il-bayt kabi:r — البيت كبير

the car is small
is-sayya:ra s̲aghi:ra — السيّارة صغيرة

Note the difference in sense between:

the big house
il-bayt il-kabi:r البيت الكبير

and:

the house is big
il-bayt kabi:r البيت كبير

So make sure that you don't say one while meaning the other. 'The house is big' is a complete sentence in itself, while 'the big house' is not.

(T) The city is old.
il-madi:na gadi:ma المدينة قديمة

The room is large.
il-ghurfa kabi:ra الغرفة كبيرة

The shop is new.
id-dukka:n jadi:d الدكان جديد

The house is small.
il-bayt s̲aghi:r البيت صغير

The apartment is expensive.
ish-shigga gha:liya الشقّة غالية

The market is nearby.
is-su:g gari:b السوق قريب

The cinema is far away.
is-si:nama ba^{c}*i:d* السينما بعيد

The car is cheap.
is-sayya:ra rakhi:s̲a السيّارة رخيصة

Of course, if you have two adjectives describing a noun, they both follow it. Generally the adjective which comes nearest the noun in English will also be nearest the noun in Arabic.

a small new house
bayt jadi:d s̲aghi:r بيت جديد صغير

the expensive new house
il-bayt il-jadi:d il-gha:li البيت الجديد الغالي

If the noun is feminine, you must add a *ta:' marbu:t̲a* to both the adjectives.

A small new car
sayya:ra jadi:da s̲aghi:ra سيارة جديدة صغيرة

The large new car
is-sayya:ra il-jadi:da il-kabi:ra السيارة الجديدة الكبيرة

Make up combinations of nouns with two adjectives from the vocabulary at your disposal. Pay attention to the feminine nouns.

2 This

There are two words for 'this' in Arabic, one for use with masculine nouns, the other with feminine nouns.

this (m) *ha:dha*	هٰذا	this (f) *ha:dhi*	هٰذي

Note the *dagger alif* written above the *ha:'* in these words. It is a feature of written Arabic that has survived in only a few words today. You have seen it once before in the Arabic word for 'God'. It is not always necessary to indicate the *dagger alif* when writing these words, but you must be aware of the effect it has on pronunciation. The transliteration represents it as an ordinary *alif,* /a:/.

Notice also the spelling of the feminine form, where the final *ha:'* ه is not pronounced. For pronunciation purposes in spoken Arabic this word is considered as ending with the *kasra* (the short *i* sound) which precedes the *ha:'*.

If the noun is masculine, use the masculine form of 'this':

This is Ahmad
ha:dha ahmad هٰذا أحمد

This is a new house
ha:dha bayt jadi:d هٰذا بيت جديد

If the noun is feminine, use the femine form:

This is Fatima
ha:dhi fa:tima هٰذي فاطمة

This is an old building
ha:dhi bina:ya gadi:ma هٰذي بناية قديمة

Substitution drill Ⓣ

Model sentence
ha:dha mat^cam jadi:d هٰذا مطعم جديد
This is a new restaurant.

Example substitution
cue *madi:na jadi:da* مدينة جديدة

response *ha:dhi madi:na jadi:da* هٰذي مدينة جديدة

Cues

1 *madi:na jadi:da* مدينة جديدة

2 *aḫmad* احمد

3 *sha:ri^c jadi:d* شارع جديد

4 *fundug gha:li* فندق غالي

5 *bina:ya kabi:ra* بناية كبيرة

6 *madi:na kabi:ra* مدينة كبيرة

7 *sayya:ra s̱aghi:ra* سيّارة صغيرة

8 *shigga rakhi:s̱a* شقّة رخيصة

9 *bayt kabi:r* بيت كبير

10 *maṯ^cam rakhi:s̱* مطعم رخيص

The other kind of sentence in which 'this' is most commonly used has this pattern: 'This (noun) is (adjective)', for example, 'This house is new.' In the Arabic for sentences of this pattern, you must use *il*, 'the' with the noun.

This house is new
ha:dha l-bayt jadi:d هٰذا البيت جديد

This literally means, 'This the house new.'

This flat is big
ha:dhi sh-shigga kabi:ra هٰذي الشقّة كبيرة

This literally means, 'This the flat big'.

Notice that both words for 'this' end in a vowel and that when they are followed by *il* 'the', the written /i/ of *il* is neither pronounced nor reflected in transliteration.

This feature often poses a problem for native speakers of English. Contrast these pairs of sentences. In both English and Arabic each pair of sentences means much the same thing, but they provide a choice of expression.

This house is large
ha:dha l-bayt kabi:r هٰذا البيت كبير

This is a large house
ha:dha bayt kabi:r — هٰذا بيت كبير

This flat is new
ha:dhi sh-shigga jadi:da — هٰذي الشقّة جديدة

This is a new flat
ha:dhi shigga jadi:da — هذي شقّة جديدة

Substitution drill Ⓣ

Model sentence
ha:dhi l-madi:na kabi:ra — هٰذي المدينة كبيرة
This town is large.

Example substitution
cue: *bayt* —— *jadi:d* — بيت —— جديد

response: *ha:dha l-bayt jadi:d* — هٰذا البيت جديد

Cues

1 *sayya:ra* —— *gha:liya* — سيّارة —— غالية

2 *maktab* —— *ṣaghi:r* — مكتب —— صغير

3 *madi:na* —— *jadi:da* — مدينة —— جديدة

4 *bayt* —— *kabi:r* — بيت —— كبير

5 *shigga* —— *rakhi:ṣa* — شقّة —— رخيصة

6 *bina:ya* —— *gadi:ma* — بناية —— قديمة

7 *maṭ[c]am* —— *gha:li* — مطعم —— غالي

8 *bayt* —— *ṣaghi:r* — بيت —— صغير

9 *madi:na* —— *kabi:ra* — مدينة —— كبيرة

10 *sayya:ra* —— *jadi:da* — سيّارة —— جديدة

3 Colours

Vocabulary B
Masculine forms

Ⓣ

red *aẖmar*	أَحْمَر	white *abyaḏ*	أَبْيَض
green *akhḏar*	أَخْضَر	blue *azrag*	أَزْرَق
yellow *as̱far*	أَصْفَر	brown *bunni*	بُنِّي
black *aswad*	أَسْوَد	orange *burtuga:li*	بُرْتُقالي

Note The first six colour adjectives all share a common pattern.

a They all begin with an *alif* which is the 'bearer' for the *fatẖa*.
b They all have a *suku:n* on the second letter.
c They all have a *fatẖa* on the third letter.

Feminine

The above are the masculine forms of the colour adjectives. To make the feminine form of most adjectives you simply add *ta:' marbu:ṯa* to the masculine form. The colour adjectives, however, have their own distinctive pattern for the feminine forms.

Ⓣ

red *ẖamra*	حَمْراء	black *sawda*	سَوْداء
green *khaḏra*	خَضْراء	white *bayḏa*	بَيْضاء
yellow *s̱afra*	صَفْراء	blue *zarga*	زَرْقاء

It is only these six colours which have this special form. They all have a common pattern.

a They all have *fatẖa* on the first letter.
b They all have *suku:n* on the second letter.
c They all end in *alif* with a *hamza* written on the line.

Note that in pronunciation the *hamza* at the end of a word is rarely heard in speech at normal conversational speed. When such a word is spoken in isolation, or uttered with particular clarity for the sake of a foreigner, you may hear the *hamza*. This is a catch in the throat rather like the sound at the end of the word 'ticket' when the final 't' is not pronounced. In transliteration, an *alif* followed by a final *hamza* will usually appear simply as /a/, with no allowance made for the rarely pronounced *hamza*. In written Arabic, on the other hand, the final *hamza* will always appear. (See *Macmillan Arabic Book 1*, Unit 9.)

The other colour adjectives make their feminine by adding /-yya/.

brown (describing feminine object)
bunniyya — بُنِّيَّة

orange (describing feminine object)
burtaga:liyya — بُرْتَقَالِيَّة

The importance of gender in Arabic can cause problems for English learners since English does not have this feature.

For example, a white car is:

white car
sayya:ra bayḏa — سيّارة بيضاء

Car is feminine, so white, in this case, is also feminine. However, should you incorrectly say:

white car
sayya:ra abyaḏ — سيّارة أبيض

using the masculine form of white, you will be understood. Don't forget that although Arabic makes distinctions between genders, such distinctions do not change the meaning. So if you make a slip like the above example, and although the phrase may jar on the ear of a native speaker of Arabic, the phrase is not unintelligible. Our advice is, always aim to speak as correctly as possible, since something mis-learned in the early stages of language learning takes a long time to un-learn later on, but if you make slips and realize it, go back and correct what you have just said.

Structured conversation

With your teacher or Arabic speaking friend, play the roles of two strangers meeting for the first time. First greet each other and enquire about each other's health. Remember that these formal preliminaries are very important in Arabic, so prolong this phase of the conversation and try to use a variety of the courtesy phrases you have learned.

Next try to find out as much as possible about each other, your names, where you are from, your jobs, where you work, where you live, etc, using structures and vocabulary you have learned from the book together with variants and any additional items you may have picked up elsewhere.

Rehearse the conversation first, stopping to check items you are unsure of, then run through it several times entirely in Arabic.

Supplementary section 6.1 Colours

To help you remember these colour adjectives, we have selected a number of common phrases, names and titles that you will hear used in everyday speech which include a colour.

Red

Everyday uses

a watermelon
batti:kh ahmar بَطِّيخ احمر

This literally means 'red melon'. Other common words in the Peninsula for melon are:

watermelon (particularly in the Gulf and eastern Peninsula)
juhh جُحّ

watermelon (in North Yemen)
habhab حَبحَب

b tea without milk
sha: ahmar شاي احمر

This means 'red tea'. In English we sometimes say 'black tea'.

Names

a The Red Crescent
il-hila:l il-ahmar اِلْهلال الاحمر

This is the corresponding organization in the Islamic countries to the Red Cross.

b The Red Sea
il-bahr il-ahmar البحر الاحمر

The sea between the east coast of Africa and the Arabian Peninsula.

Points of interest

a Alhambra is the name of the superb 11th century palace in Granada, Spain, built by the Muslim conquerors of Spain. The English name is derived from the Arabic name:

Alhambra
il-hamra الحمراء

It literally means 'the red (palace)'. It is also the name of numerous cinemas throughout the West and the Middle East.

b Hamra
il-ḫamra الحمراء

'Hamra' is also the name of the major shopping street and commercial quarter in Beirut, Lebanon.

Green

Everyday uses

green pepper
filfil akhḏar فِلْفِل اخضر

Names

a The Green Mountain
il-jabal il-akhḏar اِلْجَبَل الاخضر

This is the highest mountain in the Arabian Peninsula, in Oman.

b The Green Valley
il-wa:di il-akhḏar اِلْوادي الاخضر

This is a supermarket chain with branches in most peninsular countries.

Points of interest
The Arabic for 'vegetables' is based on the word for 'green'. There are a couple of versions of this word you may hear:

vegetables
khuḏa:r خُضار *khaḏra:wa:t* خَضْراوات

Yellow

Everyday uses

honeydew melon
baṯṯi:kh aṣfar بطيخ اصفر

This literally means 'yellow melon'. Another common word you will hear used for this kind of melon is:

honeydew melon
shamma:m شَمّام

An aid to remembering the Arabic word for 'yellow' is its similarity to 'saffron', a yellow spice.

Black

Everyday uses

black pepper
filfil aswad فلفل اسود

Points of interest
The name of the country 'Sudan' is based on the word for 'black':

the Sudan
is-su:da:n السودان

White

Everyday uses

eggs
bayḏ بَيْض

This literally means 'white things'.

Names

a The Mediterranean
il-baḫr il-abyaḏ البحر الابيض

b Casablanca. The name of the seaport in western Morocco is in Arabic:

id-da:r il-bayḏa الدار البيضاء

da:r is a classical alternative to *bayt* for 'house', and is a feminine noun, hence the use of the feminine form of the colour adjective. The same word is also used for the White House, the seat of the American Presidency in Washington DC.

Supplementary section 6.2
Adjectives

(T)

open		
maftu:ḥ	مَفْتوح	
mafku:k	مَفْكوك	
closed		
mubannad	مُبَنَّد	
mughallag	مُغَلَّق	
clean		
nadhi:f	نَظيف	
dirty		
wasikh	وَسِخ	
long, tall		
ṭawi:l	طَويل	
short		
gaṣi:r	قَصير	
thick		
thakhi:n	ثَخين	
fat		
sami:n	سَمين	
thin		
khafi:f	خَفيف	
beautiful, nice		
jami:l	جَميل	
deep		
ᶜami:g	عَميق	
heavy		
thagi:l	ثَقيل	
wide		
wa:siᶜ	واسِع	
narrow		
ḍayyig	ضَيِّق	
light		
khafi:f	خَفيف	
regular, ordinary		
ᶜa:di	عادي	

excellent		
mumta:z	مُمْتاز	
warm		
da:fi	دافي	
difficult		
ṣaᶜb	صَعْب	
easy		
basi:ṭ	بَسيط	
sahl	سَهْل	
empty		
fa:ḍi	فاضي	
full		
malya:n	مَليان	
square		
murabbaᶜ	مُرَبَّع	
round		
mudawwar	مُدَوَّر	
circular		
mustadi:r	مُسْتَدير	
triangular		
muthallath	مُثَلَّث	
east(ern)		
shargi	شَرْقي	
west(ern)		
gharbi	غَرْبي	
north(ern)		
shima:li	شِمالي	
south(ern)		
junu:bi	جُنوبي	
grey		
rama:di	رَمادي	

gold
dhahabi ذَهَبي

silver
fiḏḏi فِضّي

brown
asmar أَسْمَر

Supplementary section 6.3 Pronunciation variants

A further pronunciation variant to note concerns the letter *ji:m* ج normally pronounced like the 'j' in English 'juice'. In certain areas of the Gulf, the *ji:m* is pronounced like the 'y' in English 'young'. In these areas, the word for 'new' will be pronounced:

new
yadi:d جديد

In the two Yemens south of the Samarra Pass, and in parts of Oman, the *ji:m* is pronounced like the 'g' in English 'get'. Thus, you will hear the same word in these areas pronounced as:

new
gadi:d جديد

This pronunciation variant is also typical of the northern Egyptian dialect, so you should listen for it also in areas where there are concentrations of ex-patriate Egyptian Arabs.

To recap, then, you will encounter three common pronunciation variants in the Peninsula.

i ك

/ch/	in the Gulf and eastern Saudi Arabia
/k/	elsewhere

ii ق

/q/	southern YAR, and PDRY
/g/	elsewhere

iii ج

/y/	in the Gulf and eastern Saudi Arabia
/g/	southern YAR, and PDRY
/j/	elsewhere

New vocabulary in Unit 6

new *jadi:d*	جَديد	cheap *rakhi:ṣ*	رَخيص
old *gadi:m*	قَديم	expensive *gha:li*	غالي
big, old *kabi:r*	كَبير	hot *ḥa:rr*	حار
small, young *ṣaghi:r*	صَغير	cold *ba:rid*	بارِد

The Middle East *ish-sharg il-awsat*	إِلشَّرْق إِلأَوْسَط
The Gulf *il-khali:j il-^{c}arabi*	إِلْخَليج إِلْعَرَبي
The Red Sea *il-baḥr il-aḥmar*	إِلْبَحْر إِلأَحْمَر
The Empty Quarter *ir-rub^c il-kha:li*	إِلرُّبْع إِلْخالي
The Peninsula *il-jazi:ra il-^{c}arabiyya*	إِلْجزيرة إِلْعَرَبِيَّة

this (m) *ha:dha*	هٰذا	black *aswad*	أَسْوَد
this (f) *ha:dhi*	هٰذِه	white *abyaḍ*	أَبْيَض
red *aḥmar*	أَحْمَر	blue *azrag*	أَزْرَق
green *akhḍar*	أَخْضَر	brown *bunni*	بُنّي
yellow *aṣfar*	أَصْفَر	orange *burtuga:li*	بُرْتُقالي

Unit 7

1 Family and friends

Vocabulary A Ⓣ

husband		friend (female)	
zawj	زَوْج	*ṣadi:ga*	صَديقَة
wife		*ṣa:ḥiba*	صاحِبَة
zawja	زَوْجَة	with	
ḥurma	حُرْمَة	*ma^ca*	مَعَ
friend (male)			
ṣadi:g	صَديق		
ṣa:ḥib	صاحِب		

When a word ending in *ta:' marbu:ṭa* is followed by one of the personal suffixes, the *ta:' marbu:ṭa* is 'opened' and both pronounced and written like a regular *ta'*.

my wife					
zawjat-i	زوجتي	=	ي	+	زوجة
ḥurmat-i	حرمتي	=	ي	+	حرمة
her friend (female)					
ṣadi:gat-ha	صديقتها	=	ها	+	صديقة
ṣa:ḥibat-ha	صاحبتها	=	ها	+	صاحبة

Translation Ⓣ Translate the sentences below into Arabic. Check vocabulary, spelling and structural accuracy carefully before comparing your efforts with the key at the end of the book.

1 My friend Aziza is at home.
2 Adil isn't here. He's in the Ministry.
3 Ahmad's in America with his wife.
4 Where's Muhammad? He's at the office with Hasan.
5 Are you busy? (addressing a woman)
6 What's your job? (addressing a man)
7 He's a doctor at the new hospital.
8 She's a student at the University.
9 Samira isn't at home, she's in the market with Shaykha.
10 Is there a restaurant near here?

2 More about possession

One way to indicate possession is to attach a personal suffix (my, your, his, her) to a noun.

my name
ism-i اسمي

her house
bayt-ha بيتها

your job (addressing a man)
shughl-ak شغلك

his wife
zawjat-a زَوْجَتَه

In English, when we want to refer to something belonging to someone by their name or title, we indicate possession by adding an apostrophed *s* to the last letter of the name or title. For example, *Muhammad's house* or *the ambassador's house*. To convey this kind of possession in Arabic, you simply replace the personal suffix with a noun in the same position.

my house ('house my')
bayt-i بيتي

Muhammad's house ('house Muhammad')
bayt muḫammad بيت محمد

the ambassador's house ('house the ambassador')
bayt is-safi:r بيت السفير

Note

a In English the possessor precedes the thing possessed.

b In Arabic, the 'thing possessed' *always* comes before the possessor.

c When a noun ending in *ta:' marbu:ṯa* is followed by a personal suffix, the *ta:' marbu:ṯa* is 'opened' and both written and pronounced like a regular *ta:'*.

his wife
zawjat-a زوجته

her friend (f)
ṣadi:gat-ha صديقتها

If the personal suffix in phrases such as these is replaced by a noun, the *ta:' marbu:ṯa* is 'opened' in pronunciation only.

Ⓣ Muhammad's wife
zawjat muḫammad زوجة محمد

Jamila's friend (f)
ṣadi:gat jami:la صديقة جميلة

Ahmad's car
sayya:rat aḫmad سيّارة احمد

Aziza's flat
shiggat ʿazi:za شقّة عزيزة

Sometimes the second noun, the possessor, is itself followed by a personal suffix.

Ⓣ his wife's job
shughl zawjat-a شغل زوجته

her husband's name
ism zawj-ha اسم زوجها

my friend's house (m)
bayt ṣadi:g-i بيت صديقي

your wife's name
ism zawjat-ak اسم زوجتك

The same construction is used in Arabic to translate English phrases on the pattern:

the . . . of . . .

For example:

Ⓣ The capital of Lebanon ('capital Lebanon')
ᶜa:ṣimat lubna:n عاصمة لبنان

The capital of Egypt ('capital Egypt')
ᶜa:ṣimat maṣr عاصمة مصر

The Bank of Dubai ('Bank Dubai')
bank dubayy بنك دبي

The Ministry of Petroleum ('Ministry the Petroleum')
wiza:rat an-nafṯ وزارة النفط

The Ministry of Health ('Ministry the Health')
wiza:rat aṣ-ṣiḥḥa وزارة الصحة

The Arabic word order is the same as the English, but

a In Arabic the first noun never has the definite article الـ *il* 'the'.

b The second noun must always be definite. Note that all place names are intrinsically definite, whether or not they are preceded by the definite article. All other nouns must be made definite by the addition of الـ *il* in phrases of this kind.

c If the first of the two nouns ends in ة *ta:' marbu:ta,* the ة is 'opened' and pronounced like regular ت *ta:',* but this change is not reflected in the way the word is written.

You will find that the names of most government departments are formed according to this pattern. We include a more exhaustive list in supplementary section 7.1.

The same construction is commonly used in two other situations:

i In the Arabic equivalent for English phrases on the pattern: *the* + *noun* + *noun*; for example, the post office:

Ⓣ the post office ('office the post')
maktab il-bari:d مكتب البريد

the company office ('office the company')
maktab ish-sharika مكتب الشركة

the door key ('key the door')
mifta:ẖ il-ba:b مفتاح الباب

the car key ('key the car')
mifta:ẖ is-sayya:ra مفتاح السيّارة

ii In Muslim men's names consisting of the noun عبد *abd* 'servant', followed by one of the '99 names of God'.

Abd Allah ('servant (of) Allah')
ᶜabd alla:h عبد الله

Abd il-Qadir ('servant (of) the Omnipotent')
ᶜabd il-qa:dir عبد القادر

Abd ir-Rahman ('servant (of) the Compassionate')
ᶜabd ir-raẖma:n عبد الرحمن

You should note that it is not customary to abbreviate names of this kind, except sometimes when a fair degree of familiarity has been established with the person in question. Steer clear of the common European tendency to shorten such names to 'Abdul', it is both incorrect and discourteous.

'Abd Allah' in Arabic

3 How to describe family relationships

Here is the vocabulary you will need to describe the nuclear family. Using this vocabulary we want to explore the different ways of explaining family relationships.

Vocabulary B Ⓣ

father *abu*	أَبو	brother *akh*	أَخ
mother *umm*	أُمّ	sister *ukht*	أُخْت

Ⓣ 1 Ahmad is Qassim's father.
aḫmad abu ga:sim احمد ابو قاسم

2 Fatima is Nouria's mother.
fa:ṯima umm nu:riya فاطمة امّ نورية

3 Ahmad is Nouria's father.
aḫmad abu nu:riya احمد ابو نورية

4 Fatima is Qassim's mother.
fa:ṯima umm ga:sim فاطمة امّ قاسم

5 Qassim is Nouria's brother.
ga:sim akh nu:riya قاسم اخ نورية

6 Nouria is Qassim's sister.
nu:riya ukht ga:sim نورية اخت قاسم

Note
In the Arab world it is customary to call a man after the name of his first born son. Thus the father 'Ahmad' in this example would be called

abu ga:sim ابو قاسم

by friends and family. A mother is often referred to in a similar way. Thus the mother 'Fatima' in this example would be called

umm ga:sim أُمّ قاسم

Vocabulary C Ⓣ son *walad* ولد *ibn* ابن daughter *bint* بنت

1 Ahmad is Fatima's husband.
aḫmad zawj fa:ṯima احمد زوج فاطمة

2 Fatima is Ahmad's wife.
fa:ṯima zawjat aḫmad فاطمة زوجة احمد

3 Qassim is Ahmad and Fatima's son.
ga:sim walad aḫmad wa fa:ṯima قاسم ولد احمد وفاطمة

4 Nouria is Ahmad and Fatima's daughter.
nu:riya bint ahmad wa fa:tima نورية بنت احمد وفاطمة

See supplementary section 7.1 at the end of this unit for vocabulary relating to the extended family.

4 Adjectives for the mind and body

These are adjectives describing various states of mind and body. All are given in their masculine form.

Vocabulary D Ⓣ

hungry
jaw^c^a:n جَوْعان

thirsty
^c^atsha:n عَطْشان

tired
ta^c^ba:n تَعْبان

out of order
kharba:n خَرْبان

happy, pleased
farha:n فَرْحان

full (having had enough to eat or drink)
shab^c^a:n شَبْعان

wrong, mistaken
ghalta:n غَلْطان

sorry
muta'assif مُتَأَسِّف

sure, certain
muta'akkid مُتَأَكِّد

thankful, grateful
mashku:r مَشْكور

in a hurry
musta^c^jil مُسْتَعْجِل

relaxed, comfortable at ease
murta:h مُرْتاح

ill, sick
mari:d مَريض

Points to note

a The first seven examples share a common pattern.
b The word for 'tired' covers a wide range of English idioms. Other possible translations include 'under the weather', 'a bit off colour', 'not up to much', 'out of sorts' etc. In Yemen this word for 'tired' is also used to mean 'out of order' when describing machinery.

Remember these examples are all masculine singular adjectives. To make the feminine singular and masculine and feminine plurals:

a Feminine singular - add *fatha* and *ta:' marbu:ta*.
b Masculine plural (describing groups of men and mixed company) - add the 'strong' masculine suffix - *i:n*.
c Feminine plural (describing groups made up exclusively of women) - add the 'strong' feminine suffix - *a:t*.

Ⓣ I'm hungry (woman talking)
ana jaw^c^a:na انا جواعانة

She's tired.
hiya ta^cba:na هي تعبانة

We're thirsty. (talking on behalf of group of men or mixed company)
iḫna ^caṯsha:ni:n احنا عطشانين

They're in a hurry. (talking about a group of men or mixed company)
hum musta^cjili:n هم مستعجلين

We're tired. (talking on behalf of a group of women)
iḫna ta^cba:na:t احنا تعبانات

They're hungry.
hin jaw^ca:na:t هن جوعانات

All these adjectives can be made negative in the usual way. Across the Peninsula you will hear the three main versions of 'not'. These are: all over the Peninsula, but especially in central and western Saudi Arabia:

mu مو

in the the Gulf States and eastern Saudi Arabia:

mu:b موب

in Oman, Yemen and some western parts of the Peninsula you will hear:

mush مش

Use the version you hear used most around you.

Practice sentences Ⓣ

1 I'm tired. (woman talking)
ana ta^cba:na انا تعبانة

2 Are you certain? (to a man)
inta muta'akkid? انت متأكّد؟

3 We're happy. (mixed group)
iḫna farḫa:ni:n احنا فرحانين

4 Ahmad's tired.
aḫmad ta^cba:n احمد تعبان

5 She's sorry.
hiya muta'assifa هي متأسّفة

6 I'm not sure. (man talking)
ana mu muta'akkid انا مو متأكّد

5 'Very' and 'a little'

The Arabic equivalents for these two items are:

Ⓣ very *kathi:r* كَثير   a little *shwayya* شوَيَّة

You will commonly hear this word for 'a little' in spoken Arabic, but you will rarely see it written.

In English, 'very' and 'a little' (or 'a bit') are used before adjectives in order to modify their meaning. For example, 'She's very tired' or 'We're a little hungry'. The Arabic equivalents follow the adjectives they describe and, unlike the adjectives themselves, require no changes for number (singular or plural) and gender (masculine or feminine).

She's very tired.
hiya taᶜba:na kathi:r هي تعبانة كثير

We're a little hungry.
iḫna jawᶜa:ni:n shwayya احنا جوعانين شويّة

Incorporate these new words into sentences of your own built around the adjectives describing state and mood.

Sample sentences Ⓣ

1 I'm a bit thirsty. (man speaking)
ana ᶜaṯsha:n shwayya انا عطشان شويّة

2 He's very tired.
huwa taᶜba:n kathi:r هو تعبان كثير

3 We're very busy. (mixed group)
iḫna mashghu:li:n kathi:r احنا مشغولين كثير

4 I'm a little hungry. (woman speaking)
ana jawᶜa:na shwayya انا جوعانة شويّة

5 She's very happy.
hiya farḫa:na kathi:r هي فرحانة كثير

7 We're in a hurry. (mixed group)
iḫna mustaᶜjili:n احنا مستعجلين

8 I'm not hungry. (woman talking)
ana mu jawᶜa:na انا مو جوعانة

9 Are you comfortable here? (to a mixed group)
intum murta:ḫi:n hina? انتم مرتاحين هنا؟

10 They're not in a hurry. (about a group of women)
hin mu mustaᶜjila:t هن مو مستعجلات

Translation

Translate these sentences into Arabic. Check your answers with the key at the end of the book.

1 She's not tired.
2 We're not hungry. (group of men)
3 She's in a hurry.
4 They aren't sure. (mixed group)
5 Are you thirsty? (to a man)
6 Are you certain? (to a woman)
7 We are grateful. (mixed group)
8 I'm not tired. (woman talking)
9 Is he ill?
10 They're in a hurry. (mixed group)
11 Are you comfortable? (to a man)
12 I'm sorry. (man talking)

6 Different ways of saying 'thank you'

The more Arabs you meet the wider variety of greetings and courtesy phrases you are going to hear, far more than you are going to have at your active disposal for some time. Don't be overwhelmed at this diversity. Approach your attempts at learning Arabic with a positive attitude and an open ear. Listen to people meeting and greeting whether at work, on the street, in the market, restaurant or cafe. Be attentive and you will begin to hear things you see in this book in use around you. It can be very exciting when you hear a word or phrase uttered in a real-life context that had previously been a dumb 'vocabulary item' in black and white upon the page. Conversely, it can be very rewarding suddenly to discover in print, and recognise, a word that you have heard and remembered. To help you attune your ear to a wider range of possibilities, here are various alternatives for something we hope you have already learnt and are using as part of your everyday vocabulary.

In Unit Two you saw a word for 'thank you' and its stock response:

thank you
shukran — شكراً

you're welcome
don't mention it
it's nothing
not at all
ᶜafwan — عفواً

There are other ways of saying 'thank you' and other stock responses in Arabic. One of the important things to grasp in the early stages of learning a new language is that you spend a lot of time learning to say the same thing in different ways. Language learners often assume, quite irrationally, that there is only one way of saying something, and then feel cheated to discover that not everyone uses the same expression. English of course is no different, in this context we use 'thank you', 'thanks', 'cheers', 'ta' and other alternatives all with the same meaning.

Dialogues Ⓣ

A Thank you.
shukran شكراً

B You're welcome.
ᶜafwan عفواً

A Thank you.
mashku:r مَشْكور

B Don't mention it.
mamnu:n مَمْنون

A Thanks.
mutashakkir مُتَشَكِّر

B It's nothing.
la shukr ᶜala wa:jib لا شُكْر عَلى واجِب

Note that all three alternatives for 'thank you' share the same letters *shi:n, ka:f* and *ra:'*. All the words for 'thank you' and the various responses are interchangeable.

7 More about plurals

Remember that Arabic has two kinds of plural.

1 The 'strong' plural which is used with nouns and adjectives describing people. This consists of a suffix added to the singular word. Note, there is a 'strong' plural for men and another for women.

teacher (male)
mudarris
teachers (male)
mudarrisi:n مدرّس + ين = مدرّسين
teacher (female)
mudarrisa
teachers (female)
mudarrisa:t مدرّسة + ات = مدرّسات

In a sentence like 'The teachers (m) are busy', the adjective 'busy' which describes 'the teachers' must also be given the appropriate plural suffix.

The teachers (m) are busy
il-mudarrisi:n mashghu:li:n المدرّسين مشغولين

The teachers (f) are busy
il-mudarrisa:t mashghu:la:t المدرّسات مشغولات

Translation

Translate these sentences into Arabic. Check your answers with the key at the end of the book.

1 The teachers (m) are busy.
2 The teachers (f) are busy.
3 The doctors (m) are Egyptian.
4 The engineers (m) are English.
5 The translator (f) is Palestinian.
6 The students (m) are Bahraini.
7 The manager (m) is American.
8 The doctor (f) is Iraqi.
9 The students (f) are Yemeni.
10 The manager (f) isn't present.
11 Our teacher (f) is married.
12 The manager (m) is busy.
13 The students (m) are tired.
14 The secretary (f) is hungry.
15 The clerks (m) are busy.

2 The 'broken' plural, which is generally used to make the plurals of things as opposed to people (though there are a few exceptions to this, see Unit Five). We call these 'broken' plurals, because instead of adding something to the end of the singular word to make the plural, they undergo internal vowel changes which affect the pronunciation of the word considerably.

street
sha:ri^c شارع

streets
shawa:ri^c شوارع

house
bayt بيت

houses
buyu:t بيوت

Don't bother to learn the plurals of words you don't think you will have use of in the plural. Be selective.

Remember, words ending *ta:' marbu:ṯa* sometimes take the 'strong' feminine plural suffix *-a:t*:

car
sayya:ra سيّارة

cars
sayya:ra:t سيّارات

or they may have a 'broken' plural:

city — *madi:na* مدينة cities — *mudun* مدن

Go back and check the 'broken' plurals of nouns you have seen in previous units.

8 Plurals and adjectives

Pay close attention to these two new points.

1 Plural adjectives on the 'strong' masculine and 'strong' feminine patterns can only be used with plural nouns referring to people. A feature of Arabic that seems very odd at first encounter is that adjectives describing the plurals of objects or things are generally feminine singular in form, even though they have a plural meaning.

بيوت كبيرة

large houses
buyu:t kabi:ra بيوت كبيرة

new cars
sayya:ra:t jadi:da سيّارات جديدة

As you can see from the examples above, it doesn't matter if the plural of the noun referring to an object is 'strong' (for example, *sayya:ra:t)* or 'broken' (for example, *buyu:t)* the same rule applies. Notice that even nouns referring to objects which are masculine in their singular form, for example,

a new house
bayt jadi:d بيت جديد

are considered grammatically *feminine singular* in their plural form:

new houses
buyu:t jadi:da بيوت جديدة

Here are some more examples:

a long street
sha:ri ṯawi:l شارع طويل

long streets
shawa:ri^c tawi:la شوارع طويلة

a big shop
dukka:n kabi:r دكّان كبير

big shops
daka:ki:n kabi:ra دكاكين كبيرة

a new car
sayya:ra jadi:da سيّارة جديدة

new cars
sayya:ra:t jadi:da سيّارات جديدة

In the last example, the adjective stays the same for both singular and plural since the singular form of *sayya:ra* is itself feminine.

Transformation drill Ⓣ

Make the following singular phrases plural.

Model

an expensive hotel
fundug gha:li فندق غالي

expensive hotels
funa:dig gha:liya فنادق غالية

1 an expensive hotel
fundug gha:li فندق غالي ——▷

2 a new house
bayt jadi:d بيت جديد ——▷

3 a big car
sayya:ra kabi:ra سيّارة كبيرة ——▷

4 a short street
sha:ri[c] gaṣi:r شارع قصير ——▷

5 a big hotel
fundug kabi:r فندق كبير ——▷

6 a new office
maktab jadi:d مكتب جديد ——▷

7 a large house
bayt kabi:r بيت كبير ——▷

8 an old car
sayya:ra gadi:ma سيّارة قديمة ——▷

9 a small hotel
fundug ṣaghi:r فندق صغير ——▷

10 a long street
sha:ri[c] ṭawi:l شارع طويل ——▷

2 A few common adjectives have 'broken' plural forms in addition to their 'strong' masculine and 'strong' feminine forms.

For example,

singular		**broken plural**	
(T) new			
jadi:d	جديد	*judud*	جُدُد
small, young			
ṣaghi:r	صغير	*ṣigha:r*	صِغار
big, old			
kabi:r	كبير	*kiba:r*	كِبار
long			
ṭawi:l	طويل	*ṭiwa:l*	طِوال

These 'broken' plural adjectives can be used to describe any plural noun, irrespective of whether the noun itself has a 'broken' or a 'strong' masculine or feminine plural, and whether the noun refers to people or objects. This gives rise to the following alternatives:

the new teachers (m)	
al-mu^{c}allimi:n al-jadi:di:n	المعلّمين الجديدين
or (more commonly)	
al-mu^{c}allimi:n al-judud	المعلّمين الجدد
the new teachers (f)	
al-mu^{c}allima:t al-jadi:da:t	المعلّمات الجديدات
or	
al-mu^{c}allima:t al-judud	المعلّمات الجدد
the new cars	
as-sayya:ra:t al-jadi:da	السيّارات الجديدة
or	
as-sayya:ra:t al-judud	السيّارات الجدد
the young students (m)	
aṭ-ṭulla:b aṣ-ṣaghi:ri:n	الطّلاّب الصغيرين
or (more commonly)	
aṭ-ṭulla:b aṣ-ṣigha:r	الطّلاّب الصّغار
the young students (f)	
aṭ-ṭa:liba:t aṣ-ṣaghira:t	الطّالبات الصّغيرات
or	
aṭ-ṭa:liba:t aṣ-ṣigha:r	الطّالبات الصّغار

the small houses
al-buyu:t aṣ-ṣaghi:ra البيوت الصّغيرة

or
al-buyu:t aṣ-ṣigha:r البيوت الصّغار

Not all adjectives have 'broken' plural forms, only those given above and a few others. These broken plurals are indicated in the final word list at the end of the book.

At first sight, plurals in Arabic do look complicated. Listen carefully for the commonest usage in your own particular area.

Supplementary section 7.1
The extended family

You will probably not be in immediate need of the vocabulary describing the extended family relationships, although if you spend any time with an Arab family you will need at least a passive understanding of it. You will meet people's grandparents and cousins because there is a tendency for three, sometimes more, generations to live together under the same roof. Notice that Arabic distinguishes between maternal and paternal uncles, aunts and cousins, in much the same way as we use the phrases 'on my father's side' and 'on my mother's side' in English.

grandfather
jadd جَدّ

grandmother
jadda جدّة

paternal uncle
ᶜamm عَمّ

paternal aunt
ᶜamma عَمَّة

maternal uncle
kha:l خال

maternal aunt
kha:la خالَة

male paternal cousin
ibn ᶜamm إبْن عَمّ *ibn ᶜamma* إبْن عَمَّة

female paternal cousin
bint ᶜamm بِنْت عَمّ

bint ᶜamma بِنْت عَمَّة

male maternal cousin
ibn kha:l إِبْن خال

ibn kha:la إِبْن خالَة

female maternal cousin
bint kha:l بِنْت خال

bint kha:la بِنْت خالَة

Examples

my cousin ie, the daughter of my mother's sister
bint kha:lat-i بنت خالتي

his cousin ie, the son of his father's brother
ibn ᶜamm-a ابن عمه

Supplementary section 7.2 'Very' and 'a little'

'Very'

You will hear a wide variety of alternatives for 'very', some used interchangeably, others more specific to one particular area.

very
kathi:r كثير

is the word given earlier in this unit and will be understood throughout the Peninsula, as will the standard Arabic

very
jiddan جِدّاً

More characteristic of the Gulf and eastern Saudi Arabia are:

very
wa:jid واجِد

very
kullish كُلِّش

Due to the influence of Egyptians throughout the area, you will also come across the more typically Egyptian:

very
gawi قَوي

'A little'

In addition to the word given earlier in the unit:

a little
shwayya شوَيّة

You will also hear the more standard:

a little
gali:l قَليل

Supplementary section 7.3 Ministries and government departments

1 Ministry of Information
wiza:rat il-iʿla:m وِزارَة إلإعْلام

2 Ministry of the Economy
wiza:rat il-igtis̲a:d وِزارَة إلإقْتِصاد

3 Ministry of Finance
wiza:rat il-ma:liyya وِزارَة إلْمالِيّة

4 Ministry of Agriculture
wiza:rat iz-zira:ᶜa وِزارَة إلزّراعَة

5 Ministry of Education
wiza:rat it-taᶜli:m وِزارَة إلتَّعْليم

6 Ministry of Foreign Affairs
wiza:rat il-kha:rijiyya وِزارَة إلْخارِجيَّة

7 Ministry of the Interior
wiza:rat id-da:khiliyya وِزارَة إلدّاخِلِيَّة

8 Ministry of Communications
wiza:rat il-muwa:sala:t وِزارَة إلْمُواصَلات

9 Ministry of Public Transport
wiza:rat in-naql il-ᶜa:m وِزارَة إلنَّقْل إلْعامّ

10 Ministry of Health
wiza:rat is-sihha وِزارَة إلصِّحَّة

11 Ministry of Public Works
wiza:rat il-ashgha:l il-ᶜa:mma وِزارَة إلْأَشْغال إلْعامَّة

12 Ministry of Petroleum
wiza:rat in-naft وِزارَة إلنَّفط

13 Ministry of Defence
wiza:rat id:difa:ᶜ وِزارَة إلدِّفاع

14 Ministry of Wagfs
wiza:rat il-awga:f وِزارَة إلْأَوْقاف

15 Ministry of Justice
wiza:rat il-ᶜadl وِزارَة إلعَدْل

16 Ministry of Tourism
wiza:rat is-siya:ha وِزارَة إلسِّياحَة

Notes

a Terminology will vary somewhat from country to country. Among the common administrative alternatives you will encounter for 'Ministry' are:

organisation *hay'a*	هيْئَة	institute *maᶜhad*	مَعْهَد
authority *maslaha*	مَصْلَحَة	administration *ida:ra*	إدارَة

b Common alternatives for item five are:

Ministry of Education
wiza:rat it-tarbiya — وِزارَة إِلتَّرْبِيَة

wiza:rat it-tarbiya wa t-taᶜli:m — وِزارَة إِلتَّرْبِيَة وَالتَّعْلِيم

c The 'Ministry of Waqfs' controls the dispensation of religious charitable endowments (وَقْف plural أَوْقاف).

New vocabulary in Unit 7

Plurals follow the singular in brackets.

husband
zawj (azwa:j) — زَوْج (أَزْواج)

wife
zawja (zawja:t) — زَوْجَة (زَوْجات)

friend (m)
s̲adi:g (as̲diqa:') — صَديق (أَصْدِقاء)

s̲a:h̲ib (as̲h̲a:b) — صاحِب (أَصْحاب)

friend (f)
s̲adi:ga (s̲adi:ga:t) — صَديقَة (صَديقات)

s̲a:hiba (s̲a:h̲iba:t) — صاحِبَة (صاحِبات)

with
maᶜa — مَعَ

capital
ᶜa:s̲ima — عاصِمَة

father
abu — أَبو

mother
umm — أُمّ

brother
akh (ikhwa:n) — أَخ (إِخْوان)

sister
ukht (akhawa:t) — أُخْت (أَخَوات)

son	*ibn (abna:')*	إِبْن (أَبناء)
	walad (awla:d)	وَلَد (أوْلاد)
daughter	*bint (bana:t)*	بِنْت (بَنات)
hungry	*jaw^{c}a:n*	جَوْعان
thirsty	*^{c}atsha:n*	عَطْشان
tired	*ta^{c}ba:n*	تَعْبان
broken, out of order	*kharba:n*	خَرْبان
happy, pleased	*farha:n*	فَرْحان
sorry	*muta'assif*	مُتَأَسِّف
sure	*muta'akkid*	مُتَأَكِّد
grateful	*mashku:r*	مَشْكور
in a hurry	*musta^{c}jil*	مُسْتَعْجِل
relaxed	*murta:h*	مُرْتاح
ill, sick	*mari:d*	مَريض
full	*shab^{c}a:n*	شَبْعان
wrong, mistaken	*ghalta:n*	غَلْطان
very	*kathi:r*	كَثير
a little	*shwayya*	شَوَيَّة

Unit 8

1 About time

'The concepts of time and space are not viewed with such awe as in other cultures. Things take place on a human level: people are more important than events. A common Arab proverb says

Haste is from the devil
il-ᶜajla min ish-shayta:n — إِلْعَجْلَة مِن إِلشَّيْطان

Impatience is considered a sign of bad manners or lack of self-confidence.' (Dr J L Curtis *Bahrain: language, customs and people)*

People in the Middle East as a whole tend to be a great deal less exact about time than we are in the West. If you ask people what the time is they will normally round it off to the nearest five or ten minutes. You will also find that people's watches vary greatly.

To compound the problem, there are two prevalent systems of time keeping. Until the arrival of significant numbers of foreigners in the Arabian Peninsula, time was kept according to the Arabic system in which the day begins at sunset. Therefore '12 o'clock' is sunset, an hour later '1 o'clock' etc. At the moment, though the European system is gaining ascendancy, both exist side by side.

Punctuality is not as important in the Arab world as it is for us in the West. The philosophy governing appointments is that implied in the expression:

God willing
in sha:'alla:h — إِنْ شاء اللّٰه

If God wills that the appointment be kept, it will be kept, if God doesn't, it won't, and there is nothing that can be done, and no reason to be upset, it simply was not fated to happen. This can be very frustrating for Westerners who have just as mystical an attachment to a rational, ordered and controllable time frame as the Arabs do to the idea that nothing is certain. What is at conflict is not just respect for time, but a more profound difference in perception of time. So when someone arranges to meet you at 6 o'clock, God willing, it does not necessarily mean that they will not be there, but that the possibility exists. You should not complain if they are twenty minutes late. If you in your turn should be late and ready to apologise profusely, the first thing you are likely to hear is:

It doesn't matter
Never mind

ma^c^laysh مَعْلَيْش

Telling the time

To find out what the time is you ask:

What's the time?
What time is it?
('How much the hour?')
kam is-sa:^c^a? كَم إِلسّاعَة؟

In the reply the noun *sa:^c^a* is used, followed by one of the numbers one to twelve. In telling the time, however, some of the numbers have to be modified slightly.

It's one o'clock ('the hour one')
is-sa:^c^a wa:ḫida إِلسّاعَة واحِدَة

Note that the Arabic for 'one' has *ta: marbu:ṯa* in this case.
In the Arabic for '2 o'clock' you must use a special form of 'two':

It's two o'clock
is-sa:^c^a thintayn إِلسّاعَة ثِنْتَيْن

Make sure you learn these two special forms.
The numbers three to twelve remain the same as the forms you saw earlier. However, in the Gulf you may hear the numbers being used without *ta:'marbu:ṯa*. Listen and use what you hear used most around you.

Vocabulary A Ⓣ

It's 1 o'clock
is-sa:^c^a wa:ḫida السّاعة واحدة

It's 2 o'clock
is-sa:^c^a thintayn السّاعة ثنتين

It's 3 o'clock
is-sa:^{c}a thala:tha
السّاعة ثلاثة

It's 4 o'clock
is-sa:^{c}a arba^{c}a
السّاعة اربعة

It's 5 o'clock
is-sa:^{c}a khamsa
السّاعة خمسة

It's 6 o'clock
is-sa:^{c}a sitta
السّاعة ستّة

It's 7 o'clock
is-sa:^{c}a saba^{c}a
الساعة سبعة

It's 8 o'clock
is-sa:^{c}a thama:niya
السّاعة ثمانية

It's 9 o'clock
is-sa:^{c}a tisa^{c}a
السّاعة تسعة

It's 10 o'clock
is-sa:^{c}a ^{c}ashra
السّاعة عشرة

It's 11 o'clock
is-sa:^{c}a hida^{c}sh
السّاعة حدعش

It's 12 o'clock
is-sa:^{c}a ithna^{c}sh
السّاعة اثنعش

As an example of how to tell the time more exactly, here is a complete breakdown of an hour.

Vocabulary B

quarter *ruba^c*	رُبَع	half *nuss*	نُصّ
third *thulth*	ثُلْث	less, minus *illa*	إلاّ

Ⓣ

5.00
is-sa:^{c}a khamsa
السّاعة خمسة

5.05
is-sa:^{c}a khamsa wa khamsa
السّاعة خمسة وخمسة

5.10
is-sa:^{c}a khamsa wa ^{c}ashra
السّاعة خمسةوعشرة

5.15
is-sa:^{c}a khamsa wa ruba^c
السّاعة خمسة وربع

5.20
is-sa:^{c}a khamsa wa thulth
السّاعة خمسة وثلث

5.25
is-sa:^{c}a khamsa wa nuss illa khamsa السّاعة خمسة ونص الا خمسة

5.30
is-sa:^{c}a khamsa wa nuss السّاعة خمسة ونص

5.35
is-sa:^{c}a khamsa wa nuss wa khamsa السّاعة خمسة ونص وخمسة

5.40
is-sa:^{c}a sitta illa thulth السّاعة ستّة الا ثلث

5.45
is-sa:^{c}a sitta illa ruba^{c} السّاعة ستة الا ربع

5.50
is-sa:^{c}a sitta illa ^{c}ashra السّاعة ستّة الا عشرة

5.55
is-sa:^{c}a sitta illa khamsa السّاعة ستّة الا خمسة

6.00
is-sa:^{c}a sitta السّاعة ستّة

There is no need to use a word for 'minute' when telling the time in Arabic. There is, of course, an Arabic word for 'minute', and it is very frequently used alone as an exclamation equivalent to the English:

Just a minute
Hang on
Wait a bit
dagi:ga دقيقة

Reading and repetition drill Ⓣ

1.05
is-sa:^{c}a wa:hida wa khamsa السّاعة واحدة وخمسة

3.10
is-sa:^{c}a thala:tha wa ^{c}ashra السّاعة ثلاثة وعشرة

4.40
is-sa:^{c}a khamsa illa thulth السّاعة خمسة الاّ ثلث

8.30
is-sa:^{c}a thama:niya wa nuss السّاعة ثمانية ونصّ

1.45
is-sa:^{c}a thintayn illa ruba^{c} السّاعة ثنتين الا ربع

11.00
is-sa:^{c}a hida^{c}sh السّاعة حدعش

4.20
is-sa:^{c}a arba^{c}a wa thulth السّاعة اربعة وثلث

6.00 السّاعة ستّة
is-sa:ᶜa sitta

9.15 السّاعة تسعة وربع
is-sa:ᶜa tisaᶜa wa rubaᶜ

11.25 السّاعة حدعش ونصّ الاّ خمسة
is-sa:ᶜa h̲idaᶜsh wa nus̲s̲ illa khamsa

7.30 السّاعة سبعة ونصّ
is-sa:ᶜa sabaᶜa wa nus̲s̲

10.35 السّاعة عشرة ونصّ وخمسة
is-sa:ᶜa ᶜashra was nus̲s̲ wa khamsa

a Listen to the question
b Give response according to cue number
c Listen to the correct response
d Repeat the answer after the model

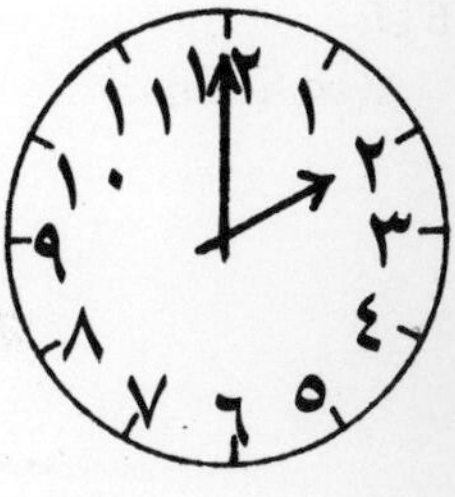
1

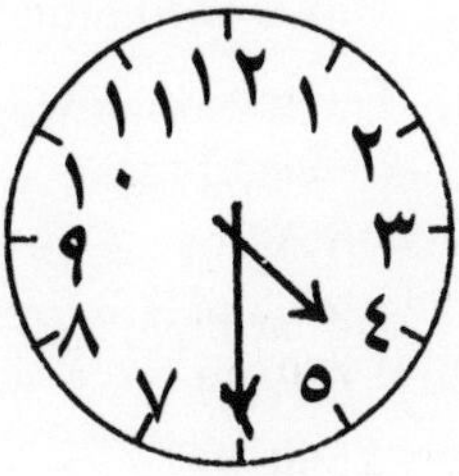
2

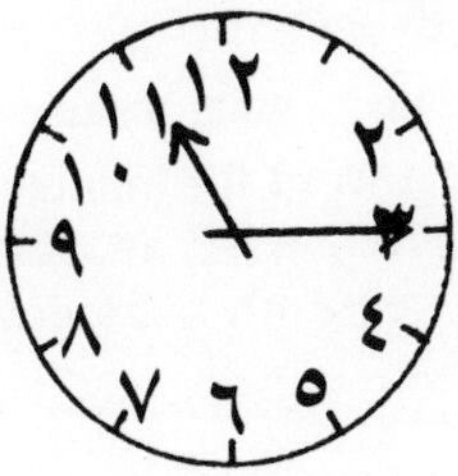
3

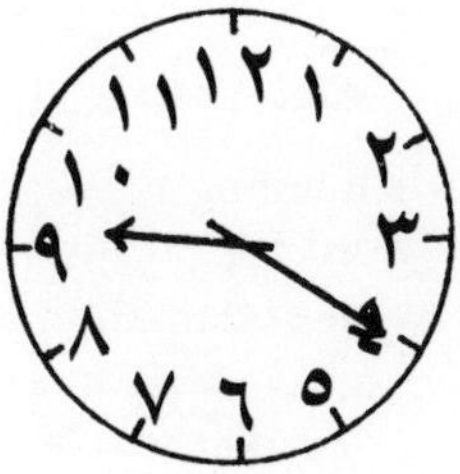
4

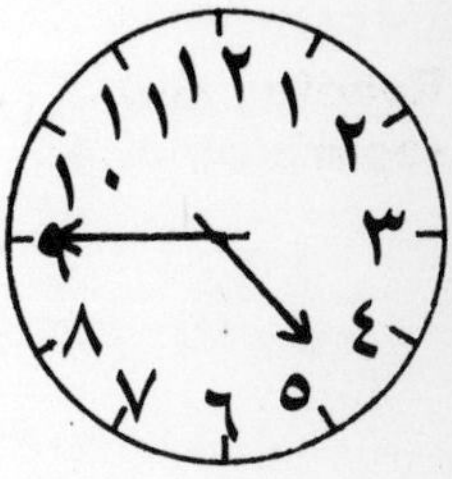
5

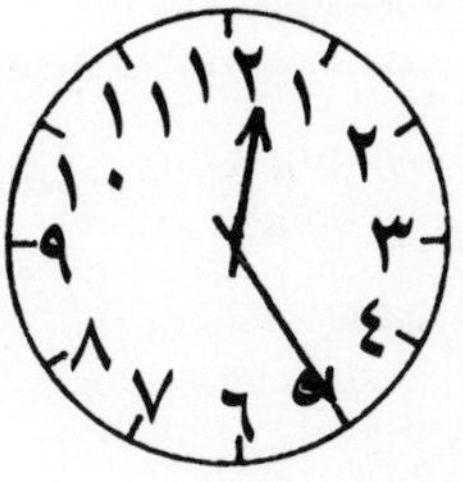
6

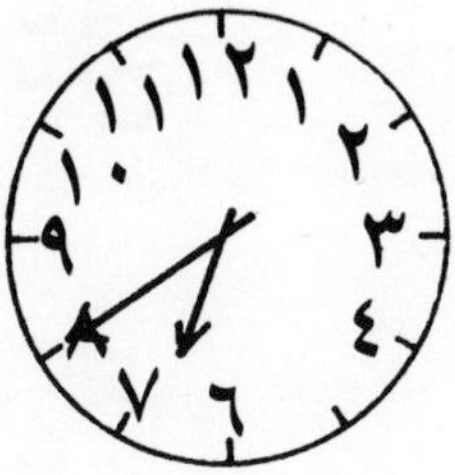
7

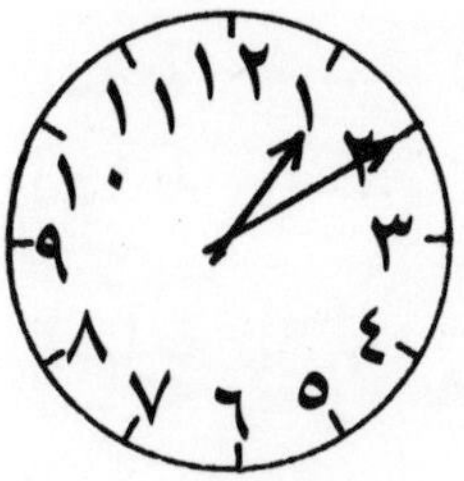
8

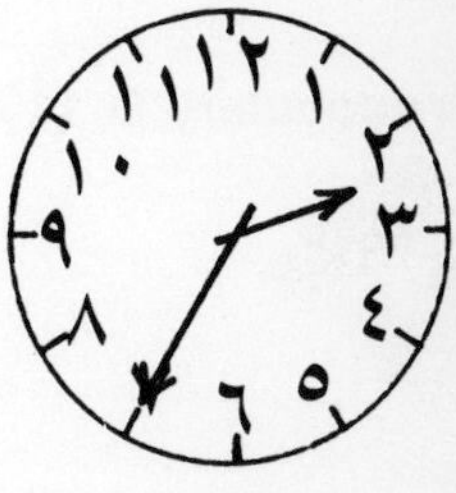
9

10

Times of the day

Though there is no exact equivalent in Arabic to English 'a.m.' and 'p.m.', there are phrases relating to different parts of the day which are often used in making more precise statements concerning the time of day.

Vocabulary C Ⓣ

a in the morning, a.m.
is̱-s̱aba:ẖ إِلصَّباح

b noon, at noon
idh-dhuhr إِلظُّهْر

c afternoon
ba^cd idh-dhuhr بَعْد ِالظُّهْر
This phrase is used from 12.00 noon until about 5.00 p.m.

d in the evening
il-masa إِلْمَساء
This is used after 5.00 p.m.

e The following word on its own means:
a (single) night
layla لَيْلَة

and 'at night' is:
fi l-layl في اللَّيْل

or:
bi-l-layl باللَّيْل

10.00 a.m.
is-sa:^ca ^cashra is̱-s̱aba:h السّاعة عشرة الصّباح

12.00 noon
idh-dhuhr الظّهر

2 p.m.
is-sa:^ca thintayn ba^cd idh-dhur السّاعة ثنتين بعد الظّهر

7 p.m.
is-sa:^ca saba^ca il-masa السّاعة سبعة المساء

Vocabulary D Ⓣ Here is a review of time-related vocabulary introduced so far and some new items.

minute *dagi:ga*	دَقيقة	day *yawm*	يَوْم
hour *sa:^ca*	ساعَة	week *usbu:^c*	أُسْبوع

month *shahr*	شَهْر	tomorrow *bukra*	بُكْرَة
year *sana*	سَنَة	about, approximately, roughly *tagri:ban*	تَقْرِيباً
ᶜa:m	عام	*h̲awa:li*	حَوالي
time *wagt*	وَقْت	now *ha:lh̲in*	هالحين
today *il-yawm*	إِلْيَوْم		

These words are fairly consistent from one area to another. You may hear both words for 'year' and 'about' used interchangeably.

The word we have given for 'tomorrow' would be understood anywhere in the Peninsula. In the Gulf States and eastern parts of Saudi Arabia you will hear:

tomorrow
ba:kir باكِر

sometimes pronounced:
ba:chir.

2 Years and months

The Gregorian calendar in Arabic

There are two calendar systems in use in the Arab world today, the Gregorian calendar which we ourselves use, and an older Muslim system based on a lunar year of about 354 days.

Arabic has two sets of names for the months of the Gregorian calendar, both of which are in common use. One consists of Arabic names, and the other of names borrowed and more or less directly transliterated into Arabic from European languages.

Vocabulary E Ⓣ

January	*yana:yir*	يَنايِر	*ka:nu:n ith-tha:ni*	كانون الثّاني
February	*fibra:yir*	فِبْرايِر	*shuba:t̲*	شُباط
March	*ma:rs*	مارْس	*a:dha:r*	آذار
April	*abri:l*	أَبْرِيل	*ni:sa:n*	نيسان

May	*ma:yu*	مايو	*ayya:r*	أيّار
June	*yu:niyu*	يونِيو	*hazi:ra:n*	حَزيران
July	*yu:liyu*	يولِيو	*tammu:z*	تَمّوز
August	*aghustus*	أَغُسْطُس	*a:b*	آب
September	*sibtambir*	سِبْتَمْبِر	*aylu:l*	أَيْلول
October	*uktu:bir*	أُكْتوبِر	*tishri:n il-awwal*	تِشْرين الأَوَّل
November	*nu:fimbir*	نوفِمْبِر	*tishri:n ith-tha:ni*	تِشْرين اِلثّاني
December	*di:simbir*	دِيسِمْبِر	*ka:nu:n il-awwal*	كانون اِلأَوَّل

For the special symbol representing initial ء *hamza* followed by ا *alif* (/a:/), see *The Macmillan Arabic Course Book 1, Write to Left.*

The four seasons

The seasons of the year in Arabic are

Ⓣ

Spring *ir-rabi:ᶜ*	إلرَّبيع	Autumn *il-khari:f*	إلْخَريف
Summer *is-sayf*	إلصَّيْف	Winter *ish-shita*	إلشِّتاء

The Muslim calendar

The Muslim era dates from 16th July, 622 AD, the date ascribed to the emigration of the Prophet Muhammad and his followers to Medina after several years of opposition to his message in his native city of Mecca. It is from this date that the years of the Muslim calendar are reckoned. Since the Muslim year has only 354 days (twelve lunar months, each of twenty-nine and a half days), it progressively outstrips the Christian year. Most of 1977 AD, for example, was 1397 AH.

The Muslim calendar is rarely used alone in the Arab world today. Newspapers and most official and business documents show the Christian date as well. For the moment, therefore, use this list for reference only.

Here are the names of the months of the Muslim year.

Ⓣ	1	*il-muharram*	إِلْمُحَرَّم
	2	*ṣafar*	صَفَر
	3	*rabi:ᶜ il-awwal*	رَبيع إِلأَوَّل
	4	*rabi:ᶜ ith-tha:ni:*	رَبيع إِلثّاني
	5	*juma:da l-awwal*	جُمادي الْأَوَّل
	6	*juma:da l-a:khira*	جمادي الْآخِرَة
	7	*rajab*	رَجَب
	8	*shaᶜba:n*	شَعْبان
	9	*ramaḏa:n*	رَمَضان
	10	*shawwa:l*	شَوّال
	11	*dhu l-qaᶜda*	ذو الْقَعْدَة
	12	*dhu l-hijja*	ذو الحِجَّة

In order to make clear which calendar is being used, dates of the Muslim era are often followed by an initial *ha:'* هـ, short for:

in the year of the Emigration هِجْرِيَّةً
hijriyyatan

Dates of the Christian era are followed by an initial *mi:m* مـ short for:

in the year of the Birth ميلاديّاً
mi:la:diyyan

The 'Birth', of course, refers to the birth of Christ.

Look at these headings from Arabic newspapers showing the Muslim date alongside its Christian equivalent.

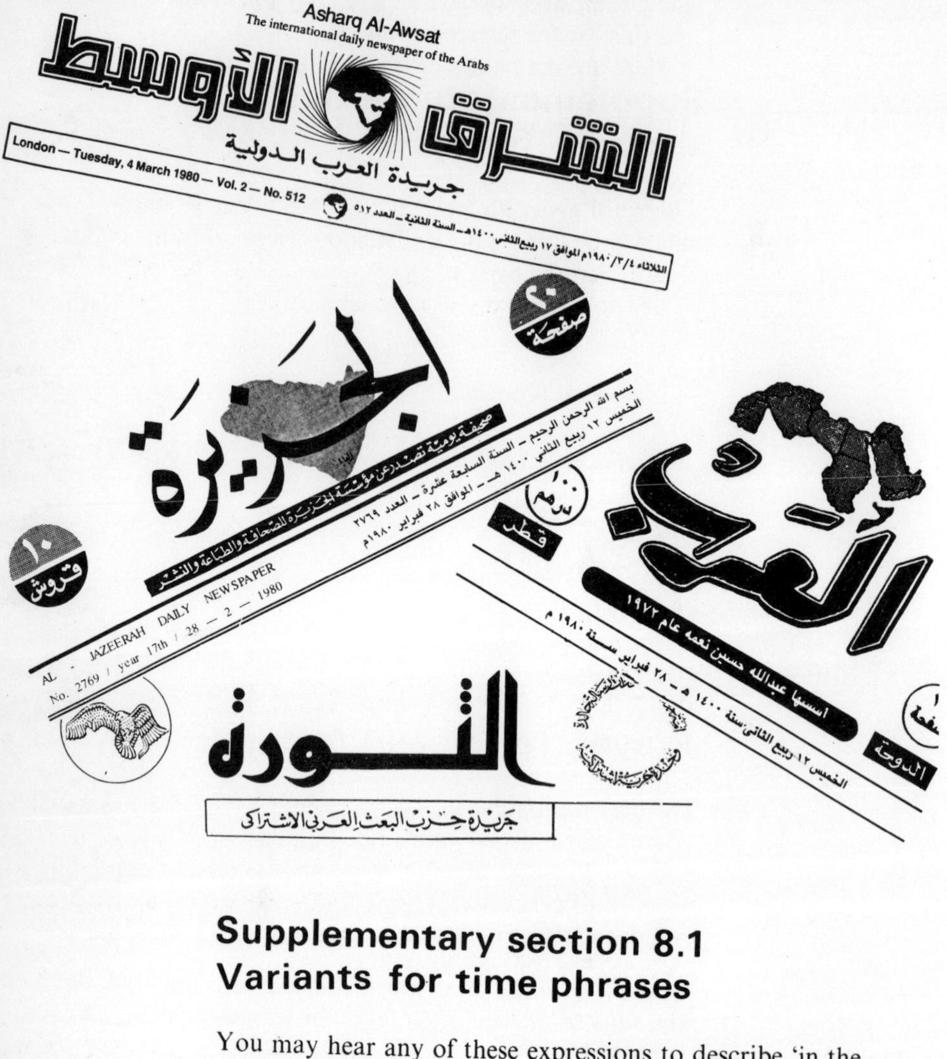

Supplementary section 8.1
Variants for time phrases

You may hear any of these expressions to describe 'in the morning', depending on where you are in the Peninsula. They are all variations on the same word.

iṣ-ṣaba:ḥ   إلصّباح   ṣaba:han   صَباحاً

fi ṣ-ṣaba:ḥ   في الصّباح   fi ṣ-ṣubḥ   في الصُّبْح

As an alternative to the more universal phrase for afternoon,

ba'd dh-dhuhr   بَعْد إلظُّهْر

given earlier in the unit, you may hear in the Gulf and eastern Saudi Arabia,

ʿugb i<u>dh</u>-<u>dh</u>uhr عُقْب إِلظُّهر

Supplementary section 8.2
Variants for 'now'

The word given for 'now' in the vocabulary of this unit will be universally understood. Here are some variants used in various parts of the Peninsula, the first two are closely related to the word you have already seen.

il-ḫi:n إِلْحين

da:lḫi:n دالحين

tawa تَوا

hassa هَسَّة

Supplementary section 8.3
Prayer, feasts and festivals

The day in the Arab world is very closely related to the times of the call to prayer, heard five times a day. They occur between 4.00 a.m. and 7.00 p.m. approximately, depending on the time of year and local time. The names of the five prayers are given below; they are not essential vocabulary, but are included for general interest.

The sunset prayer
ṣala:t il-maghrib صَلاة إِلْمَغْرِب

The night prayer
ṣala:t il-ʿasha صَلاة إِلْعَشاء

The dawn prayer
ṣala:t il-fajr صَلاة إِلْفَجْر

The noon prayer
ṣala:t i<u>dh</u>-<u>dh</u>uhr صَلاة إِلظُّهْر

The afternoon prayer
ṣala-t il-ʿaṣr صَلاة إِلْعَصْر

Calligraphic representation of Muslim at prayer

Islamic prayer and ritual

'The most important of the ritual and moral duties incumbent on all Muslims are prayer, almsgiving, fasting and pilgrimage. Custom and tradition have supplied the gaps which the Qur'an leaves, and have welded its prescriptions into a well-defined system, based theoretically on the practice of the Prophet himself. For the broad outlines doubtless the prophet's example was faithfully recorded and adopted . . .. The Qur'an appears to require only three prayers a day, but tradition insists on five; the first begins at sunset, and is followed by the night, dawn, noon and afternoon prayers. The faithful are called to prayer by the muadhdhin, who . . . cries with a powerful and penetrating voice: "God is most great. I testify that there is no God but God. I testify that Muhammad is God's apostle. Come to prayer, come to security. God is great". Each clause is repeated at least once and the morning call reminds Muslims that "prayer is better than sleep".
(A Guillaume *Islam*)

The two major festivals in the Muslim year lend their names to the months of the Muslim calendar in which they fall.

Ramadan, the month of fasting

ramaḏa:n رَمَضان

Hajj, the time of the annual pilgrimage to Mecca and Medina

il-ḫajj إِلْحَجّ

Pilgrims at the Great Mosque in Mecca

Unlike many of our festivals which are governed by a solar calendar and fall on a definite date each year, Muslim festivals, governed by a lunar calendar, advance by approximately 10 days each year, taking 33 years to complete a cycle.

The Qur'an expressly orders that the fast continues throughout the month of Ramadan. Fasting can be a very great strain, especially when it falls in the summer months when temperatures over 100 degrees must be coped with. The fast begins before dawn of the day after the new moon of the month of Ramadan appears. Each country has its own moon viewers, who on sighting the new moon telephone or telegraph the news so that the beginning of the fast can be broadcast nationally. In some countries the news is announced by the firing of a cannon.

Fasting means abstaining from all food and drink, smoking and sexual intercourse from that moment in the early morning when it is possible to distinguish a black thread from a white thread, and continues through the hours of daylight until the sun sinks below the horizon. Often cannons are used to announce the beginning and end of each day's fast.

Certain people are exempt from fasting; the sick, pregnant women, young children, and travellers. Travellers are expected to fast an equal number of days later at their convenience.

The rhythm of the days is slower in Ramadan, daytime activity is kept to a minimum, some shops may close and ministries and offices work shorter hours. People often sleep through the long afternoons. However, after the cannon goes off to mark the end of the day's fasting the fast is broken with a meal, people take to the streets and markets, visit friends and relatives and for a month evenings and nights are as active as the normal daytime. Many people stay up all night, maybe taking a second meal and breakfast before the beginning of the next day's fasting.

The meal at sunset is called

il-ifṯa:r — إلإفْطار

and often consists of special foods and delicacies especially prepared during Ramadan. The end of Ramadan is celebrated by a holiday known as

ᶜi:d il-fiṯr — عيد إلْفِطْر

or

il-ᶜi:d iṣ-ṣaghi:r — الْعيد إلصَّغير

which usually lasts for three days. It is customary to wear new clothes for this *ᶜi:d,* visit friends and relatives and give alms to the poor.

The second major event in the Muslim year is

the pilgrimage

il-ḫajj — إلْحَجّ

which takes place in the twelfth month of the Muslim calendar. It is incumbent on every Muslim to attempt to try to make the pilgrimage to Mecca at least once in his or her lifetime, and today with modern means of communications, more than a million Muslims of all nationalities make the pilgrimage annually.

The feast on the tenth day of the month of the Hajj is called

Feast of the Sacrifice

ᶜi:d il-aḏḫa — عيد إلأَضْحى

or

il-ᶜi:d il-kabi:r — الْعيد إلْكَبير

The name of this feast relates to the custom of killing and eating a sheep to celebrate the end of the Pilgrimage. This is the central feast of Islam, and is derived from the feast of the Atonement, Abraham's substitute sacrifice.

Various greetings can be used before and during holidays and feasts:

Happy holiday

ᶜi:d muba:rak — عيد مُبارَك

('blessed holiday')

and these variations,

ᶜi:d-ak muba:rak عيدَك مُبارك

ᶜi:d muba:rak ᶜalay-k عيد مُبارَك عَلَيْك

These can be used for the end of both Ramadan and Hajj feasts.

New Year, according to both the Gregorian and Muslim calendar is:

New Year ('head of the year')
ra:s is-sana راس إِلسَّنَة

Common New Year greetings are:

Happy New Year
kull sana wa intum bi-khayr كل سنة وانتم بخير

kull sana wa intum ṭayyib كل سنة وانتم طيّب

kull ᶜa:m wa intum bi-khayr كل عام وانتم بخير

New vocabulary in Unit 8

never mind *maᶜlaysh*	مَعْلَيْش	evening *masa*	مَساء
how many? how much? *kam?*	كَم؟	night *layla*	لَيْلَة
quarter *rubaᶜ*	رُبع	minute *dagi:ga (daga:'ig)*	دَقيقة (دَقائِق)
third *thulth*	تُلْث	hour *sa:ᶜa (sa:ᶜa:t)*	ساعَة (ساعات)
half *nuṣṣ*	نُصّ	day *yawm (ayya:m)*	يَوْم (أَيّام)
minus, less *illa*	إِلاّ	week *usbu:ᶜ (asa:bi:ᶜ)*	أُسْبوع (أَسابيع)
morning *ṣaba:ḥ*	صَباح	month *shahr (ashhur)*	شَهْر (أَشْهُر)
noon *dhuhr*	ظُهْر	year *sana (sanawa:t/sini:n)* *ᶜa:m*	سَنَة (سَنَوات سِنين) عام
after *baᶜd*	بَعد	time *wagt*	وَقْت

today
il-yawm إِلْيَوْم

tomorrow
bukra بُكْرَة

ba:kir باكِر

approximately
tagri:ban تَقْريباً

h̲awa:li حَوالي

now
ha:lh̲i:n هالْحين

January
yana:yir يَنايِر

February
fibra:yir فِبْرايِر

March
ma:rs مارْس

April
abri:l أَبْريل

May
ma:yu مايو

June
yu:niyu يونيو

July
yu:liyu يوليو

August
aghusṯus أَغُسْطُس

September
sibtambir سِبْتَمْبِر

October
uktu:bir أُكْتوبِر

November
nu:fimbir نوفِمْبِر

December
di:sambir ديسَمْبِر

afternoon
ba^{c}|d idh̲-dh̲uhr بَعْد اِلظُّهْر

Unit 9

1 'Have' and 'have got'

You have learnt to express possession by adding a personal suffix to a noun to convey the equivalent of the English 'my, your, his, her, our, their'. For example,

my name
ism-i اسمي

our house
bayt-na بيتنا

your job (f)
shughl-ik شغلك

These suffixes are usually written as part of the word they describe, joined directly to the last letter. However, if the last letter of the word is a non-connector, the suffix will stand alone. For example,

their son
walad-hum ولدهم

These personal suffixes also function as the equivalents to the English 'me, you, him, her, us, them'.

An immediate practical application of this use of the personal suffixes is to allow us to form the Arabic equivalent to the verb 'have/have got'. This is conveyed in Arabic by the use of:

near
ᶜand عِنْد

with the relevant personal suffix to show who is talking, being addressed or referred to. Thus:

I have
ᶜand-i عِنْدي

This translates literally as 'near me', but expresses in Arabic the same idea of possessing, owning or having as 'I have ...' and 'I've got . . .' do in English.

Vocabulary A (T)

I have *ᶜand-i*	عنْدي	we have *ᶜand-na*	عنْدنا
you have (to a man) *ᶜand-ak*	عنْدك	you have (mp) *ᶜand-kum*	عنْدكم
you have (to a woman) *ᶜand-ik*	عنْدِك	you have (fp) *ᶜand-kin*	عنْدكِن
he has *ᶜand-a*	عنْدَه	they have (m) *ᶜand-hum*	عنْدهُم
she has *ᶜand-ha*	عنْدها	they have (f) *ᶜand-hin*	عنْدهِن

Points to note

a Pay attention to the pronunciation of the letter *ᶜayn* at the beginning of this word.

b Note that because the last letter of *ᶜand* is a non-connector, all the personal suffixes stand alone.

c Remember that if you are in the Gulf and eastern parts of the Peninsula you will hear the /-ik/ of 'you have' when addressing a woman pronounced as /-ich/.

d You will also hear the /-a/ of 'he has' pronounced alternatively as /-u/ in different parts of the Peninsula. In both these cases imitate the pronunciation you hear used around you.

You may also hear a 'helper' vowel between *ᶜand* and some personal suffixes to make the combination easier to say.

(T)

we have *ᶜanda-na*	عنْدَنا	they have (m) *ᶜanda-hum*	عنْدَهُم
you have (mp) *ᶜanda-kum*	عنْدَكُم	they have (f) *ᶜanda-hin*	عنْدَهِن
you have (fp) *ᶜanda-kin*	عنْدَكِن		

Vocabulary B

These new words will allow you to make some common idiomatic phrases in combination with *ᶜand*.

idea *fikra*	فِكْرَة	money *flu:s*	فلوس
appointment *mawᶜid*	موْعِد	time *wagt*	وَقْت

Practice Sentences (T)

1 I've got an idea.
ᶜand-i fikra
عندي فكرة

2 She's got a large family.
ᶜand-ha ᶜa:ila kabi:ra
عندها عائلة كبيرة

3 We've got a small apartment.
ᶜand-na shigga ṣaghi:ra عندنا شقّة صغيرة

4 He's got an appointment.
ᶜand-u mawᶜid عنده موعد

5 They've got a big house.
ᶜanda-hum bayt kabi:r عندهم بيت كبير

Questions

Pay close attention to the tape models. Repeat the examples until you can imitate the interrogative tone to your own satisfaction.

(T) 1 Have you got a car? (to a man)
ᶜand-ak sayya:ra? عندك سيّارة؟

2 Has he got an appointment?
ᶜand-a mawᶜid? عنده موعد؟

3 Have they got a new house?
ᶜanda-hum bayt jadi:d? عندهم بيت جديد؟

4 Have you got a large family? (to a woman)
ᶜand-ik ᶜa:ila kabi:ra? عندك عائلة كبيرة؟

5 Have you (m) got time? (Are you free?)
ᶜand-ak wagt? عندك وقت؟

Negatives

The negative is made by putting *ma* in front of *ᶜand.*

(T) 1 I haven't got a lot of time.
ma ᶜand-i wagt kathi:r ما عندي وقت كثير

2 He hasn't got a big car.
ma ᶜand-u sayya:ra kabi:ra ما عنده سيّارة كبيرة

3 She hasn't got a job.
ma ᶜand-ha shughl ما عندها شغل

4 I haven't got any idea. (I haven't got a clue.)
ma ᶜand-i fikra ما عندي فكرة

5 I haven't got any money.
ma ᶜand-i flu:s ما عندي فلوس

There is no equivalent in Arabic for 'any', which therefore remains untranslated.

Translation

Translate these sentences into Arabic. Check your answers with the key at the end of the book.

1 I've got a new car.
2 She has a son and a daughter.
3 We have an apartment in Jedda.
4 My wife's got a job in the bank.
5 I haven't got time.
6 Have you an appointment? (to a woman)
7 Do you have a car? (to a man)
8 Do you have any children? (to a couple)
9 I have an appointment with the doctor.
10 They have a house in London.

Transformation drill Ⓣ

Make the following sentences negative.

1 I have an appointment.
ᶜand-i mawᶜid عندي موعد

2 We have a car.
ᶜanda-na sayya:ra عندنا سيّارة

3 He's got a lot of money.
ᶜand-u flu:s kathi:r عنده فلوس كثير

4 They've got a large house.
ᶜanda-hum bayt kabi:r عندهم بيت كبير

5 I've got a lot of work today.
ᶜand-i shughl kathi:r il-yawm عندي شغل كثير اليوم

2 Some common food items

Probably one of the most recurrent uses you will have for Arabic in the early stages of living (and learning) in an Arab country is going to the shops and markets. This is an activity that gives you an excellent opportunity to practise your Arabic. Of course, in most cities in the Peninsula where you are likely to be living, there are supermarkets catering for foreigners where the owners and assistants speak English. But if you really want to speak some Arabic, do some of your shopping at small shops where there is less chance of the shopkeeper knowing any English, and go to the same shops regularly. What you need is practice where you must repeat the same things time and again; shopping provides this kind of constant repetition. Address the owner in Arabic, this is an ideal opportunity to practise the different greetings. Ask for things in Arabic, and even if he addresses you in English, reply, if you can, in Arabic.

The following dialogues cover various shopping situations and will provide you with a model to base your shopping expeditions around. It is impossible to predict and cater for all prospective learners' needs so we have chosen some very basic items for drills and examples, and included a wider range of everyday food, fruit, drink and grocery items as supplementary vocabulary to be learnt as and when required.

Market Stall

Vocabulary C

Since the Arabic for many of these very common items varies from area to area in the Peninsula we try to give you some idea of the range you will encounter. In many cases the difference is one of pronunciation only, in other cases completely different words are used. You must find out by listening and asking which particular version is used most where you are living. If you are asking Arab friends (in English) what a word is in Arabic, insist on their telling you the word that people use when they *speak*. Many people when asked tend to give the standard or classical word, ignoring the everyday word which they and everyone else uses. In many cases the classical and the colloquial word are the same, but in other cases completely different words are used.

The first word given is one which would be understood anywhere in the Peninsula, the alternatives are given with a rough guide to countries where they are used. You may find further alternatives; if so, note them and use them. As always, use what you hear used around you.

Ⓣ tea

sha:i شاي

In the Gulf States, eastern Peninsula and Iraq this is pronounced:

sha:i شاي

in Yemen:

sha:hi شاهي

coffee

gahwa قَهْوَة

in Yemen:

bunn بُنّ

bread

khubz خُبْز

There are many names for different kinds of bread in Arabic, often particular to a small area. This word will be understood anywhere. Find out if there are any local words for bread, note them and use them.

The word for 'butter' is an example of one of those words with a wide variety of pronunciation depending on vowel changes. Use what you hear used around you.

Ⓣ butter

zubud زُبُد *zibid* زِبِد *zibda* زِبْدَة

In the Gulf and eastern parts of the Peninsula you will hear this variant:

butter

dihin دِهِن

The word for 'cheese' also has a variety of pronunciations:

Ⓣ cheese

jubun جُبُن

jiban جِبَن

juban جُبَن

jibin جِبِن

jubna جُبْنَة

milk

ḫali:b حَليب

also heard:

laban لَبَن

eggs

bayḏ بَيْض

apples

tuffa:ḫ تُفّاح

or:

tiffa:ḫ تِفّاح

oranges

burtuga:l بُرْتُقال

juice

ᶜaṣi:r عَصير

bananas
mawz موز

sugar
sukkar سُكَّر

In the Gulf and eastern parts of the Peninsula you will hear

shakar شَكَر

3 Dialogues to help you shop

In Arabic when asking the questions 'Have you any . . .?', 'Have you got any . . .?' or 'Do you have any . . .?' in combination with any of the new vocabulary above, there is no equivalent for 'any'.

Very often when enquiring about the availability of something in a shop, for example, the question 'Have you got . . .?' is expressed by:

fi: ᶜand-kum في عندكم ؟

The use of the plural personal suffix *-kum* 'you' is often used as a polite form when addressing an individual. Compare with the French 'vous'. A literal translation of the Arabic would be 'Is there near you?' to which you will hear all these possible replies:

naᶜam fi: نعم في

Yes, we have
naᶜam ᶜand-na نعم عندنا

aywa fi: ᶜand-na ايوا في عندنا

No, we haven't
la ma fi: لا ما في

la ma fi: ᶜand-na لا ما في عندنا

la ma ᶜand-na لا ما عندنا

Remember that you will hear several different words for 'Yes'. In the Gulf States and eastern Saudi Arabia you will hear *aku* and other alternatives for *fi,* meaning 'there is/are/'. See Unit Four.

Dialogue Ⓣ **A** Good morning.
ṣaba:ḥ il-khayr صباح الخير

B Good morning.
ṣaba:ḥ in-nu:r صباح النور

A Have you got any sugar?
fi:ʿand-kum sukkar? في عندكم سكّر؟

B Yes, we have.
aywa ʿand-na ايوا عندنا

A And are there any oranges today?
wa fi: burtuga:l il-ˌyawm? وفي برتقال اليوم؟

B Yes, there are.
i: naʿam fi: اي نعم في

A O.K. A kilo of sugar
ṭayyib. ki:lu sukkar طيّب كيلو سكّر

and a kilo of oranges please.
wa ki:lu burtuga:l min faḏl-ak وكيلو برتقال من فضلك

B Here you are.
tafaddal تفضّل

A Thank you.
shukran شكراً

B Don't mention it.
ʿafwan عفواً

The Arabic word for 'kilogram', 'kilo' is transliterated directly from the word used in most European languages. In the Arabic of phrases like 'a kilo of sugar' and 'a kilo of oranges' there is no equivalent to the English 'of'. You simply say '(a) kilo sugar', '(a) kilo oranges' etc.

Substitution drill Ⓣ

Model sentence
fi ʿand-kum sukkar? في عندكم سكر؟
Do you have any sugar?

Example substitution
cue *ʿaṣi:r* عصير

response *fi ʿand-kum ʿaṣi:r?* في عندكم عصير؟

cues

1	*sha:i*	شاي	5	*gahwa*	قهوة
2	*zibda*	زبدة	6	*khubz*	خبز
3	*jubna*	جبنة	7	*bayḏ*	بيض
4	*mawz*	موز	8	*ḥali:b*	حليب

9 *tuffa:ḥ* تفاح 10 *burtuga:l* برتقال

To ask 'How much is . . .?' in Arabic you use

How much? كَم ؟
kam

which you saw in Unit Seven when learning to tell the time.

Remember that in the Gulf States and eastern Saudi Arabia you will hear this word pronounced:

cham? كم ؟

In both instances the word is sometimes prefixed by *bi* making:

How much? بِكَم ؟
bi-kam?

bi-cham? بِكَم ؟

A common alternative for *kam?* is:

How much? قَدَّيْش ؟
gaddaysh?

Dialogue (T)

A How much are the oranges today? كم البرتقال اليوم ؟
kam il-burtuga:l il-yawm?

B Six riyals a kilo. ستة ريال الكيلو
sitta riya:l il-ki:lu

A And how much are the bananas? والموز بكم ؟
wa l-mawz bi-kam?

B Five riyals a kilo. خمسة ريال الكيلو
khamsa riya:l il-ki:lu

A A kilo of oranges كيلو برتقال
ki:lu burtuga:l

and a kilo of bananas please. وكيلو موز من فضلك
wa ki:lu mawz min faḍl-ak

B Here you are. تفضّل
tafaḍḍal

A Thank you. شكراً
shukran

B You're welcome. عفواً
ᶜafwan

The word order in Arabic is optional, *kam* can come at the beginning or end of the question.

Substitution drill Ⓣ

Model sentence

kam il-burtuga:l? كم البرتقال؟

How much are the oranges?

Example substitution

cue *tuffa:ḫ* تفاح

response *kam it-tuffa:ḫ?* كم التفّاح؟

Cues

1	*ḫali:b*	حليب	6	*gahwa*	قهوة
2	*sukkar*	سكّر	7	*ᶜaṣi:r*	عصير
3	*zibda*	زبدة	8	*jubna*	جبنة
4	*mawz*	موز	9	*khubz*	خبز
5	*bayḏ*	بيض	10	*sha:i*	شاي

4 Money

Talking about money in the Peninsula can be confusing. There is no unified currency in the Gulf, and different names abound, usage varying from country to country. The UAE's main unit is the Dirham; Bahrain and Kuwait use Dinars; North Yemen, Saudi Arabia, Qatar and Oman have Riyals (sometimes spelt Rials), and the word for the Indian unit of currency, the rupee, is still heard. At the moment all currencies are freely convertible.

dirham(s)
dirham (dara:him) (دَراهِم) دِرْهَم

dinar(s)
di:na:r (dana:ni:r) (دَنانير) دينار

riyal(s)
riya:l (riya:la:t) (رِيال) رِيال

These are the main units of currency corresponding to the 'pound' or 'dollar'. In each case these basic units of currency are divided into 'fils',

fils
fils فِلْس

which correspond to 'pennies' and 'cents'.

The Riyal in Saudi Arabia, North Yemen, Qatar, and the Dirham in the UAE consists of 100 fils. The Dinar in Bahrain and Kuwait consists of 1000 fils. For rough conversion in the Gulf, one UAE Dirham = one Qatari Riyal = one Bahraini Dinar.

The Arabic words for 'pound' and 'dollar' are:

pound(s)
junayh (junayha:t) — جُنَيْه (جُنَيْهات)

dollar(s)
du:la:r (du:la:ra:t) — دولار (دولارات)

Always try to decipher the writing on bank notes and coins that pass through your hands.

5 Weights and measures

Remember that when you talk about the quantity or weight of a commodity, there is no equivalent to 'of' in expressions like:

a kilo of sugar
ki:lu sukkar — كِيلو سكّر

a kilo of oranges
ki:lu burtuga:l — كيلو برتقال

When asking for different kinds of produce you need to have quite a wide range of vocabulary describing weights, measures and containers at your disposal. We will point out some of the local variants you may hear. As in the examples above there is no equivalent to the English 'of' when asking for the following items.

Vocabulary D

a 1/4 kilo of
ruba^c ki:lu رُبَع كيلو

a 1/2 kilo of
nuṣṣ ki:lu نُصّ كيلو

a kilo of
ki:lu كيلو

In some areas you will find a weight used equivalent to the English pound:

a pound of
raṭal رَطَل

a dozen
darzan دَرْزَن

There are several words for 'tin' or 'can'. Widely used is:

a tin of, a can of
^cilba عِلْبَة

In eastern parts of the Peninsula you will hear:

gu:ṭi قوطي

and in Yemen:

giṣa^ca قِصَعَة

a packet of
a pack of
a box of
ba:kit با كِت

a carton of
kartu:n كَرْتون

a bottle of
buṭil بُطِل

and in some areas:
shi:sha شيشَة

or
ga:ru:ra قارورَة

In phrases like:

a can of juice
^cilbat ^caṣi:r علبة عصير

a bottle of water
shi:shat ma:y شيشة ماي

the *ta:' marbu:ṯa* is 'opened' in pronunciation and pronounced like a regular /t/.

Ⓣ 1 A kilo of apples
ki:lu tuffa:ẖ كيلو تفاح

2 Half a kilo of sugar
nuṣṣ ki:lu sukkar نصّ كيلو سكّر

3 A quarter kilo of cheese
ruba^c ki:lu juban ربع كيلو جبن

4 A pound of butter
raṯal zibid رطل زبد

5 A packet of cigarettes
ba:kit sija:ra باكت سجارة

6 A box of matches
^cilbat kibri:t علبة كبريت

7 A bottle of water
buṯil ma:y بطل ماي

8 A tin of milk
giṣa^cat ẖali:b قصعة حليب

9 A dozen eggs
darzan bayd درزن بيض

10 A carton of cigarettes
kartu:n sija:ra كارتون سجارة

Another extremely versatile word which can be used to denote an item of something is:

ẖabba حبّة

Note the opening of the *ta:' marbu:ṯa*.

A loaf of bread
ẖabbat khubz حبّة خبز

A bar (cake) of soap
ẖabbat ṣa:bu:n حبّة صابون

This word is also used to denote 'a' or 'an' when talking about fruit. For example, 'a banana', 'an apple', 'an orange'.

an orange
ẖabbat burtuga:l حبّة برتقال

a banana
ẖabbat mawz حبّة موز

Substitution drill

Model sentence
ki:lu sukkar min fadl-ak كيلو سكّر من فضلك
A kilo of sugar, please.
Example substitution
cue *habbat sa:bu:n* حبّة صابون

response *habbat sa:bu:n min fadl-ak* حبّة صابون من فضلك

Cues
1 *ga:ru:rat ʿasi:r* قارورة عصير
2 *ba:kit saja:yir* باكت سجاير
3 *nuss ki:lu jubna* نصّ كيلو جبنة
4 *habbat burtuga:l* حبّة برتقال
5 *ʿilbat kibri:t* علبة كبريت
6 *ratal gahwa* رطل قهوة
7 *habbat tuffa:h* حبّة تفاح
8 *ʿilbat ʿasi:r* علبة عصير
9 *nuss ratal sha:y* نصّ رطل شاي
10 *habbat khubz* حبّة خبز

Supplementary section 9.1
Food

Here is a list of supplementary vocabulary relating to food items you might want to buy in a shop or in the market. These words are not given for you to learn all at once, but for you to learn as and when you need them. Any of these words which we use subsequently as an integral part of a drill or exercise will be introduced as relevant vocabulary for you to learn at the appropriate time. If you want to practise any of these items you can substitute them for the vocabulary items used in the two previous drills.

Listen for local variants and try to learn them.

flour
dagi:g دَقيق

salt
milh مِلْح

yoghourt
laban لَبَن

black pepper
filfil aswad فِلْفِل أَسْوَد

carrots
jazar جَزَر

aubergines
ba:dhinja:n باذِنْجان

cabbage
malfu:f مَلْفوف

okra
ba:miya بامِيَة

oil	*zayt*	زَيْت
olives	*zaytu:n*	زَيْتون
vinegar	*khall*	خَلّ
rice	*ruz*	رُز
honey	*^{c}asal*	عَسَل
coffee (beans)	*bunn*	بُنّ
mustard	*khardal*	خَرْدَل
pickles	*t̲urshi*	طُرْشي
jam	*murabba*	مُرَبّى
soup	*shurba*	شُرْبَة
chocolate	*shuku:la:ta*	شُكولاتَة
biscuits	*bisku:t*	بسكوت
fruit	*fawa:kih*	فَواكِه
watermelon	*juh̲h̲*	جُحّ
honeydew melon	*shamma:m*	شَمّام
apricot	*mishmish*	مِشْمِش
peach	*khu:kh*	خوخ
plum	*bargu:g*	بَرْقوق

cauliflower	*garnabi:t̲*	قَرْنَبيط
potatoes	*bat̲a:t̲a*	بَطاطا
courgettes	*ku:sa*	كوسَة
beans	*fa:s̲u:liya*	فاصوليا
peas	*bizilla*	بِزِلّة
salad	*s̲ala:t̲a*	صلاطَة
tomatoes	*t̲ama:t̲*	طَماط
cucumber	*khiya:r*	خِيار
onions	*bas̲al*	بَصَل
lettuce	*khass*	خَسّ
green pepper	*filfil akhd̲ar*	فِلفِل أخْضَر
meat	*lah̲am*	لَحَم
lamb	*lah̲am ghanami*	لَحَم غَنَمي
beef	*lah̲am bagari*	لَحَم بَقَري
liver	*kibda*	كِبْدَة
kidney	*kila:wi*	كِلاوِي
brains	*mukh*	مُخ
chicken	*daja:j*	دَجاج

lemon	*laymu:n*	لَيْمون
lime	*li:m*	ليم
pineapple	*ana:na:s*	أَناناس
grapes	*ᶜanab*	عَنَب
cigarettes	*saja:yir*	سَجايِر
matches	*kabri:t*	كَبْريت
soap	*s̱a:bu:n*	صابون
water	*ma:i*	ماي
	moya	موية

Supplementary section 9.2 'Loan words'

One of the features of Arabic which makes it a rather daunting undertaking for the absolute beginner is the lack of any substantial body of vocabulary shared with European languages. In learning Arabic you have to start from scratch, whereas if you picked up a French or Spanish newspaper, for example, you would recognise many words, even though you may not have studied those languages at all.

Arabic has, however, borrowed and adapted a number of common words from European languages; they are known as 'loan words' or 'cognates'. This gives you the opportunity of considerably expanding your vocabulary without having to learn totally new words. When using loan words you must 'Arabicise' your pronunciation, otherwise you won't be understood.

camera	*ka:mira*	كامِرا
radio	*ra:diyu*	راديو
television	*talifizyu:n*	تِلفِزْيون
telephone	*talifu:n*	تِلفون
restaurant	*ristawra:n*	رِسْتوْران
hotel	*u:ti:l*	أُوتيل
cinema	*si:nama*	سينَما
film	*film*	فِلْم
taxi	*taksi*	تَكْسي
bus	*ba:s̱*	باص
garage	*kara:j*	كَراج
tyre	*ṯayyar*	طَيَّر

battery
baṯṯariyya بَطَّرِيَّة

toilet
twa:lit تواِلت

jacket, vest
ja:kit جاكِت

trousers, pants
banṯalu:n بَنْطَلون

'Telephone' in Arabic

These are just a few of the commoner loan words which are more or less universally used throughout the Arab world. In most cases there are purely Arabic equivalents which are often used, particularly in more formal situations. You can make the task of learning the language considerably easier by incorporating loan words into your active vocabulary. Listen for others and note them as they occur.

New vocabulary in Unit 9

idea
fikra (afka:r) فِكْرَة (أَفْكار)

appointment
mawᶜid (mawa:ᶜid) موْعِد (مَواعِد)

money
flu:s فلوس

family
ᶜa:'ila عائِلَة

coffee	*gahwa*	قَهْوَة
coffee beans	*bunn*	بُنّ
bread	*khubz*	خُبْز
butter	*zibda*	زُبْدَة
cheese	*jubna*	جُبْنَة
milk	*ḥali:b*	حَليب
	laban	لَبَن
eggs	*bayḍ*	بَيْض
sugar	*sukkar*	سُكَّر
	shakar	شَكَر
juice	*ʿaṣi:r*	عَصير
orange	*burtuga:l*	بُرْتُقال
apple	*tuffa:ḥ*	تُفّاح
banana	*mawz*	مَوْز
Dirham	*dirham*	دِرْهَم
Dinar	*di:na:r*	دينار
Riyal	*riya:l*	ريال
kilogram	*ki:lu*	كِيلو
pound (lb)	*raṭl*	رَطْل
dozen	*darzan*	دَرْزَن
can, tin	*ʿilba (ʿilab)*	عِلْبَة (عُلَب)
	gu:ṭi	قوطي
packet	*ba:kit*	باكِت
carton	*kartu:n*	كَرْتون
bottle	*buṭil*	بُطِل
	shi:sha	شيشَة
	ga:ru:ra	قارورَة

Unit 10

1 More about possession

In Unit Seven you saw that there is no equivalent in Arabic to the English apostrophe *s* that indicates possession. To show possession in such cases you simply put the thing possessed in front of the possessor. For example,

Ahmad's house
bayt a<u>h</u>mad — بيت احمد

the sheikh's house
bayt ish-shaykh — بيت الشيخ

But what happens in Arabic, when in reply to the question 'Whose is this?' you want to give the bare answer 'Ahmad's' or 'The sheikh's', without specifying the thing possessed? Since Arabic has no equivalent to the apostrophe *s*, you must use something in its place. What Arabic does in such cases is to supply a noun, the literal meaning of which is 'property'.

property
<u>h</u>agg — حقّ

Ahmad's
<u>h</u>agg a<u>h</u>mad — حقّ احمد

the sheikh's
<u>h</u>agg ish-shaykh — حقّ الشّيخ

Similarly 'mine, yours, his, hers, ours, theirs' are expressed in spoken Arabic by using *<u>h</u>agg* with the relevant personal suffixes.

Vocabulary A Ⓣ

mine
<u>h</u>agg-i — حقّي

yours (ms)
<u>h</u>agg-ak — حقَّك

yours (fs)
<u>h</u>agg-ik — حقِّك

his
<u>h</u>agg-a — حقّه

hers
<u>h</u>agg-ha — حقّها

ours
<u>h</u>agg-na — حقّنا

yours (mp) *hagg-kum*	حقّكُم	theirs (m) *hagg-hum*	حقّهُم
yours (fp) *hagg-kin*	حقّكِن	theirs (f) *hagg-hin*	حقّهِن

You must distinguish between addressing a man and a woman, thus there are two forms of 'yours' when addressing both individuals and groups. Remember, when talking to mixed company you use *hagg-kum*. There are also two forms of 'theirs', one for talking about groups of men and the other for groups of women. Remember, when you are talking about mixed company you use *hagg-hum*.

Questions

You need the following vocabulary to form the questions 'Whose is this?' and its alternative in English 'Who does this belong to?'

Vocabulary B

who? *man?*	مَن ؟	this (f) *ha:dhi*	هٰذي
whose? *hagg man?*	حقّ مَن ؟	these (joint m & f) *ha:dhi:l*	هٰذيل
this (m) *ha:dha*	هٰذا		

Points to note

a *man* 'who' is distinguished from *min* 'from' by a *fatha*. This difference is only apparent in written Arabic when the short vowel signs are indicated. In spoken Arabic, of course, there is no difficulty in differentiating between these two words.

b Although the Arabic equivalent for 'whose' consists of two words, try to remember it as an inseparable unit.

c Remember that in Arabic you must distinguish between men and women and feminine objects and masculine objects when using the word 'this'. However, when referring to something unspecified the masculine form is used.

d Note the *'dagger alif* written above the *ha:'* in

this (m) *ha:dha*	هٰذا	this (f) *ha:dhi*	هٰذي

This is a feature of the writing system which has survived in only a few words in use today. You have seen this feature in the word

God *alla:h*	اللّٰه

It is not always necessary to indicate the *dagger alif* when writing these words, but you must be aware of the effect it has on pronunciation. It is a rare feature and you will only encounter it in three or four other words.

e These words for 'this' will serve you anywhere in the Peninsula . You mav find some local variation in the pronunciation of the /dh/. In some areas you will hear it pronounced as a /d/making:

ha:da   هٰذا   ha:di   هٰذي

Is this yours? (to a man)
ha:dha ḥagg-ak?   هٰذا حقّك؟

Is this Ahmad's?
ha:dha ḥagg aḥmad?   هٰذا حقّ احمد؟

Is this yours? (to a group)
ha:dha ḥagg-kum?   هٰذا حقّكم؟

Are these hers?
ha:dhi:l ḥagg-ha?   هٰذيل حقّها؟

Is this yours? (to a woman)
ha:dha ḥagg-ik?   هٰذا حقّك؟

Remember that questions on this pattern are distinguished from their corresponding statements in speech only by rising intonation. In written Arabic the only difference between the question and the statement is the question mark at the end of the sentence.

Arabic covers both these ways of asking the same question in English:

Whose is this?
Who does this belong to?

ha:dha ḥagg man?   هٰذا حقّ مَن؟

The position of *ḥagg man?* is optional, it can go either at the beginning of the question or the end. You will hear both

ha:dha ḥagg man?   هٰذا حقّ مَن؟

and

ḥagg man ha:dha?   حقّ من هٰذا؟

Practice sentences

Ⓣ Use the sentences for writing practice.

1 Who does this belong to?
ḥagg man ha:dha?   حقّ من هٰذا؟

2 These are mine.
ha:dhi:l h̲agg-i هٰذيل حقّي

3 Is this yours? (to a man)
ha:dha h̲agg-ak? هٰذا حقّك؟

4 Whose is this? (indicating car)
h̲agg man ha:dhi? حقّ من هٰذا؟

5 This is ours.
ha:dha h̲agg-na هٰذا حقنا

6 Is this yours? (addressing a group)
ha:dha h̲agg-kum? هٰذا حقّكم؟

7 Is this hers?
ha:dha h̲agg-ha? هٰذا حقّها؟

8 Whose are these?
ha:dhi:l h̲agg man? هٰذيل حقّ من؟

9 This is Ahmad's.
ha:dha h̲agg ah̲mad هٰذا حقّ احمد

10 Does this belong to you? (to a woman)
ha:dha h̲agg-ik? هٰذا حقّك؟

Question and answer drill

Model:

Q Whose is this?
h̲agg man ha:dha? حقّ من هٰذا؟

A Mine
h̲agg-i حقّي

Substitute the following for 'mine'.

1 Ahmad's
2 ours
3 theirs (m)
4 his
5 yours (mp)
6 the doctor's
7 mine
8 Muhammad's
9 Khadija's
10 theirs (f)
11 the engineer's
12 theirs (f)
13 hers
14 yours (mp)
15 the teacher's
16 yours (fp)
17 his
18 Fatima's
19 ours
20 yours (ms)

In the Gulf and eastern Saudi Arabia a word which is sometimes used as an alternative to *hagg* حقّ is:

ma:l مال

The two words are used in exactly the same way.

mine *ma:l-i*	مالي	theirs (m) *ma:l-hum*	مالهم
his *ma:l-u*	ماله	Is this yours? *ha:dha ma:l-ak?*	هذا مالك ؟
ours *ma:l-na*	مالنا	Whose is this? *ha:dha ma:l man?*	هٰذا مال من ؟

2 Prepositions and personal suffixes

In Unit Nine you saw the personal suffixes used as the equivalents to the English 'me, you, him, her, us' and 'them' in the Arabic for 'have/have got'.

I have ('near me') *^{c}and-i*	عندي	we have ('near us') *^{c}and-na*	عندنا

The personal suffixes can be used in this way with any preposition. One preposition you will find frequent use for with the personal suffixes is:

with
ma^c مَع

Vocabulary C Ⓣ

with me *ma^c-i*	مَعْي	with us *ma^c-na*	مَعْنا
with you (m) *ma^c-ak*	مَعَك	with you (mp) *ma^c-kum*	مَعْكُم
with you (f) *ma^c-ik*	مَعِك	with you (fp) *ma^c-kin*	مَعْكِن
with him *ma^c-a*	مَعَه	with them (m) *ma^c-hum*	مَعْهُم
with her *ma^c-ha*	مَعْها	with them (f) *ma^c-hin*	مَعْهِن

Note that 'with you' (f) in the Gulf and eastern parts of the Peninsula is:

ma^c-ich معك

For 'with him' you may hear:

ma^c-u معه

depending on where you are in the Peninsula.

The most unusual feature of these personal suffixes to us is that they are written as part of the word they follow, thus 'with me' which must be written as two words in English appears as a single entity in Arabic.

An alternative for 'have/have got'

You are already aware that the concepts of personal possession conveyed in English by the verbs 'have/have got' are in Arabic conveyed not by a verb, but by the word عند ('near') with the relevant personal suffix. When talking about personal possession in English it is quite common to use the words 'on' or 'with' to specify possession on the body or about the person, or in the sense of accompaniment. For example, I haven't got any money *on* me, I have a car *with* me, I've got my family *with* me. In Arabic, these somewhat more specific forms of possession are conveyed by the use of مع *ma^{c}a* 'with' plus the relevant personal suffix, in place of عند

I haven't got any money on me
ma ma^c-i: flu:s ما معي فلوس

Contrast with:
I haven't got any money (ie 'I'm broke')
ma ^{c}and-i: flu:s ما عندي فلوس

I have a car with me (not necessarily implying that you actually own the car, you may have borrowed it from a friend)
ma^c-i: sayya:ra معي سيّارة

Contrast with:
I have a car (ie 'I own a car')
^{c}and-i: sayya:ra عندي سيّارة

I've got my family with me
ma^c-i: ^{c}a:'ilat-i: معي عائلتي

Contrast with:

^{c}and-i: 'a:'ila عندي عائلة

I've got a family
(ie 'I'm married with children)

Sometimes Arabic uses مع to indicate personal possession in cases where English doesn't need 'on' or'with' because it is quite obvious that possession on the body or about the person is being referred to.

Have you got a cigarette (on you)?
ma^c-ak sija:ra? معك سجارة ؟

Have you got any matches (on you)?
ma^c-ak kabri:t? معك كبريت ؟

Have you got a watch?
ma^c-ak sa:'a? معك ساعة ؟

3 Nationalities

You have already seen how to use the Arabic names for a number of Arab and western countries in reply to such questions as 'Where are you from?' and 'Where is he from?'

Where are you (m) from?
inta min wayn? انت من وين ؟

I'm from London
ana: min lundun انا من لندن

Where's he from?
huwa min wayn? هو من وين ؟

He's from Qatar.
huwa min gatar هو من قطر

We now want to show you how to form adjectives from the names of countries so that in addition to saying 'I'm from England', 'He's from Qatar', you can say 'I'm English', 'He's Qatari'.

In English, adjectives describing nationality are formed from the names of countries in a variety of ways,

Name of country	**Adjective**
England	English
France	French
America	American
Lebanon	Lebanese
Qatar	Qatari

It can be difficult for foreign learners of English to predict the form of an adjective of nationality, even if they know the English version of the country name. The task is far easier for learners of Arabic, since most such adjectives are formed simply by adding the letter /ya:'/ to the country name. This gives the masculine singular form of the adjective. Remember that a long vowel at the end of a word is transliterated as its short vowel equivalent, in this case /i/.

	Masculine singular of adjective				Name of country	
Qatari	قطري *gaṯari*	=	ي	+	قطر *gaṯar*	Qatar
Lebanese	لبناني *lubna:ni*	=	ي	+	لبنان *lubna:n*	Lebanon

The feminine adjective is formed by adding the suffix /iyya/ to the name of the country:

	Feminine singular of adjective				Name of country	
Qatari	قطريّة *gaṯariyya*	=	يّة	+	قطر *gaṯar*	Qatar
Lebanese	لبنانيّة *lubna:niyya*	=	يّة	+	لبنان *lubna:n*	Lebanon

Do not try to learn all the adjectives describing nationality that are given in the following pages which cover all Arab and major western nations. You will probably need only half a dozen as active vocabulary, but since they are all closely based on the names of the countries you saw in the maps in Unit Three no new vocabulary learning is involved. Those that you do not learn to use actively should form part of your passive vocabulary, so that when you hear them used in conversation or see them written in street signs, names, titles or advertisements, you can identify them.

Here is a list of countries from which adjectives of nationality are formed in this way.

Feminine singular of adjective		Masculine singular of adjective		Name of country
لبنانيّة *lubna:niyya*	Lebanese	لبناني *lubna:ni*	لبنان *lubna:n*	Lebanon
عمانيّة *ʿuma:niyya*	Omani	عماني *ʿuma:ni*	عمان *ʿuma:n*	Oman
مصريّة *masriyya*	Egyptian	مصري *maṣri*	مصر *masr*	Egypt

قطريّة *gatariyya*	Qatari	قطري *gatari*	قطر *gatar*	Qatar
تونسيّة *tu:nisiyya*	Tunisian	تونسي *tu:nisi*	تونس *tu:nis*	Tunisia
إيرانية *i:ra:niyya*	Iranian	ايراني *i:ra:ni*	ايران *i:ra:n*	Iran
فلسطينية *filastinniyya*	Palestinian	فلسطيني *filasti:ni*	فلسطين *filasti:n*	Palestine

Countries whose Arabic names begin with the prefixed definite article *il* 'the' lose this prefix when the adjective of nationality is formed.

Feminine singular of adjective		**Masculine singular of adjective**		**Name of country**
بحرينيّة *bahrayniyya*	Bahraini	بحريني *bahrayni*	البحرين *il-bahrayn*	Bahrain
كويتيّة *kuwaytiyya*	Kuwaiti	كويتي *kuwayti*	الكويت *il-kuwayt*	Kuwait
اردنيّة *'urduniyya*	Jordanian	اردني *'urduni*	الاردن *il-urdun*	Jordan
يمنيّة *yamaniyya*	Yemeni	يمني *yamani*	اليمن *il-yaman*	Yemen
باكستانيّة *ba:kista:niyya*	Pakistani	باكستاني *ba:kista:ni*	الباكستان *il-ba:kista:n*	Pakistan
سودانيّة *su:da:niyya*	Sudanese	سوداني *su:da:ni*	السّودان *is-su:da:n*	Sudan
مغربيّة *maghribiyya*	Moroccan	مغربي *maghribi*	المغرب *il-maghrib*	Morocco
عراقيّة *ᶜira:qiyya*	Iraqi	عراقي *ᶜiraqi*	العراق *il-ᶜiraq*	Iraq

The names of certain countries are modified before the addition of the adjectival suffixes:

Feminine singular of adjective		Masculine singular of adjective		Name of country
سوريّة *su:riyya*	Syrian	سوري *su:ri*	سوريا *su:riya*	Syria
فرنساويّة *fransa:wiyya*	French	فرنساوي *fransa:wi*	فرنسا *fransa*	France
امريكيّة *amri:kiyya*	American	امريكي *'amri:ki*	امريكا *amri:ka*	America
انجليزيّة *ingli:ziyya*	English	انجليزي *ingli:zi*	انجلترا *ingilterra*	England
سعوديّة *suᶜu:diyya*	Saudi	سعودي *suᶜu:di*	السعودية *is-suᶜu:diyya*	Saudi Arabia

The names of a number of Gulf states do not lend themselves to the formation of adjectives of nationality. They are:

Ras al-Khayma
ra:s il-khayma راس الخيمة

Abu Dhabi
abu dabi أبو ظبي

Dubai
dubay دبي

Umm al-Qaywan
umm il-gaywa:n ام القيوان

Sharja
sha:riga شارقة

Fujayra
il-fujayra الفجيرة

It is more usual to use من *min* ('from') and the name of the country when describing someone from these countries.

He's from Abu Dhabi.
huwa min abu dhabi هو من أبو ظبي

She's from Ras al-Khayma.
hiya min ra:s il-khayma هي من راس الخيمة

Transformation drill

Change the sentences below on the following pattern:

Ⓣ **Model sentence**

He's Saudi. ◁—— He's from Saudi Arabia.

هو سعودي ◁—— هو من السّعودية

Listen to each sentence and make the transformation in the gap provided:

١ احمد من البحرين

٢ هي من قطر

٣ هو من امريكا

٤ فاطمة من مصر

٥ محمّد من ايران

٦ انا من عُمان

٧ جون من انجلترّا

٨ انتَ من ايمن؟

٩ هو من الكويت

١٠ انا من السّعودية

١١ هي من فلسطين

١٢ المدرّس من مصر

١٣ هي من فرنسا

١٤ المهندس من الاردن

١٥ ماري من امريكا

١٦ قاسم من السّعودية

When you have completed the tape drill, use these sentences and the transformations you produce from them for reading and writing practice.

Most adjectives of nationality form their plurals on the 'strong masculine' and 'strong feminine' patterns, for example:

Masculine plural		**Masculine singular**
لبنانيين		لبناني
lubna:niyi:n	Lebanese	*lubna:ni*
بحرينيين		بحريني
bah̲rayniyi:n	Bahraini	*bah̲rayni*

Feminine plural		**Feminine singular**
yamaniyya:t	Yemeni	*yamaniyya*
يمنيّات		يمنيّة
amri:kiyya:t	American	*amri:kiyya*
امريكيّات		امريكيّة

The one notable exception to this rule is 'English', the masculine plural of which is irregular:

Masculine plural		**Masculine singular**
انجليز		انجليزي
ingli:z	English	*ingli:zi*

The feminine plural is quite regular:

Feminine plural		**Feminine singular**
انجليزيّات		انجليزيّة
ingli:ziyya:t	English	*ingli:ziyya*

Notice also:

Masculine plural		**Masculine singular**
عرب		عربي
ᶜarab	Arab	*ᶜarabi*
Feminine plural		**Feminine singular**
عربيّات		عربيّة
ᶜarabiyya:t	Arab	*ᶜarabiyya*

4 Ordinal numbers

	Masculine		**Feminine**	
first	*awwal*	أوَّل	*u:la*	أُولى
second	*tha:ni*	ثاني	*tha:niya*	ثانِيَة
third	*tha:lith*	ثالِث	*tha:litha*	ثالِثَة
fourth	*ra:bi*^{c}	رابِع	*ra:bi*^{c}*a*	رابِعَة
fifth	*kha:mis*	خامِس	*kha:misa*	خامِسَة
sixth	*sa:dis*	سادِس	*sa:disa*	سادِسَة
seventh	*sa:bi*^{c}	سابِع	*sa:bi*^{c}*a*	سابِعَة
eighth	*tha:min*	ثامِن	*tha:mina*	ثامِنَة
ninth	*ta:si*^{c}	تاسِع	*ta:si*^{c}*a*	تاسِعَة
tenth	^{c}*a:shir*	عاشِر	^{c}*a:shira*	عاشِرَة

With the exception of 'first', the feminine form is in all cases made by the addition of *ta:' marbu:ṯa* to the masculine.

The ordinal numbers in Arabic may either precede or follow the noun. When the ordinal precedes the noun, both ordinal and noun stand alone without the definite article, and the ordinal is always in its masculine form:

the first building
awwal bina:ya أوَّل بِناية

the third car
tha:lith sayya:ra ثالِث سيّارة

When the ordinal follows the noun, both noun and number take the definite article, and the number must agree in gender with the noun:

the first building
il-bina:ya il-u:la البِناية الأولى

the third car

is-sayya:ra ith-tha:litha السيّارة الثّالثة

Points to note

a The Arabic for 'second' can also mean 'other' or 'another'. In this case the number follows the noun and agrees with it in gender, but neither noun nor adjective take the definite article:

another car

sayya:ra tha:niya سيّارة ثانية

(This literally means 'a second car').

b An Arabic ordinal may also be used to translate an English ordinal without an accompanying noun, where the ordinal may be either definite:

the first	*il-'awwal*	الأوّل	the third	*ith-tha:lith*	الثّالث

or indefinite. In this case the ordinal is frequently preceded by *wa:ḫid* 'one':

a second/another (one)

wa:ḫid tha:ni واحد ثاني

a third (one)

wa:ḫid tha:lith واحد ثالث

Translation

1 The third building.
2 Another house.
3 The first car.
4 The fourth street.
5 Another one.
6 The first.
7 The third week.
8 Another idea.
9 The other student (m).
10 The second apartment.
11 The third.
12 The fourth office.
13 The fifth book.
14 The second building.
15 Another company.

5 Body language

Arabs are so fond of gestures that it has often been said it is possible to conduct a conversation in Arabic without uttering a single word. Gestures tend to be similar throughout the Arab world, though as with language in the more conventional sense, you will encounter some localised variation. Be observant and incorporate gestures into your general language performance, try not to be self-conscious, and above all do not feel that you are being pretentious. Body language is as fundamental a part of communication as words. Here are a few of the more frequently used gestures.

1 Putting together the tips of the fingers and thumb and moving the hand up and down signifies 'Be patient', and is a gesture much used by drivers.

2 Tugging the point of the chin between horizontal thumb and forefinger of the right hand signifies disapproval of an action or statement, and is often accompanied by the word *ᶜayb* عَيْب 'shame'. In this gesture the point of the chin is symbolic of the beard, traditionally associated with honour in Arab culture.

3 Blinking with both eyes simultaneously, sometimes accompanied by a barely perceptible nod of the head, signifies 'yes'.

4 Raising both eyebrows simultaneously, sometimes accompanied by a slight upward movement of the head and a clicking sound made by the tip of the tongue against the back of the upper teeth, signifies 'no'.

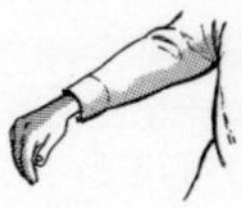

5 To beckon someone you should hold your hand downwards with the fingers together and motion towards yourself. Beckoning with one finger held up has an offensive connotation for Arabs.

Supplementary section 10
Travel

passport
jawa:z (jawa:za:t)   جَواز (جَوازات)

ba:sbu:r   باسْبور

visa
ta'shi:r (ta'shi:ra:t)   تَأْشير (تَأْشيرات)

fi:sa   فيزا

consul
gunsul   قُنْصُل

consulate
gunṣuliyya   قُنْصُليَّة

ticket
tadhkira (tadha:kir)   تَذْكِرة (تَذاكِر)

embassy
sifa:ra (sifa:ra:t)   سِفارَة (سِفارات)

airport
maṭa:r   مَطار

'plane
ṭayya:ra (ṭayra:n)   طَيّارَة (طَيَران)

suitcase; bag
shanṭa (shanaṭ)   شَنْطة (شَنَط)

customs
jama:rik   جَمارك

New vocabulary in Unit 10

who *man*	مَن؟	Palestinian *filasṭi:ni*	فِلَسْطيني
whose *ḥagg man*	حَقّ مَن؟	Bahraini *baḥrayni*	بَحْرَيْني
these *ha:dhi:l*	هٰذيل	Kuwaiti *kuwayti*	كُوَيْتي
God *alla:h*	الله	Jordanian *urduni*	أُرْدُني
English *ingli:zi*	إنْجليزي	Yemeni *yamani*	يَمَني
American *amri:ki*	أمريكي	Pakistani *ba:kista:ni*	بَاكِسْتاني
Qatari *gaṭari*	قَطَري	Sudanese *su:da:ni*	سوداني
Lebanese *lubna:ni*	لُبْناني	Moroccan *maghribi*	مَغْرِبي
Omani *ᶜuma:ni*	عُماني	Iraqi *ᶜira:qi*	عِراقي
Egyptian *maṣri*	مَصْري	Syrian *su:ri*	سوري
Tunisian *tu:nisi*	تونسي	French *fransa:wi*	فَرْنساوي
Iranian *i:ra:ni*	إيراني	Saudi *suᶜu:di*	سُعودي

Unit 11

1 An introduction to verbs

With the lack of an equivalent in Arabic for 'am, is' and 'are' and the use of *ʿand* together with the personal suffixes to express 'have, have got', you have been able to learn to say a lot of simple but very useful Arabic without using a verb. Verbs should not pose you too many problems. There are only two forms of the verb in spoken Arabic: one for talking about present time and future time, and the other for talking about past time. In this and following units we want to show you how the verb form for talking about present time works. From now on we will call this the 'present tense'.

The present tense in Arabic obeys a regular and predictable system. Each verb consists of a 'stem', which carries the meaning of the verb, to which are added prefixes and suffixes which indicate the different persons 'I, you, he, she', etc, and are absolutely constant from one verb to another.

The prefixes are added to the stem by one of the short vowels which we shall refer to as the 'helper' vowel. Thus, once you know a verb stem and the helper vowel that joins the prefixes to the stem, you can form any verb.

Set out below is the verb 'do' in all the singular persons. Note that there are two forms of 'you', one for addressing a man, the other for addressing a woman.

Listen carefully to the models on the tape several times, then read the notes below.

Vocabulary A Ⓣ

The stem of 'do' is:
ʿmal عمل

I do
aʿmal أعْمَل

you do (m)
taʿmal تَعْمَل

you do (f)
taʿmali:n تَعْمَلين

he does
yaʿmal يَعْمَل

she does
taʿmal تَعْمَل

Points to note

a 'I' in pronunciation is indicated by a short /a/. In written Arabic the *alif* is merely a bearer for the *fatḫa* and consequently is not pronounced.

Remember that *alif* is a non-connector and therefore always stands alone at the beginning of a word. This means that the first letter of the stem, in this case the *ᶜayn,* appears in its initial form.

b 'You'(addressing a man) is indicated by the letter *ta:'* joined to the first letter of the stem.

Note the change in the appearance of the stem. The first letter, the *ᶜayn,* now appears in its medial form because *ta:'* joins to following letters.

c 'You' (addressing a woman) is indicated by the letter *ta:'* joined to the first letter of the stem, and *i:n* joined to the last letter of the stem .

d 'He' is indicated by the letter *ya:'* joined to the first letter of the stem.

e 'She' is indicated by the letter *ta:'* joined to the first letter of the stem.

Note that 'you' (addressing a man) and 'she' are identical in form. Context will usually show if a man is being addressed or a woman referred to.

f As a rule, the helper vowel with any verb is going to be either /a/ or /i/.

It is very difficult to be categoric about which of the two you will hear used with any one verb. Since it is points like this which distinguish the Arabic of one area from that of another, you are just as likely to hear:

he does
yiᶜmal يِعْمَل

as:

he does
yaᶜmal يَعْمَل

depending on where you happen to be in the Peninsula. In fact this helper vowel is very fluid, and it does not really matter which you use, both pronunciations are used and would be understood all over the Peninsula; it is only a very minor pronunciation difference. Remember that it is the letters of the stem and the prefixes which convey the important information about the verb; whether the helper vowel is /a/ or /i/ is of little consequence. But, as you can see and hear in the model above, the helper vowel remains constant within a verb, so if you use /a/, use it with all the persons, and if you use /i/, use it with all the persons. If you are living in an Arab country, listen to what people around you say, and imitate their pronunciation in your own speech.

Here is a table showing the different prefixes and suffixes that make up the singular persons of the present tense.

I	a . . .	أَ
you (m)	t . . .	تـ
you (f)	t . . . i:n	تـ . . . ين
he	y . . .	يـ
she	t . . .	تـ

Note that 'I' is always indicated by /a/ in pronunciation of all verbs, whatever the helper vowel.

Generally it is not necessary to use:

I	*ana*	انا	he	*huwa*	هو
you (m)	*inta*	انتَ	she	*hiya*	هي
you (f)	*inti*	انتِ			

with verbs. The prefixes perform the same function and convey the same information to the listener.

In some areas, the final /n/ of the 'you' (feminine) form of verbs is dropped:

you (f) do
ta^c^mali:n تعملين

or
ta^c^mali تعملي

Use the form that is used most commonly in your area.

The verbs 'go' and 'want'

Vocabulary B (T) The stem of 'go' is *ru:ẖ* روح

The helper vowel is /i/.

I go *aru:ẖ*	أَروح	he goes *yiru:ẖ*	يِروح
you go (m) *tiru:ẖ*	تِروح	she goes *tiru:ẖ*	تِروح
you go (f) *tiru:ẖi:n*	تِروحين		

Although the transliteration shows the helper vowel as /i/, depending on where you are in the Peninsula, you may hear:

he goes
yaru:h̠ يَروح

Very often there is no helper vowel at all and you will hear:

you go (m)
tru:h̠ تروح

he goes
yru:h̠ يروح

As always, listen to Arabic being spoken, and imitate in your speech what you hear used around you.

Vocabulary C Ⓣ The stem of 'want' is *bgha*
The helper vowel is /i/.

I want
abgha أَبْغى

he wants
yibgha يِبغى

you want (m)
tibgha تِبْغى

she wants
tibgha تِبغى

you want (f)
tibghi:n تِبْغين

The last letter of the stem is an *alif maqṣu:ra*. This is the name given to a final *alif* when it is represented by a *ya:'* without dots. It occurs only at the end of a word. It is pronounced and transliterated exactly like a regular *alif* at the end of a word, ie as /a/.

Pay attention to verbs where the last letter of the stem is a vowel. There are not that many, but several very common verbs have this feature.

When making 'you' for addressing a woman, the final vowel is dropped, and the *i:n* is joined directly to the second letter of the stem, making:

you want (f)
tibghi:n تِبْغين

This is not a random change, any verb whose stem ends in a vowel will behave in exactly the same way.

'Want' and 'do' are very common verbs. There are a number of alternatives for *yibgha* and *ya'mal* in use throughout the Peninsula. Check with supplementary section 11.1 at the end of this unit, where the most common of these variants are listed, and concentrate on those which are most typical of your area.

Lack of the infinitive

There is no equivalent in Arabic to the infinitive form of verbs in English, eg, 'to do', 'to go', 'to want'. Thus sentences like 'I want to go', 'She wants to go', are rendered:

I want to go
abgha aru:h̲ ابغى اروح

This literally means 'I want I go'.

She wants to go
hiya tibgha tiru:h̲ هي تبغى تروح

This literally means 'She wants she goes.'
Note the use of *hiya* 'she' to distinguish between 'you' (m) and 'she', which are identical in form.

Likewise, asking questions like 'What do you (f) want to do?' 'Where does he want to go?' are rendered in Arabic:

What do you (f) want to do?
aysh tibghi:n taᶜmali:n? ايش تبغين تعملين؟

This literally means 'What you want you do?'

Where does he want to go?
wayn yibgha yiru:h̲? وين يبغى يروح؟

This literally means 'Where he wants he goes?'

The following dialogues and drills practise these three verbs in all the singular persons together with a selection of familiar vocabulary from earlier units. Before going on to the first dialogue, go back and listen to and repeat the tape models of these three verbs again.

Dialogue

Since Arabic distinguishes between addressing a man and a woman, we include dialogues for men or women talking to a man, and for men or women talking to a woman. Listen to both dialogues and repeat whichever is appropriate to you.

Vocabulary D Ⓣ OK
t̲ayyib طيّب

Let's go! Come on!
yalla يَلاّ

Addressing a man
A Hello.
marh̲aba مرحبا

B Hello. اهلا
ahlan

How are you? كيف حالك ؟
kayf ḥa:l-ak?

A Very well, thanks. بخير الحمد لله
bi-khayr il-ḥamdu li-lla:h

B What do you (m) want to do? ايش تبغى تعمل ؟
aysh tibgha taᶜmal?

A I want to go to the market. ابغى اروح السوق
abgha aru:h is-su:g

B OK, let's go. طيب يلا
ṭayyib yalla

Points to note

a What do you (m) want to do? ايش تبغى تعمل ؟
aysh tibgha taᶜmal?

The Arabic literally translated is 'What you want you do?' Remember that there is no Arabic equivalent to the English '*to* do', '*to* go'.

b I want to go to the market. ابغى اروح السوق
abgha aru:ḥ is-su:g

Literally translated, the Arabic means 'I want I go the market'. Remember that not only is the 'to' of the English infinitive not translated, but neither is the preposition 'to' generally translated when talking about going somewhere, for example, 'to the market'.

Addressing a woman
Foreign men living in the Middle East will not, in the normal run of affairs, have many opportunities to talk to Arab women, but of course European women have the chance to mix socially with Arab women. So, it is European women learners who must concentrate on the special feminine forms of the language. Men should have at least a slight understanding and knowledge of them so that they can use them if the necessity arises.

The dialogue above has been re-written for a woman talking to a woman. Men can of course use this exercise, taking the part of **B** asking the questions, and using **A**'s replies as listening comprehension.

Ⓣ **A** Hello.

marhaba مرحبا

B Hello. How are you?
ahlan kayf ha:l-ik? اهلا. كيف حالك؟

A Very well, thanks.
bi-khayr il-hamdu li-lla:h بخير الحمد لله

B What do you (f) want to do?
aysh tibghi:n taᶜmali:n ايش تبغين تعملين؟

A I want to go to the market
abgha aru:h is-su:g ابغى اروح السّوق

B OK, let's go.
tayyib yalla طيّب. يلاّ

Points to note

What do you want to do?
aysh tibghi:n taᶜmali:n ايش تبغين تعملين؟

Remember the suffix /-i:n/ indicates that a woman is being addressed.

Substitution drill

To give you practice asking and hearing the two common questions 'What do you want to do?' and 'Where do you want to go?' we include these two drills using the three verbs introduced in this unit and some familiar vocabulary items from previous units.

Q *aysh tibgha taᶜmal?* ايش تبغى تعمل؟

aysh tibghi:n taᶜmali:n? ايش تبغين تعملين

A *abgha aru:h* *il-bayt* ابغى اروح البيت

il-bahr البحر

is-su:g السّوق

il-bank البنك

Q *wayn tibgha tiru:h?* وين تبغى تروح؟

wayn tibghi:n tiru:hi:n? وين تبغين تروحين؟

A *abgha aru:h̲* *il-maṯcam* ابغى اروح المطعم

is-si:nama السّنما

il-bah̲r البحر

il-fundug الفندق

il-maktab المكتب

is-sifa:ra السّفارة

We do not include an English key to these drills since all the vocabulary is familiar.

For further writing and comprehension practice, write these questions and answers out in your own hand and then translate them into English. If you want to extend the drills to practise other vocabulary, you can substitute other places in your answers to the questions.

Questions

Asking questions which are not introduced by a 'question word', for example, 'what' and 'where', is very straightforward in Arabic. Remember that in Arabic the order of the words in a sentence remains the same for both statements and questions. You indicate that you are asking a question by using 'rising intonation'.

Do you (f) want to go home?
tibghi:n tiru:h̲i:n il-bayt? تبغين تروحين البيت ؟

Does he want to go?
yibgha yiru:h̲? يبغى يروح ؟

Note that in writing the only difference between a question and a statement is the question mark at the end of the sentence.

Do you (m) want to go?
tibgha tiru:h̲? تبغى تروح ؟

Do you (f) want to go?
tibghi:n tiru:h̲i:n? تبغين تروحين؟

Does he want to go?
yibgha yiru:h̲? يبغى يروح ؟

Does she want to go?
hiya tibgha tiru:h̲? هي تبغى تروح ؟

Repetition drill Ⓣ Listen and repeat after the models, paying particular attention to how you ask the questions.

1 *tibghi:n tiru:h̲i:n is-su:g?* تبغين تروحين السوق ؟

2 *yibgha yiru:h̲ is-si:nama?* يبغى يروح السّينما ؟

3 *tibgha tiru:h̲ il-maṯᶜam?* تبغى تروح المطعم ؟

4 *hiya tibgha tiru:h̲ il-bah̲r?* هي تبغى تروح البحر؟

5 *tibgha tiru:h̲?* تبغى تروح ؟

6 *tibghi:n tiru:h̲i:n?* تبغين تروحين؟

7 *yibgha yiru:h̲?* يبغى يروح ؟

8 *hiya tibgha tiru:h̲?* هي تبغى تروح ؟

9 *tibghi:n tiru:h̲i:n il-bayt?* تبغين تروحين البيت ؟

10 *tibgha tiru:h̲ il-madi:na?* تبغى تروح المدينة ؟

Write out these questions and then translate them into English.

Negatives

To make a statement negative you simply put

ma ما

in front of the verb.

I don't want to go.
ma abgha aru:h̲ ما ابغى اروح

He doesn't want to go.
ma yibgha yiru:h̲ ما يبغى يروح

She doesn't want to go.
hiya ma tibgha tiru:h̲ هي ما تبغى تروح

Transformation drill (T)

1 *abgha aru:h̲* ابغى اروح

2 *hiya tibgha tiru:h̲ il-bayt* هي تبغى تروح البيت

3 *tibgha tiru:h̲?* تبغى تروح ؟

4 *abgha aru:h̲ is-si:nama* ابغى اروح السّينما

5 *yibgha yiru:h̲* يبغى يروح

6 *tibghi:n tiru:h̲i:n?* تبغين تروحين ؟

7 *yibgha yiru:h̲ il-maktab* يبغى يروح المكتب

8 *abgha aru:h̲ il-mat̲ᶜam* ابغى اروح المطعم

9 *hiya tibgha tiru:h̲ il-bah̲r* هي تبغى تروح البحر

10 *abgha aru:h̲ il-bayt* ابغى اروح البيت

Use the tape for dictation practice, then translate the sentences into English.

Short answers to questions

In English we tend to answer questions with short answers rather than with a blunt 'Yes' or 'No'. For example:

Q Do you want to go?
A Yes, I do./No, I don't.
and
Q Does she want to go?
A Yes, she does./No, she doesn't.

Arabic, however, does not have equivalents to our short answers, and the usual way to reply to questions like the examples above would be either 'Yes' or 'No'. This might seem a little abrupt to an English speaker unconsciously used to short answer forms, but it is perfectly natural to a native Arabic speaker.

Remember that you will hear a variety of words for 'Yes' used throughout the Peninsula; check them in Unit Two.

Substitution drill (T) This drill practises the verbs you have just learned with 'with' and the suffix pronouns.

Model sentence

abgha aru:ẖ maᶜ-ak ابغى اروح معك

I want to go with you.

Example substitution

cue *huwa* —— *inti* هو —— انت

he —— you (fs)

response *yibgha yiru:ẖ maᶜ-ik* يبغى يروح معك

Cues

1 *huwa* —— *ana* هو —— انا

2 *hiya* —— *ana* هي —— انا

3 *ana* —— *huwa* انا —— هو

4 *ana* —— *inti* انا —— انت

5 *hiya* —— *inta* هي —— انت

6 *huwa* —— *hiya* هو —— هي

7 *huwa* —— *inti* هو —— انت

8 *ana* —— *hiya* انا —— هي

9 *ana* —— *inta* انا —— انت

10 *huwa* —— *inti* هو —— انت

2 Numbers 101 to infinity

We are including the following information on the higher numbers in the main part of the text because it is very likely that most students will need to use them, however rarely, in the early stages of learning the language. At this stage it will be sufficient for you to acquaint yourself with the general principles governing the use of the higher numbers. Later you can return to this section as often as it takes for you to feel confident in using the full range of numbers.

Ⓣ 101	*miya wa wa:ẖid*	مية وواحد
102	*miya wa ithnayn*	مية وإثنين
103	*miya wa thala:tha*	مية وثلاثة
120	*miya wa ^{c}ashri:n*	مية وعشرين
124	*miya wa arba^{c}a wa ^{c}ashri:n*	مية وأربعة وعشرين
128	*miya wa thama:niya wa ^{c}ashri:n*	مية وثمانية وعشرين
200	*miyat-ayn*	ميتين
256	*miyat-ayn wa sitta wa khamsi:n*	ميتين وستة وخمسين
300	*thala:thmiya*	ثلاثمية
400	*arba^c miya*	أربعمية
500	*khamsmiya*	خمسمية
527	*khamsmiya wa saba^{c}a wa ^{c}ashri:n*	خمسمية وسبعة وعشرين
600	*sittmiya*	ستّمية

700 *saba^c^miya* سبعمية

800 *thama:nmiya* ثمانمية

900 *tisa^c^miya* تسعمية

Points to note

a Two or more numbers are always joined by *wa* و 'and', (sometimes pronounced /u/).
b The dual form is used for 200. The *ta:' marbu:ta* of *miya* is untied before the addition of the dual suffix.
c The hundreds from 300 to 900 are written as one word.
d Notice the Arabic word order in compound numbers: hundreds—▷units—▷tens.

Ⓣ

1000 *alf* ألْف

1979 *alf wa tisa^c^miya wa saba^c^a wa tis^c^i:n* ألف وتسعمية وسبعة وتسعين

1980 *alf wa tisa^c^miya wa thama:ni:n* ألف وتسعمية وثمانين

1981 *alf wa tisa^c^miya wa wa:hid wa thama:ni:n* ألف وتسعمية وواحد وثمانين

2000 *alf-ayn* ألفين

3000 *thala:that a:la:f* ثلاثة آلاف

4000 *arba^c^at a:la:f* أربعة آلاف

etc.

Points to note

a 1000 in Arabic is simply '(a) thousand'.
b The dual form is used for 2000.
c Notice the Arabic word order: thousands—▷hundreds —▷ units—▷tens.
d The plural of *alf* ألف (*a:la:f* آلاف) is used with numbers 3000 upwards.

Ⓣ 1 million *milyu:n* مِلْيون

2 million *milyu:n-ayn* مليونين

3 million *thala:tha mala:yi:n* ثلاثة ملايين

4 million *arba^c^a mala:yi:n* أربعة ملايين

5,785,962

khamsa mala:yi:n wa saba^cmiya wa khamsa wa thama:ni:n alf wa tisa^cmiya wa ithnayn wa sitti:n

خمسة ملايين وسبعمية وخمسة وثمانين ألف وتسعمية وإثنين وستين

Points to note

a 1 million in Arabic is simply '(a) million'.
b The dual form is used for 2 million.
c The plural form of *milyu:n* مليون (*mala:yi:n* ملايين) is used with numbers of three to ten million.

Numbers followed by nouns

A noun directly preceded by a number between three and ten in Arabic is in its plural form, as you would expect. However, a curious feature of the language is that a noun will take the *singular* form when preceded by any number greater than ten.

1 house
bayt — بيت

2 houses
bayt-ayn — بيتين

3 houses
thala:tha buyu:t — ثلاثة بيوت

4 houses
arba^ca buyu:t — أربعة بيوت

5 houses
khamsa buyu:t — خمسة بيوت

6 houses
sitta buyu:t — ستّة بيوت

7 houses
saba^ca buyu:t — سبعة بيوت

8 houses
thama:niya buyu:t — ثمانية بيوت

9 houses
tisa^ca buyu:t — تسعة بيوت

10 houses
^cashra buyu:t — عشرة بيوت

11 houses
h̲ida^{c}sh bayt حدعش بيت

20 houses
^{c}ashri:n bayt عشرين بيت

27 houses
saba^{c}a wa ^{c}ashri:n bayt سبعة وعشرين بيت

50 houses
khamsi:n bayt خمسين بيت

59 houses
tisa^{c}a wa khamsi:n bayt تسعة وخمسين بيت

100 houses
miyat bayt مية بيت

101 houses
miya wa bayt مية وبيت

102 houses
miya wa bayt-ayn مية وبيتين

103 houses
miya wa thala:tha buyu:t مية وثلاثة بيوت

104 houses
miya wa arba^{c}a buyu:t مية وأربعة بيوت

118 houses
miya wa thama:nta^{c}sh bayt مية وثمانتعش بيت

a The Arabic forms for '101 houses' and '102 houses' follow logically from information already given, but may appear curious at first sight.

b Pay special attention to the Arabic for '103 houses' and '104 houses'. The plural form is used *whenever* a noun is immediately preceded by a number between three and ten, no matter what other number may occur before them.

Re-cap on numbers

1 In Arabic there are three forms of the noun; singular, dual and plural.

2 The plural form is used whenever a noun is immediately preceded by any of the numbers three to ten, no matter what other number may occur before them.

3 The singular form of the noun is used elsewhere.

4 Two or more numbers are joined by *wa*.
5 Numbers occur in the order millions—▷thousands—▷ hundreds—▷units—▷tens.

Translation

1	30 students	11	28 years
2	4 books	12	1951
3	1965	13	75 dinars
4	2 buildings	14	102 dollars
5	105 employees	15	3,975
6	3 cars	16	18 months
7	1978	17	8 months
8	10 days	18	12 cities
9	7 weeks	19	250 kilometres
10	6 years	20	1984

Supplementary section 11.1
Variants for 'want' and 'do'

As a native English speaker you are well aware of the numerous common vocabulary variations between American and British usage: sidewalk/pavement, garbage/rubbish, pants/trousers, and so on. When dealing with spoken Arabic in such a large area as the Peninsula, you must accustom yourself to a similar situation. We have already pointed out some of the common variants for nouns, question words and adjectives, and we now want to mention briefly some of the variants you are likely to encounter with two of the most common verbs: 'want' and 'do'.

'Want'

You will hear four common variants in the Peninsula. It is important that you maintain at least a passive awareness of all four since the large number of expatriate Arabs working throughout the Peninsula ensures that you may encounter all of them at some time, irrespective of the variant which is predominant in your own particular area.

i The most common verb in Saudi Arabia, and the one which we use throughout this book, is *yibgha* يبغى which we introduced earlier in this unit.

ii In parts of Saudi Arabia and the Gulf, you will hear this common alternative:

I want *abi*	أَبي	he wants *yibi*	يِبي
you (m) want *tibi*	تِبي	she wants *tibi*	تِبي
you (f) want *tibi:n*	تِبين		

iii Another common variant is the Standard Arabic verb which will be understood, though not always actively used, throughout the area:

I want *ari:d*	أَريد	he wants *yiri:d*	يِريد
you (m) want *tiri:d*	تِريد	she wants *tiri:d*	تِريد
you (f) want *tiri:di:n*	تِريدين		

iv The most common variant in the two Yemens is also heard throughout the Peninsula since North Yemenis constitute a substantial part of the expatriate Arab work force, particularly in Saudi Arabia:

I want *ashti*	أَشْتي	he wants *yishti*	يِشْتي
you (m) want *tishti*	تِشْتي	she wants *tishti*	تِشْتي
you (f) want *tishti*	تِشْتي		

'Do'

i Probably the most common variant, and certainly one that will be understood throughout the area, is the verb which we have already introduced in this unit:

ya^c^mal يعمل

ii An alternative which is primarily used in the two Yemens, but also in other areas throughout the Peninsula, is:

I do
asawwi أَسَوّي

you (m) do
tisawwi تِسَوّي

you (f) do
yisawwi تِسوي

he does
tisawwi يِسَوّي

she does
tisawwi تِسَوّي

Do not attempt to acquire active control of all these variants, but use the one which is used in your area.

Supplementary section 11.2
The home

door	*ba:b (abwa:b)*	باب (أَبْواب)
floor	*ard̲*	أَرْض
ceiling	*sagf*	سَقْف
roof	*sat̲h̲*	سَطْح
wall	*h̲a:'it̲*	حائِط
	jida:r	جِدار
window	*diri:sha*	دِريشَة
	t̲a:ga	طاقَة
television	*talifizyu:n*	تِلِفِزْيون
radio	*ra:diyu*	راديو
lamp	*lamba*	لَمبَة
plug	*fi:sha*	فيشَة
transformer	*muh̲a:wila*	مُحاوِلَة
tape recorder	*musajjila*	مُسَجِّلَة
cupboard	*khazza:na*	خَزّانَة
bed	*takht*	تَخْت
	sari:r	سَرير
curtain	*sita:ra*	سِتارَة
carpet	*sija:da*	سِجادَة
furniture	*sa:ma:n*	سامان
chair	Kursi (*kara:si*) pl.	كُرْسي
table	*amya:z*	ميز
bedroom	*h̲ujrat nawm*	حُجْرَة نَوْم
sitting room	*majlis*	مَجْلِس
kitchen	*mat̲bakh*	مَطْبَخ
bathroom	*h̲amma:m*	حَمّام

garden *ḫadi:ga*	حَديقَة	washing machine *ghassa:la*	غَسّالَة
refrigerator *thalla:ja*	ثَلّاجَة		

New vocabulary in Unit 11

he does *yaᶜmil*	يَعْمِل	OK *ṯayyib*	طَيِّب
he goes *yiru:ḫ*	يِروح	let's go! come on! *yalla!*	يَلّا !
he wants *yibgha*	يِبْغى		

Unit 12

1 Six new verbs

In this unit you will learn six new verbs. We present them in the singular persons, 'I', 'you', masculine and femine forms, 'he' and 'she'.

'See'

The stem of 'see' is *shu:f* شوف
The helper vowel is /i/.

Vocabulary A Ⓣ

I see *ashu:f*	أَشوف	he sees *yishu:f*	يِشوف
you see (m) *tishu:f*	تِشوف	she sees *tishu:f*	تِشوف
you see (f) *tishu:fi:n*	تِشوفين		

Note that although the tape models and transliteration give the helper vowel as /i/, depending on where you are in the Peninsula you may hear:

he sees
yashu:f يشوف

Very often it is difficult to distinguish any helper vowel at all and you will hear:

he sees
yshu:f يشوف

Practice sentences Ⓣ

1 He wants to see Ahmad.
yibgha yishu:f ahmad يبغى يشوف احمد

2 Who do you (m) want to see?
man tibgha tishu:f? من تبغى تشوف؟

3 I want to see the desert.
abgha ashu:f iṣ-ṣaḥra ابغى اشوف الصّحراء

4 What do you (f) want to see?
aysh tibghi:n tishu:fi:n? ايش تبغين تشوفين؟

5 She wants to see the house.
hiya tibgha tishu:f il-bayt هي تبغى تشوف البيت

Use these simple sentences for further practice.
Write them out using other persons of the verb.
Use other vocabulary from previous units.
Read your attempts aloud to yourself, get used to saying this new verb.
Record yourself.
Listen for this verb in people's speech.

Substitution drill

Ⓣ **Model sentence**
abgha ashu:f aḥmad ابغى اشوف احمد
I want to see Ahmad.

Example substitution

cue *hiya* —— *il-maktab* هي —— المكتب
she —— the office

response *tibgha tashu:f il-maktab* تبغى تشوف المكتب
she wants to see the office

Cues

1 *huwa* —— *il-bayt* هو —— البيت

2 *ana* —— *is-su:g* انا —— السّوق

3 *hiya* —— *il-mudi:r* هي —— المدير

4 *ana* —— *id-duktu:r* انا —— الدّكتور

5 *huwa* —— *muḥammad* هو —— محمد

6 *hiya* —— *il-fundug* هي —— الفندق

7 *huwa* —— *il-muhandis* هو —— المهندس

8 *ana* —— *il-madi:na* انا —— المدينة

9 *huwa* —— *il-maktab* هو —— المكتب

10 *hiya* —— *fa:ṭima* هي —— فاطمة

'Speak'

The stem of 'speak' is *tkallam* تكلّم
The helper vowel is /i/.

Vocabulary B (T)

I speak *atkallam*	أَتْكَلَّم	he speaks *yitkallam*	يِتْكَلَّم
you (m) speak *titkallam*	تِتْكَلَّم	she speaks *titkallam*	تِتْكَلَّم
you (f) speak *titkallami:n*	تِتْكَلَّمين		

Note that this is the first verb stem of more than three letters that you have seen.

You may hear /a/ as the helper vowel in some areas. For example:

yatkallam يَتْكَلَّم

Look at this sentence:

I want to speak to Ahmad.
abgha atkallam maᶜa aḥmad ابغى اتكلّم مع احمد

The Arabic, literally translated, is 'I want I speak *with* Ahmad'. The Arabic equivalent for 'to' is never used in this context.

Practice sentences (T)

1 Do you (m) speak Arabic?
titkallam ᶜarabi? تتكلّم عربي ؟

2 He wants to speak to Muhammad.
yibgha yitkallam maᶜa muḥammad يبغى يتكلّم مع محمّد

3 Do you (f) speak English?
titkallami:n ingli:zi? تتكلّمين انجليزي ؟

4 I speak a little Arabic.
atkallam shwayya ᶜarabi اتكلّم شويّة عربي

5 I want to speak to Ali.
abgha atkallam maᶜ ᶜali ابغى اتكلّم مع علي

Now write out these sentences using the different persons of the verb. Read them out loud to get used to pronouncing this new verb, paying attention to the *shadda* over the /l/.

'Come'

The stem of 'come' is *ji* جي
The helper vowel is /i/.

Vocabulary C Ⓣ

I come
aji أَجي

he comes
yiji يِجي

you come (m)
tiji تِجي

she comes
tiji تِجي

you come (f)
tiji:n تِجين

Note that the stem of 'come' consists of only two letters.

Remember that when making 'you' (addressing a woman) with verbs ending in a vowel, the vowel is dropped and the /i:n/ is joined directly to the preceding letter. Since the stem of 'come' consists of only two letters, the /i:n/ is joined to the one remaining letter of the stem, the *ji:m*.

This is not a random change, any verb whose stem ends in a vowel behaves in exactly the same way.

You will also hear /a/ as the helper vowel in some areas, for example:

he comes
yaji يَجي

Practice sentences Ⓣ

1 I want to come.
abgha aji ابغى اجى

2 He's coming at six o'clock.
yiji as-sa:ᶜa sitta يجي السّاعة ستّة

3 Do you (m) want to come?
tibgha tiji? تبغى تجي؟

4 She wants to come to the restaurant.
hiya tibgha tiji ila l-maṯᶜam هي تبغى تجي الى المطعم

5 Do you (f) want to come?
tibghi:n tiji:n? تبغين تجين؟

2 Talking about the future

Though there are ways of modifying the present tense of a verb in various dialect areas for talking about the future, it is universally acceptable to use the simple present tense together with future time phrases ('tomorrow', etc). In any case, context will usually indicate beyond doubt that an utterance is concerned with the future rather than the present.

Substitution drill

Model sentence

aji bukra — اجي بكرة

I'll come tomorrow.

Example substitution

cue *huwa* —— *il-yawm* — هو —— اليوم

he —— today

response *yiji il-yawm* — يجي اليوم

he'll come today

Cues

1 *hiya* —— *bukra* — هي —— بكرة

2 *ana* —— *ba^cdi <u>dh</u>-<u>dh</u>uhr* — انا —— بعد الظهر

3 *inta* —— *mu kida?* — انت —— اليوم موكدا؟

4 *huwa* —— *is-sa:^ca wa:<u>h</u>ida* — هو —— الساعة واحدة

5 *ana* —— *il-<u>h</u>i:n* — انا —— الحين

6 *inti* —— *mu kida?* — انت —— الصّباح موكدا؟

7 *ana* —— *yawm il-khami:s* — انا —— يوم الخميس

8 *huwa* —— *gabl i<u>dh</u>-<u>dh</u>uhr* — هو —— قبل الظّهر

9 *hiya* —— *mu kida?* — هي —— بكرة موكدا؟

10 *ana* —— *bukra is-sa:^ca sitta* — انا —— بكرة السّاعة ستّة

'Say' and 'tell'

The same verb in Arabic covers both the English verbs.
The stem of 'say, tell' is *gu:l* — قول
The helper vowel is /i/.

Vocabulary D Ⓣ

I say *agu:l*	أَقول	he says *yigu:l*	يِقول
you say (m) *tigu:l*	تِقول	she says *tigu:l*	تِقول
you say (f) *tigu:li:n*	تِقولين		

Note that although the tape models and transliteration give the helper vowel as /i/, depending on where you are in the Peninsula you may also hear:

he says
yagu:l — يَقول

Very often it is difficult to distinguish any helper vowel at all, and you will hear something like:

he says
ygu:l — يقول

If you have an Arab friend who speaks some English, you can ask him or her how you say a word you do not know or have forgotten in Arabic:

How do you (m) say 'today'?
kayf tigu:l 'today'? — كيف تقول اليوم today ؟

in Arabic
bi-l-ᶜarabi — بالعربي

bi, a less frequent alternative for *fi* ('in') is always used in this phra
This now allows you to say:

How do you (m) say 'today' in Arabic?

kayf tigu:l 'today' bi-l-ᶜarabi? — كيف تقول today بالعربي ؟

Use this question to widen your vocabulary whenever possible.

3 'Why' and 'when'

With these two question words you can extend your use of the present tense.

Vocabulary E (T)

why?
laysh? — لَيْش؟

when?
mata? — مَتى ؟

Practice sentences (T)

1 When do you (m) want to come?
mata tibgha tiji? — متي تبغى تجي ؟

2 Why do you (f) want to do that?
laysh tibghi:n taᶜmali:n ha:dha? — ليش تبغين تعملين هٰذا؟

3 Why do you (m) want to go?
laysh tibgha tiru:ẖ? — ليش يبغى يروح ؟

4 When do you (m) want to see Ahmad?
mata tibgha tishu:f ahmad? — متي تبغى تشوف احمد؟

For further practice write out these or similar sentences using all the relevant persons of the verb.

Transformation drill

Make the following sentences negative.

For example:

He wants to go.
yibgha yiru:h — يبغى يروح

He doesn't want to go.
ma yibgha yiru:h — ما يبغى يروح

1 She wants to come.
hiya tibgha tiji — هي تبغى تجي

2 I want to go.
abgha aru:h — ابغى اروح .

3 He speaks English.
yitkallam ingli:zi — يتكلّم انجليزي

4 I want to come.
abgha aji — ابغى اجي

5 He speaks Arabic.
hiya titkallam ʿarabi — هي تتكلّم عربي

For extra practice write out these sentences in all the other relevant persons of the verb. Always read your attempts out loud, paying special attention to any of the new sounds.

Translation

Translate the following sentences into Arabic. Take care over your spelling, look up anything you are not sure of. Check your answers a couple of times before looking at the key at the back of the book.

1 Does he want to come?
2 Who does she want to see?
3 When are you (f) coming?
4 I want to see the doctor.
5 Do you (f) want to come?
6 I speak a little Arabic.
7 Where do you (m) want to go?
8 What do you (m) want to do?
9 Why do you (m) want to go?
10 Do you (f) speak Arabic?
11 Who do you (m) want to see?
12 Do you (m) speak English?
13 When do you (m) want to go?
14 What does he want to do?
15 She speaks a little Arabic.
16 What are you (m) doing?
17 What are you (f) doing?
18 Where is he going?
19 Why is she coming?
20 He's coming with her.

Use these sentences for further practice. Change them to other persons, where they make sense. Answer the questions, write them out and then read them out loud, paying attention to rising intonation.

If you are living in an Arab country try to use your Arabic at every opportunity, make all the statements and ask all the questions that your present knowledge allows you to. Listen to the Arabic you hear spoken around you. You should be recognising quite a lot of words and whole phrases by now. Always listen for the new things you have just learned in the speech of people around you.

4 Asking questions politely

In English we have many ways of introducing a polite question or making a request, for example, 'can', 'could', 'may', 'is it possible'. One word in Arabic, used with a verb, conveys these words in most circumstances:

mumkin مُمْكِن

Practice sentences (T)

1 Can I come?
mumkin aji? ممكن اجي ؟

2 Can you (m) come tomorrow?
mumkin tiji bukra? ممكن تجي بكرة ؟

3 Could I see Muhammad?
mumkin ashu:f muḥammad? ممكن اشوف احمد؟

4 May I speak to Ahmad please?
mumkin atkallam maʿa aḥmad? ممكن اتكلّم مع احمد؟

5 Can I go?
mumkin aru:ḥ? ممكن اروح ؟

Experiment with these sentences and, using them as models, make up other sentences using different persons of the verbs and alternative vocabulary.

Notice that whatever person of the verb is used, *mumkin* never changes.

Another useful phrase for introducing polite requests is 'Can you tell me . . .?' In Arabic this question is expressed in the form: 'Can you say to me . . .?' In this context 'to' is translated by the prefix /l/ ي followed by the personal suffix /i/ ل 'me'.

Can you (m) tell me . . .?
mumkin tigu:l l-i . . .? ممكن تقول لي...؟

Can you (f) tell me . . .?
mumkin tigu:li:n l-i . . .? ممكن تقولين لي...؟

This Arabic phrase also covers other English equivalents such as 'Could you tell me . . .?', 'Would you mind telling me . . .?' etc.

Practice sentences

1 Can you (m) tell me what the time is?
mumkin tigu:l l-i kam is:sa:ᶜa? ممكن تقول لي كم السّاعة؟

2 Can you (f) tell me where the post office is?
mumkin tigu:li:n l-i wayn maktab il-bari:d? ممكن تقولين لي وين مكتب البريد؟

3 Could you (m) tell me what his name is?
mumkin tigu:l l-i aysh ism-u? ممكن تقول لي ايش اسمه؟

4 Can you (f) tell me who she is?
mumkin tigu:li:n l-i man hiya? ممكن تقولين لي من هي؟

5 Could you (m) tell me when you're coming?
mumkin tigu:l l-i mata tiji? ممكن تقول لي متى تجي؟

5 'Must'

In English we have a wide range of alternatives to express necessity and obligation. These are: 'must', 'have/has to', 'should', 'ought to', 'have/has got to', 'had better', 'it is necessary' and 'needs to'. One word in Arabic, used with a verb conveys these alternatives in most circumstances.

la:zim لازِم

Different shades of meaning are indicated in context by intonation, stress, facial and hand gestures.

Practice sentences Ⓣ

1 I must go at 10 o'clock.
la:zim aru:h̲ is-sa:ᶜa ᶜashra لازم اروح السّاعة عشرة

2 You (m) should go with Ahmad.
la:zim tiru:h̲ maᶜ ahmad لازم تروح مع احمد

3 He has to go tomorrow.
la:zim yiru:h̲ bukra لازم يروح بكرة

4 She ought to go home.
hiya la:zim tiru:h̲ il-bayt هي لازم تروح البيت

5 I've got to go.
la:zim aru:h̲ لازم اروح

6 You (f) had better go.
la:zim tiru:h̲i:n لازم تروحين

Note that whatever the person of the verb, *la:zim* remains the same. It never changes.

Questions

Questions, unless introduced by a question word, are indicated by rising intonation.

Practice sentences (T)

1 Do you (m) have to go?
la:zim tiru:h̲? لازم تروح؟

2 Must you (f) go at six?
la:zim tiru:hi:n as-sa:ʿa sitta? لازم تروحين السّاعة ستّة؟

3 Why must you (m) go to London?
laysh la:zim tiru:h̲ lundun? ليش لازم تروح لندن؟

4 When have you (f) got to go?
mata la:zim tiru:h̲i:n? متى لازم تروحين؟

Negatives

Depending on where you are living, you will hear one of the following put in front of *la:zim* to make the negative:

mu la:zim مو لازم *mush la:zim* مش لازم

mu:b la:zim موب لازم

Use whichever you hear used most around you.

Substitution drill Ⓣ **Model sentence**

la:zim tiru:ẖ ma^c-u لازم تروح معه

You must go with him.

Example substitution

cue *inti* —— *hiya* انت —— هي

you (fs) —— her

response *la:zim tiru:ẖi:n ma^c-ha* لازم تروحين معها

You must go with her.

cues

1 *ana* —— *hum* انا —— هم

2 *huwa* —— *ana* هو —— انا

3 *huwa* —— *iẖna* هو —— احنا

4 *hiya* —— *inta* هي —— انت

5 *hiya* —— *ana* هي —— انا

6 *ana* —— *huwa* انا —— هو

7 *ana* —— *inti* انا —— انتِ

8 *inti* —— *ana* انتِ —— انا

9 *inta* —— *ana* انتَ —— انا

10 *huwa* —— *inta* هو —— انتَ

'Drink'

The stem of 'drink' is *shrab* شرب

The helper vowel is /i/.

Vocabulary F Ⓣ

I drink *ashrab*	أَشْرَب	he drinks *yishrab*	يِشْرَب
you drink (m) *tishrab*	تِشْرَب	she drinks *tishrab*	تِشْرَب
you drink (f) *tishrabi:n*	تِشْرَبين		

Note that you may also hear /a/ as the helper vowel in some areas:

he drinks
  yashrab يَشْرَب

Use whichever you hear used around you.

This verb is also used to mean 'smoke'. Thus the question,

tishrab? تشرب ؟

when offering a cigarette is equivalent to the English 'Do you smoke?'

Practice sentences (T)

1 What do you (f) want to drink?
  aysh tibghi:n tishrabi:n? ايش تبغين تشربين؟

2 Would you (m) like to drink some coffee?
  tibgha tishrab gahwa? تبغى تشرب قهوة؟

3 What does he want to drink?
  aysh yibgha yishrab? ايش يبغى يشرب؟

4 I want to drink some cold water.
  abgha ashrab ma:i ba:ríd ابغى اشرب ماي بارد

5 What does she want to drink?
  aysh hiya tibgha tishrab? ايش هي تبغى تشرب؟

'Pepsi-cola' in Arabic

'Eat'

The stem of 'eat' is *a:kul* اكل

Since the first letter of the stem is a vowel, it does not need a helper vowel.

Notice that the short /a/ of the prefix and the long /a:/ which is the first letter of the stem are run together in the 'I' person of the verb and pronounced simply as /a:/. Instead of writing two *alifs* together, the first *alif* (the 'bearer' of the short /a/ of the prefix) is written as a *madda* over the second *alif*. (Refer to *Macmillan Arabic Book 1*, Unit 15.)

Vocabulary G Ⓣ

I eat
a:kul آكُل (instead of أأكُل)

you eat (m)
ta:kul تاكُل

he eats
ya:kul ياكُل

you eat (f)
ta:kuli:n تاكُلين

she eats
ta:kul تاكُل

Note that in some areas you may hear an /i/ instead of an /u/ in the stem of this verb:

he eats
ya:kil ياكِل

Imitate what you hear used most around you.

Practice sentences Ⓣ

1 What do you (m) want to eat?
aysh tibgha ta:kul?
ايش تبغى تاكل؟

2 What would you (f) like to eat?
aysh tibghi:n ta:kuli:n?
ايش تبغين تاكلين؟

3 I'd like to eat some meat.
abgha a:kul laham
ابغى آكل لحم

4 He wants to eat in the restaurant.
*yibgha ya:kul fi l-mat*ᶜ*am*
يبغى ياكل في المطعم

5 She wants to eat some fish.
hiya tibgha ta:kul samak
هي تبغى تاكل سمك

Substitution drill Ⓣ

Model sentence
*yibgha yitkallam ma*ᶜ*-ak*
He wants to talk to you (m).
يبغى يتكمّم معك

Example substitution

cue *ana* —— *inti*   انا —— انتِ
I —— you (f)

response *abgha atkallam ma^c-ik*   ابغى اتكلّم معِك
I want to talk to you (f).

cues

1 *ana* —— *hum*   انا —— هم

2 *ana* —— *il-mudi:r*   انا —— المدير

3 *huwa* —— *inta*   هو —— انتَ

4 *huwa* —— *muẖammad*   هو —— محمد

5 *hiya* —— *ana*   هي —— انا

6 *hiya* —— *hum*   هي —— هم

7 *ana* —— *inta*   انا —— انت

8 *hiya* —— *iẖna*   هي —— احنا

9 *huwa* —— *hum*   هو —— هم

10 *ana* —— *intum*   انا —— انتم

Substitution drill (T)

Model question
mumkin tiji ma^c-i?   ممكن تجي معي ؟
Can you (ms) come with me?

Example substitution

cue *huwa* —— *iẖna*   هو —— احنا
he —— us

response *mumkin yiji ma^c-na?*   ممكن يجي معنا ؟
Can he come with us?

cues

1 *ana* —— *intum*   انا —— انتم

2 *ana* —— *inta*   انا —— انتَ

3 *inta* —— *iẖna*   انتَ —— احنا

4 *inta* —— *ana*   انتَ —— انا

5 *huwa* —— *inta*		هو—— انتَ
6 *hiya* —— *hum*		هي—— هم
7 *inti* —— *huwa*		انتِ—— هو
8 *ana* —— *inti*		انا—— انتِ
9 *huwa* —— *iḫna*		هو—— احنا
10 *hiya* —— *iḫna*		هي—— احنا

6 Eating out

It would be difficult to give a concise description of the food available in the restaurants and hotels of the Arabian Peninsula which would be relevant to the area as a whole. At the time of writing, the picture varies widely from the sophisticated coastal cities of Saudi Arabia and the Gulf to the still relatively traditional culinary fastnesses of the interiors of those same states, and of whole countries such as North Yemen and Oman. In all the capital cities of the Peninsula it is nowadays possible to find at least a representative selection of western styles of cooking, while in some areas the choice is positively comprehensive. Bahrain, for example, offers French, Italian, Indian, Chinese, Persian and Lebanese food, along with hamburger bars and fried chicken stands. At the other extreme, cities such as Sana'a in the Yemen Arab Republic (North Yemen) still offer a predominantly traditional culinary environment, though the larger hotels and one or two restaurants do cater for the homesick western palate, and of course the supermarkets are well-stocked with a wide range of western foods from the banal (baked beans and corn flakes) to the positively hedonistic (truffles and quail).

On the whole it can be said that the more culinarily chauvinistic need have no fears of being deprived of their daily staples wherever they travel in the Peninsula, while those who take the plunge and sample the delights of local cuisine will rarely return to the West with their preconceptions of European culinary supremacy intact.

An excellent and comprehensive account of Arabic food, together with the traditions and lore surrounding it, is given by Claudia Roden in *A Book of Middle Eastern Food* (Penguin

Books, London, 1970). Though it does not deal specifically with the Peninsula (it does contain some recipes from Saudi Arabia and Yemen), it paints an edifying portrait of the culinary traditions of the northern Arab countries which have had a powerful influence on eating habits throughout the Arabic speaking world and beyond.

Arabs eating out

Vocabulary H Ⓣ You will find the following words useful in a restaurant and for eating out in general.

knife
sikki:n سِكّين

fork
shawka شَوْكَة

spoon
mal^{c}aqa مَلْعَقَة

plate
s̲ah̲n صَحْن

glass
galas̲ قَلَص

cup
ku:b كوب

finja:n فِنْجان

table
mi:z ميز

t̲a:wila طاوِلَة

ti:bil تيبل

chair
kursi كُرْسي

Where we have given alternatives it is likely that you will hear them used interchangeably. Some of the words are obviously Arabicised English words: *ti:bil, ku:b* and *galas̲.*

In the Gulf and eastern parts of the Peninsula you will hear these local alternatives:

fork
chinga:l كِنقال

spoon
gafsha قَفْشَة

glass
ja:m جام

As always where there are several alternatives for common items, find out what is used locally and use that.

Supplementary section 12
Parts of the body

head	*ra:s*	راس
forehead	*jabi:n*	جَبين
face	*wajh*	وَجْه
mouth	*fam*	فَم
eye	*ʿayn*	عَين
ear	*idhn*	إِذْن
tooth	*sinn*	سِنّ
moustache	*shawa:rib*	شَوارِب
lip	*shifa*	شِفَة
nose	*anf*	أَنْف
	khashm	خَشْم
tongue	*lisa:n*	لِسان
chin	*dhign*	ذِقْن
cheek	*khad*	خَد
neck	*ʿunug*	عُنُق
beard	*lih̲ya*	لِحْيَة
throat	*h̲alg*	حَلْق
arm	*dhira:ʿ*	ذِراع
hand	*yad*	يَد
shoulder	*kitf*	كِتْف
finger	*is̲baʿ*	إِصْبَع
foot, leg	*rijl*	رِجْل
chest	*s̲adr*	صَدْر
heart	*galb*	قَلْب
back	*dh̲uhr*	ظُهْر
blood	*dam*	دَم
skin	*jild*	جِلْد
bone	*ʿadh̲m*	عَظْم
body	*jism*	جِسْم

New vocabulary in Unit 12

to see	*yashu:f*	يَشوف
to speak	*yitkallam*	يِتْكلَّم
to come	*yiji*	يِجي
to say	*yagu:l*	يقَول
why	*laysh*	لَيْش ؟
when	*mata*	متَى ؟
can	*mumkin*	مُمكِن
must, should	*la:zim*	لازِم
to drink	*yishrab*	يِشْرَب
to eat	*ya:kul*	ياكُل

knife	*sikki:n (saka:ki:n)*	سِكّين (سكاكين)
fork	*shawka (shawak)*	شَوْكَة (شوَك)
spoon	*milᶜaga (milᶜaga:t)*	مِلْعَقَة (مِلْعَقات)
plate	*s̲ah̲n (s̲uh̲u:n)*	صَحْن (صُحون)
glass	*galas̲*	قَلَص
cup	*ku:b (akwa:b)*	كوب (أَكْواب)
table	*mi:z (amya:z)*	ميز (أَمْياز)
	t̲a:wila (t̲a:wila:t)	طاوِلَة (طاوِلات)
chair	*kursi (kara:si)*	كُرْسي (كَراسي)

Unit 13

1 Masculine and feminine nouns

In the previous units you have seen 'he' and 'she' used when referring to people. 'He' and 'she' are also used in Arabic when referring to objects or things where in English we would use 'it'. 'It' never changes in English because we do not distinguish between masculine and feminine nouns. In Arabic, where we must make a clear distinction between masculine and feminine nouns,
huwa, 'he', is used to mean 'it' when referring to masculine nouns,
hiya, 'she', is used to mean 'it' when referring to feminine nouns

In order to give you some practice in using this feature, we have anticipated some of the vocabulary you may use with the verbs that we introduce later in the unit.

Vocabulary A Ⓣ

reception, party *ḥafla*	حَفْلَة	plane *ṯa:'ira*	طائِرَة
meeting *ijtima:ᶜ*	إجْتِماع	ship, boat *safi:na*	سَفِينَة
department *gism*	قِسْم	lunch *ghada*	غَداء
programme *barna:mij*	بَرْنامِج	dinner, supper *ᶜasha*	عَشاء
film *film*	فِلْم		

Remember that most feminine nouns are easily recognisable in written Arabic since they end in *ta:ʿ marbu:ṯa*. In pronunciation they end with the short vowel sound /a/ represented by *fatḥa* which usually precedes the *ta:' marbu:ṯa*.

2 Six new verbs

From now on when we introduce a new verb we will give it in the 'he' form. This shows you the stem and the helper vowel.

Vocabulary B

start, begin
yibda يِبْدا

close, shut
yibannid يَبنِّد

finish, end, stop
yikhalliṣ يِخَلّص

arrive
yu:ṣal يوصَل

open
yiftaḥ يفْتَح

depart, leave
yigu:m يِقوم

You may hear /a/ as the helper vowel with some of these verbs in some parts of the Peninsula, or even no helper vowel at all, as in these examples:

finish, end, stop
ykhalliṣ يَخَلِّص

depart
ygu:m يقوم

close, shut
ybannid يبَنِّد

Practice sentences

1 When does the film begin?
mata yibda l-film? متى يبدا الفلم ؟

This literally means, 'When (he) begins the film?' Note that the initial vowel of *il* is dropped after the final vowel of *yibda*.

2 When does it begin?
mata yibda? متى يبدأ؟

This literally means 'When (he) begins?' referring to any masculine noun.

3 When does the party finish?
mata tikhalliṣ il-ḥafla? متى تخلّص الحفلة ؟

This literally means 'When (she) finishes the party?'

4 When does it begin?
mata tikhalliṣ? متى تخلّص ؟

This literally means 'When (she) begins?' referring to any feminine noun.

Note that in Arabic the verbs 'begin' and 'finish' come before the subjects 'film' and 'party', the opposite of the English. If you put the subject first:

When does the film begin?
mata il-film yibda? متى الفلم يبدا؟

When does the party finish?
mata il-ḥafla tikhalliṣ?

متى الحفلة تخلّص؟

you will be understood, but it is not the correct practice. The drill below practises this feature with the new vocabulary introduced in this unit.

Practice sentences   ⓣ

1 When does the bank shut?
mata yibannid il-bank?

متى يبنّد البنك؟

2 When does the film begin?
mata yibda l-film?

متى يبدا الفلم؟

3 When does the office open?
mata yiftaḫ il-maktab?

متي يفتح المكتب؟

4 When does the party begin?
mata tibda l-ḥafla?

متي تبدا الحفلة؟

5 When does the plane arrive?
mata tu:ṣal iṭ-ṭa:'ira?

متى توصل الطائرة

6 When does the department open?
mata yiftaḫ il-gism?

متى يفتح القسم؟

7 When does the plane depart?
mata tigu:m iṭ-ṭa:'ira?

متى تقوم الطائرة؟

8 When does the programme finish?
mata yikhalliṣ il-barna:mij?

متى يخلّص البرنامج؟

9 When does the restaurant close?
mata yibannid il-maṭʿam?

متى يبند المطعم؟

10 When will the party finish?
mata tikhalliṣ il-ḥafla?

متى تخلّص الحفلة؟

11 When does lunch begin?
mata yibda l-ghada?

متى يبدا الغداء؟

12 When will the ship arrive?
mata tu:ṣal is:safi:na?

متى توصل السفينة؟

13 When will the meeting finish?
mata yikhalliṣ il-ijtima:ʿ?

متى يخلّص الاجتماع؟

14 When will dinner begin?
mata yibda l-ʿasha?

متى يبدا العشاء؟

15 When will the plane arrive?
mata tu:ṣal iṭ-ṭa:'ira?

متى تجي الطائرة؟

For extra practice you can make new sentences using these verbs and nouns.

3 Plurals of verbs

Until now we have concentrated on practising the singular persons of verbs.

The plural persons of the verb, 'we', 'you' and 'they', are indicated by prefixes and suffixes, absolutely constant from one verb to another, which are joined to the stem of the verb by a helper vowel. The helper vowel remains constant throughout any one verb. It is the same for the plural persons and for the singular persons.

A distinction is made in the plurals of verbs between:

a 'You', addressing a group of men and mixed male/female groups, which we shall in future refer to as 'you (mp)'.

b 'You', addressing groups made up exclusively of women, which we shall in future refer to as 'you (fp)'.

c 'They', talking about groups of men or mixed male/female groups, which we shall refer to as 'they (mp)'.

d 'They', talking about groups made up exclusively of women, which we shall in future refer to as 'they (fp)'.

For all practical purposes, male and female learners alike need only concentrate on learning to use the masculine plural forms, since all of these forms refer to mixed company which is the most likely way you will meet women socially. Men have little need to learn the exclusive feminine forms of 'you' and 'they'; women learners, however, who have social contacts with Arab women or jobs which bring them into contact with groups of women, ought to make the attempt to learn these exclusive feminine forms.

In some areas you may find that no distinction is made between masculine and feminine forms, in which case 'you' (mp) and 'they' (mp) are the only forms used.

In the following tables the exclusive feminine forms are included in the notes.

Here are two verbs in the plural.

'Drink'

The stem of 'drink' is *shrab* شَرب

The helper vowel is /i/.

Ⓣ we drink
nishrab نِشْرَب

you drink (mp)
tishrabu:n تِشْرَبون

they drink (m)
yishrabu:n يِشْرَبون

Points to note

a 'We' is indicated by the letter *nu:n* joined to the first letter of the stem.

b 'You' (mp) is indicated by the letter *ta:'* joined to the first letter of the stem, and *u:n* joined to the last letter of the stem.

c 'They' (m) is indicated by the letter *ya:'* joined to the first letter of the stem and *u:n* joined to the last letter of the stem.

d 'You' (fp) is indicated by the letter *ta:'* joined to the first letter of the stem, and *in* joined to the last letter of the stem.

Ⓣ you drink (fp)
tishrabin تِشْرَبِن

e 'They' (f) is indicated by the letter *ya:'* joined to the first letter of the stem, and *in* joined to the last letter of the stem.

Ⓣ they drink (f)
yishrabin يِشْرَبِن

Here is a table showing the different prefixes and suffixes that make up the plural persons of the present tense.

we			they (m)		
n ———		نـ . . .	*y* ———	*u:n*	يـ . . . ون
you (mp)			they (f)		
t ———	*u:n*	تـ . . . ون	*y* ———	*in*	يـ . . . ن
you (fp)					
t ———	*in*	تـ . . . ن			

Write out this verb as many times as you need to learn the different plural prefixes and suffixes.

In some areas the final /n/ of the 'you' and 'they' masculine plural forms of verbs is dropped:

you (mp) drink		they (m) drink	
tishrabu:n	تشربون	*yishrabu:n*	يشربون
or		or	
tishrabu	تشربو	*yishrabu*	يشربو

Use the form which is most frequently used in your area.

'Come'

The stem of 'come' is *ji* جي

The helper vowel is /i/.

(T)

we come		they come (m)	
niji	نِجي	*yiju:n*	يِجون
you come (mp)			
tiju:n	تِجون		

Points to note

a In verbs where the last letter of the stem is a vowel, when making 'you' (mp) and 'they' (m), the vowel is dropped and the *u:n* is joined directly to the preceding letter. Since the stem of 'come' consists of only two letters, the *u:n* is joined directly to the one remaining letter, the *ji:m*.

b Exclusively feminine forms:

(T) you come (fp)

tijin تجن

they come (f)

yijin يجن

When making 'you' (fp) and 'they' (f) the final vowel /i/ is dropped and the suffix *in* is joined directly to the preceding letter.

These are not random changes, any verb whose stem ends in a vowel will behave in exactly the same way. For example:

Ⓣ

you want (mp) *tibghu:n*	تبغون	they want (m) *yibghu:n*	يبغون
you want (fp) *tibghin*	تبغن	they want (f) *yibghin*	يبغن

Here is a list of all the verbs you have seen so far (including local variants for 'want' and 'do') given in the 'he' form to show you what the helper vowel is. Write them out in the plural persons. Leave the exclusively feminine forms unless you have special need for them.

want *yibgha*	يبغى	say, tell *yigu:l*	يقول
yabi	يبي	drink *yishrab*	يشرب
yiri:d	يريد	eat *ya:kul*	ياكل
yishti	يشتي	start, begin *yibda*	يبدا
do *ya^cmal*	يعمل	finish, end, stop *yikhalliṣ*	يخلّص
yisawwi	يسوي	open *yiftaḥ*	يفتح
go *yiru:ḥ*	يروح	close, shut *yibannid*	يبنّد
see *yishu:f*	يشوف	arrive *yu:ṣal*	يوصل
speak, talk *yitkallam*	يتكلّم	depart *yigu:m*	يقوم
come *yiji*	يجي		

Pay attention to the 'you' and 'they' forms of verbs whose stems end in vowels, /a/ or /i/. Go back and check with the model of the verb 'come' to see what happens.

4 Adverbs of time

One of the major uses of the present tense is talking about regular habits, occurrences and actions.

Vocabulary C Ⓣ

always	*da:'iman*	دائِماً	usually	*ᶜa:datan*	عادَةً
sometimes	*ahya:nan*	أَحْياناً	often, a lot	*kathi:r*	كَثير
never	*abadan*	أَبَداً	once	*marra*	مَرَّة

Points to note

a The Arabic for 'always', 'sometimes' and 'never' share a common feature, they end in *an* represented by double *fatha* written above an *alif* which is not pronounced but acts merely as a bearer.

b The Arabic for 'usually' shares the same feature, but the double *fatha* is written above the *ta:' marbu:ta* which is heard as an ordinary *ta:'* in pronunciation. The opening of the *ta:' marbu:ta* is apparent only in the pronunciation, not in the writing.

c *kathi:r* meaning 'often', 'a lot' also covers the English words 'very often', 'much', 'very much'. You will hear the alternative:

wa:jid واجد

used with the same range of meanings in the Gulf States and eastern Saudi Arabia.

d These words go either at the beginning or end of a sentence, or after the verb.

The following vocabulary which you first saw in Unit Eight:

Ⓣ

day	*yawm*	يوم	year	*sana*	سنة
week	*usbu:ᶜ*	اسبوع			
month	*shahr*	شهر			

together with the new word:

each, every *kull* كُلّ

allows you to make the following expressions:

Ⓣ

every day	*kull yawm*	كلّ يوم	every month	*kull shahr*	كلّ شهر
every week	*kull usbu:ᶜ*	كلّ اسبوع	every year	*kull sana*	كلّ سنة

Practice sentences

Ⓣ These sentences give you practice using the new vocabulary above with the new verbs introduced in this unit. Use them for reading, writing, pronunciation and comprehension practice. Make up your own sentences using different combinations of the same vocabulary.

1 She comes every week.
hiya tiji kull usbu:[c]
هي تجي كلّ اسبوع

2 They (m) go to London every year.
yiru:ḫu:n ila lundun kull sana
يروحون الى لندن كلّ سنة

3 Is he always around?
huwa mawju:d da:'iman?
هو موجود دائماً

4 We go to the cinema every week.
niru:ḫ is-si:nama kull usbu:[c]
نروح السينما كلّ اسبوع

5 I usually go to the beach every day.
[c]a:datan aru:ḫ il-baḫr kull yawm
عادةً اروح البحر كلّ يوم

6 We sometimes go to the restaurant.
aḫiya:nan niru:ḫ ila l-maṯ[c]am
احياناً نروح الى المطعم

7 I never talk Arabic.
ma atkallam [c]arabi abadan
ما اتكلّم عربي ابداً

8 She comes every month.
hiya tiji kull shahr
هي تجي كلّ شهر

9 He never eats at home.
ma ya:kul fi l-bayt abadan
ما ياكل في البيت ابداً

10 Does it open every day? (referring to a masculine noun)
yiftaḫ kull yawm?
يفتح كلّ يوم؟

Note that when using *abadan* 'never' you must make the verb negative with *ma*; see numbers 7 and 9.

With the word:

Ⓣ once
marra
مرّة

and the vocabulary above we can make the equivalent of 'once a day', 'once a week' etc. Note that the Arabic literally translated is 'once in the day', 'once in the week'.

Ⓣ once a day
marra fi l-yawm
مرّة في اليوم

once a week
marra fi l-usbu:[c]
مرّة في الاسبوع

once a month
marra fi sh-shahr مرّة في الشهر

once a year
marra fi s-sana مرّة في السنّة

The query which elicits responses which include the expressions above is:

how often?
how many times?
kam marra? كم مرّة؟

The Arabic is literally 'How many time?'

Practice sentences Ⓣ

1 I go to the cinema once a week.
aru:h ila s-si:nama marra fi l-usbu:ᶜ اروح الى السّينما مرّة في الاسبوع

2 They (m) go to London once a year.
yiru:ḥu:n lundun marra fi s-sana يروحون لندن مرّة في السنّة

3 He goes to the office once a day.
yiru:ḥ il-maktab marra fi l-yawm يروح المكتب مرّة في اليوم

4 She comes to Bahrain once a month.
hiya tiji ila l-baḥrayn marra fi sh-shahr هي تجي الى البحرين مرّة في الشهر

5 I usually go to the beach once a day.
ᶜadatan aru:ḥ ila l-baḥr marra fi l-yawm عادةً اروح الى البحر مرّة في اليوم

For extra practice, write these sentences using other singular and plural persons of the verb and different vocabulary. Read the sentences aloud to give yourself confidence in pronouncing all the persons of the verb.

With the addition of *-ayn,* which conveys the idea of 'two-ness', to *marra:*

marrat-ayn مرّتين

we convert 'once' into 'twice' or 'a couple of times'. Note the opening of the *ta:' marbu:ṭa* before the *-ayn* suffix. It is both written and pronounced as a regular *ta:'*.

Often, in answer to questions about 'how often?', we say 'once or twice'. You can say the same thing in Arabic:

once or twice
marra aw marrat-ayn مرّة او مرّتين

Translation

1 How often do you (ms) go to Jedda?
2 We go to London twice a year.
3 He goes to the market twice a day.
4 How often does she go to the cinema?
5 I go to the cinema once or twice a week.
6 They (mp) go to Bahrain once a month.
7 How often do you (mp) go to the university?
8 We go twice a week.
9 She goes to Masqat once a month.
10 I go to the bank once a week.
11 They (mp) go to the office every day.
12 She goes to the sea once or twice a week.
13 How often do you (fs) go to the market?
14 They (mp) go to America once a year.
15 How often does he go to Dubai?

Review of the present tense

The present tense in Arabic can be used in the following situations.

1 Talking about habitual actions, things you do regularly, every day, sometimes.

He comes every day at six o'clock.
yiji is-sa:ᶜa sitta kull yawm
يجي السّاعة ستّة كلّ يوم

She goes there every week.
hiya tiru:ẖ hina:k kull usbu:ᶜ
هي تروح هناك كلّ اسبوع

2 Talking about something happening at the time of speaking, or to express a continuous action.

He is coming now.
yiji halẖi:n
يجي هالحين

She is going now.
hiya tiru:ẖ halẖi:n
هي تروح هالحين

What are you (ms) doing?
aysh taᶜmal?
ايش تعمل ؟

What are you (fs) drinking?
aysh tishrabi:n?
ايش تشربين؟

What are you eating? (to a mixed group)
aysh ta:kulu:n?
ايش تاكلون؟

3 Talking about the future. The present tense can be used in conjunction with words referring to the future, very often with:

God willing
in sha:' alla:h إن شاء اللّه

This leaves you in no doubt that the future is being mentioned.

He'll come tomorrow.
yigi bukra in sha:' alla:h يجي بكرة ان شاء اللّه

We'll go on Friday.
niru:ḫ yawm il-jumaᶜa in sha:' alla:h نروح يوم الجمعة ان شاء اللّه

Will you (ms) see Ahmad tomorrow?
tishu:f a̲hmad bukra? تشوف احمد بكرة؟

When will she come?
mata hiya tiji? متى هي تجي؟

Two of a kind

The addition of the suffix *-ayn* indicating 'two-ness' or 'two of something' is an unusual feature of Arabic. It provides a short cut to phrases like 'a couple of . . .' and 'a pair of . . .'.

Here we combine some of the time vocabulary you have learned with the *-ayn* suffix to produce expressions like 'a couple of hours', 'a couple of days', etc, which are often used to convey the idea of rough, approximate time, or as an alternative to 'a few'.

a couple of, two minutes
dagi:gat-ayn دقيقتين

hours
sa:ᶜat-ayn ساعتين

days
yawm-ayn يومين

weeks
usbu:ᶜ-ayn اسبوعين

months
shahr-ayn شهرين

years
sanat-ayn سنتين

Points to note

a Note the opening of the *ta:' marbu:ta* before the addition of the *-ayn* suffix in the words for 'minute', 'hour' and 'year'. The *ta:' marbu:ta* is both written and pronounced as a regular *ta:'*.

b *usbu:ᶜayn,* 'two weeks' is the Arabic equivalent to 'fortnight'.

Supplementary section 13
Re-cap on time

You have seen several instances of one Arabic phrase covering a wide range of English expressions. When dealing with time, however, the situation is reversed, Arabic has a number of specific words to cover a variety of situations which can all be covered in English by the one word 'time'. You have already seen two of these words.

Ⓣ a *sa:ᶜa* ساعة

Used for asking and telling the time.

What time is it?
kam is-sa:ᶜa? كم السّاعة ؟

It's seven o'clock.
is-sa:ᶜa sabaᶜa السّاعة سبعة

This word also means 'clock' or 'watch'.

b *marra* مرّة

Meaning 'time' in the sense of 'occasion'.

once, on one occasion
marra مرّة

twice
marrat-ayn مرّتين

how many times?
kam marra? كم مرّة ؟

Notice also the idiomatic:

again
marra tha:niya مرّة ثانية

sometimes
marra:t مرّات

c *mudda* مدّة

Used to mean 'period of time'.

a long time
mudda ṯawi:la مدّة طويلة

How long is the contract?
(How much is the period of the contract?)
kam muddat al-ᶜaqd? كم مدّة العقد

d *wagt* وقت

Used when talking about time in a general sense.

I don't have time.
ma ᶜand-i wagt ما عندي وقت

Is there time?
fi: wagt? في وقت؟

New vocabulary in Unit 13

party
ḫafla (ḫafla:t) حَفْلَة (حَفْلات)

meeting
ijtima:ᶜ (ijtima:ᶜa:t) إجْتِماع (إجْتِماعات)

department
gism (agsa:m) قِسْم (أَقْسام)

programme
barna:mij (bara:mij) بَرْنامج (بَرامِج)

film
film (afla:m) فِلْم (أَفْلام)

'plane
ṯa:'ira (ṯayra:n) طائِرَة (طَيْران)

ship
safi:na (sufun) سَفِينَة (سُفُن)

lunch
ghada غَداء

dinner
ᶜasha عَشاء

to start, begin
yibda يبْدا

to finish, end
yikhalliṣ يخلِّص

to open
yiftaḫ يَفْتَح

to close, shut
yibannid يبنِّد

to arrive
yu:ṣal يَوصَل

to depart
yigu:m يَقوم

always *da:'iman*	دائماً	often, a lot *kathi:r*	كَثير
sometimes *ahya:nan*	أَحْياناً	all, every *kull*	كُلّ
never *abadan*	أَبَداً	once *marra*	مَرَّة
usually *ʿa:datan*	عادَةً	twice *marrat-ayn*	مَرَّتَيْن

Unit 14

1 'Can'

The fine distinctions between the different shades of meaning of 'can' are difficult to grasp in any language, even your own, if you have never had to give the matter much thought. The differences between 'can' meaning 'ability', 'know-how' and 'possibility' only really become apparent when learning a new language, or trying to explain your own to a foreign learner.

In Unit Twelve you saw *mumkin* used as the equivalent to 'can', 'may', 'could', etc when asking a polite question or making a request. Here we want to show you the Arabic equivalent to the English use of 'can' to express someone's ability to perform a skill, for example, 'He can speak Arabic' or 'She can drive'. Though this idea is perhaps most commonly expressed in English by 'can', we also use the alternative 'know how to'. For example, 'He knows how to speak Arabic', or 'She knows how to drive'.

Vocabulary A Ⓣ

can, able
yigdar يِقْدَر

know (how to)
ya^c^rif يَعْرِف

drive
yisu:g يِسوق

swim
yisbaḩ يِسْبَح

Thus the two examples above can be translated by either *yigdar* or *ya^c^rif:*

Ⓣ He can speak Arabic.
yigdar yitkallam ^c^arabi يقدر يتكلّم عربي

He knows how to speak Arabic.
ya^c^rif yitkallam ^c^arabi يعرف يتكلّم عربي

She can drive.
hiya tigdar tisu:g هي تقدر تسوق

She knows how to drive.
hiya ta^c^rif tisu:g هي تعرف تسوق

The same alternatives are used in both English and Arabic to express inability to perform a skill:

Ⓣ He can't swim.
ma yigdar yisbaẖ ما يقدر يسبح

He doesn't know how to swim.
ma yaᶜrif yisbaẖ ما يعرف يسبح

I can't drive.
ma agdar asu:g ما اقدر اسوق

I don't know how to drive.
ma aᶜrif asu:g ما اعرف اسوق

There are occasions in both Arabic and English when 'can' and 'know how to' may not be used interchangeably.

a When the ability involved is not an acquired skill, but a function of normal human activity (eg sleeping, seeing, hearing, coming, going). In such cases it is usual to use *yigdar*.

Can you (m) see Ahmad?
tigdar tishu:f aẖmad? تقدر تشوف احمد؟

She can't come tomorrow.
hiya ma tigdar tiji bukra هي ما تقدر تجي بكرة

b When someone's ability, or inability, to perform a skill is dependent on external circumstances (eg temporary physical incapacity), despite their possessing the requisite skill, *yigdar* is normally used:

I can't swim today (ie I haven't got time or I've broken my leg).
ma agdar asbaẖ il-yawm ما اقدر اسبح اليوم

He can't drive. (ie He isn't insured.)
ma yigdar yisu:g ما يقدر يسوق

In all the examples above there is an exact correspondence between 'can', 'be able' and *yigdar* on the one hand, and between 'know how to' and *yaᶜrif* on the other. Though the situation may seem complicated when examined in detail, you will find that practice and exposure to the language will give you confidence in using these new verbs. In both English and Arabic when talking about ability or inability to perform a skill, you can use the verb describing the skill on its own, without using 'can'.

Ⓣ 1 He speaks Arabic.
yitkallam ᶜarabi يتكلّم عربي

2 Do they speak English?
yitkallamu:n ingli:zi? يتكلّمون انجليزي؟

3 I don't drive.
ma asu:g ما اسوق

4 They don't swim.
ma yisbaḫu:n ما يسبحون

5 She doesn't speak Arabic.
hiya ma titkallam ᶜarabi هي ما تتكلّم عربي

2 Negative commands

To give someone an order not to do something in English we use 'Do not/don't' with the verb. In Arabic you simply put *la,* 'no' in front of the relevant 'you' form of the verb:

Don't go! (to a man)
la tiru:ḫ لا تروح

Don't go! (to a woman)
la tiru:ḫi:n لا تروحين

Don't go! (to a group of men or a mixed male-female group)
la tiru:ḫu:n لا تروحون

This applies to all the verbs you have learned so far. Obviously you are going to use some verbs in this way more than others; some verbs you will probably have no occasion to use at all. Here are some examples using verbs you have already seen:

Ⓣ 1 Don't do that. (to a man)
la taᶜmal ha:dha لا تعمل هٰذا

2 Don't open the door. (to a woman)
la tiftaḫi:n il-ba:b لا تفتحين الباب

3 Don't swim here. (to a mixed group)
la tisbaḫu:n hina لا تسبحون هنا

4 Don't speak English. (to a man)
la titkallam ingli:zi لا تتكلّم انجليزي

5 Don't come tomorrow. (to a woman)
la tiji:n bukra لا تجين بكرة

6 Don't drive on the left. (to a man)
la tisu:g ᶜala l-yasa:r لا تسوق على اليسار

7 Don't do that. (to a woman)
la taᶜmali:n ha:dha لا تعملين هٰذا

8 Don't go! (to a mixed group)
la tiru:ẖu:n لا تروحون

'No smoking' in Arabic

Here are some useful negative commands. We give them in the three forms you will need most:

Ⓣ Addressing a man:

Don't forget! *la tinsa* لا تنسى — Don't worry! *la takha:f* لا تخاف

Addressing a woman:

Don't forget! *la tinsi:n* لا تنسين — Don't worry! *la takha:fi:n* لا تخافين

Addressing a group of men or a mixed male-female group:

Don't forget! *la tinsu:n* لا تنسون — Don't worry! *la takha:fu:n* لا تخافون

3 More about the future

Vocabulary B

return *yirja^c*	يَرْجَع	after *ba^{c}d*	بَعَد

In the Gulf and eastern Saudi Arabia you will hear this variant:

after *^{c}ugub* — عُقُب

Dialogue Ⓣ Addressing a man

First read the English version of the dialogue, then try to work through the tape drill without referring to the English.

A Good morning.
B Good morning.
A I want to talk to the manager.
B He's not here at the moment.
A When will he come back?
B At ten o'clock. Please take a seat.
A No, thank you. I'm in a hurry.
What's the time now?
B Half past nine.
A OK. I'll come back in half an hour. Goodbye.
B Goodbye.

A *s̱aba:ẖ il-khayr* — صباح الخير

B *s̱aba:ẖ in-nu:r* — صباح النّور

A *abgha atkallim ma^c il-mudi:r* — ابغى اتكلّم مع المدير

B *huwa mu mawju:d hal-ẖi:n* — هو مو موجود هالحين

A *mata yirja^c?* — متي يرجع

B *is-sa:^{c}a ^{c}ashra in sha:' alla:h. tfaddal* — السّاعة عشرة ان شاء اللّه
(indicating a chair) — تفضّل

A *la shukran. ana musta^{c}jil* — لا شكراً انا مستعجل

kam is-sa:^{c}a hal-ẖi:n? — كم السّاعة هالحين؟

B *tisa^{c}a wa nus̱s̱* — تسعة ونصّ

A *tayyib arja^c ba^cd nuss sa:^ca* طيّب ارجع بعد نصّ ساعة

ma^ca s-sala:ma مع السّلامة

B *ma^ca s-sala:ma* مع السّلامة

Points to note

a In Arabic you say 'I want I talk *with* the manager'.

b Remember that there is no special form of the verb to express the future. Statements about the future are frequently accompanied by the phrase *in sha:' alla:h*, 'God willing' which, in context, corresponds to 'I hope' or 'probably'.

c 'Please take a seat' can be expressed quite simply in Arabic by *tfaddal* with a hand gesture indicating where to sit.

Further practice

Substitute alternatives for these items in the dialogue:

Different greetings
Variants for 'want'
Different times
Variants for 'now'
Different ways of saying 'Goodbye'

Your choice of variants should be governed by what is used where you live.

As you have seen, the lack of a special form of the verb to express the future in Arabic is overcome by using the present tense with the equivalent of phrases like 'tomorrow' or 'in half an hour's time'.

In the previous dialogue you saw the expression:

ba^cd nuss sa:^ca بعد نصّ ساعة

which we translated as 'in half an hour'. *ba^cd* (literally 'after') is used in a wide variety of time phrases on the pattern of 'in a/an . . .' or 'in a/an . . .'s time'. Remember that many of the phrases using the *-ayn* suffix (indicating two of something) are idiomatic expressions where the idea of 'a couple of . . .' can convey an approximate idea of time just as in English.

Vocabulary C

in half an hour's time
ba^cd nuss sa:^ca بعد نصّ ساعة

in an hour
ba^cd sa:^ca بعد ساعة

in an hour and a half
ba^cd sa:^ca wa nuss بعد ساعة ونصّ

in two hours' time
ba^c^d sa:^c^atayn بعد ساعتين

in a day's time
ba^c^d yawm بعد يوم

in two days' time
in a couple of days
ba^c^d yawm-ayn بعد يومين

in a week's time
*ba^c^d usbu:^c^* بعد اسبوع

in two weeks, in a fortnight,
in a couple of weeks' time
ba^c^d usbu:^c^-ayn بعد اسبوعين

in a month's time
ba^c^d shahr بعد شهر

in a couple of months' time
ba^c^d shahr-ayn بعد شهرين

in a year's time
ba^c^d sana بعد سنة

in two/a couple of years' time
ba^c^d sanat-ayn بعد سنتين

Three other items on the same pattern are:

in a little while
ba^c^d shwayya بعد شويّة

after, afterwards, next, later, then
(in the sense of next)
ba^c^dayn بعدين

the day after tomorrow
ba^c^d bukra بعد بكرة

Substitution drill Ⓣ

Model sentence
yiji ba^c^d usbu:^c^-ayn يجي بعد اسبوعين
He'll come in a couple of weeks' time.

Example substitution

cue *hiya* ——— *ba^c^d bukra* هي ——— بعد بكرة
she ——— the day after tomorrow

response *tiji ba^c^d bukra* تجي بعد بكرة
She'll come the day after tomorrow.

Cues

1	*iḫna* —— *bacd usbu:c-ayn*	احنا —— بعد اسبوعين
2	*hum* —— *bacd shahr*	هم —— بعد شهر
3	*ana* —— *bacdayn*	انا —— بعدين
4	*huwa* —— *bacd usbu:c*	هو —— بعد اسبوع
5	*hiya* —— *bacd sa:cat-ayn*	هي —— بعد ساعتين
6	*hum* —— *bacd yawm-ayn*	هم —— بعد يومين
7	*ana* —— *bacd shwayya*	انا —— بعد شوّية
8	*iḫna* —— *bacd bukra*	احنا —— بعد بكرة
9	*huwa* —— *bacd sa:ca*	هو —— بعد ساعة
10	*hiya* —— *bacd shahr-ayn*	هي —— بعد شهرين

An alternative in English to phrases on the pattern of 'in a/an . . .'s time' is to use an expression like 'next week', 'next month' etc. You will hear either or both of these words used in Arabic to mean:

next
ga:dim قادِم *wa:ji* واجي

next week
il-usbu:c il:wa:ji الاسبوع الواجي
(This literally means 'The week the next'.)

next month
ish-shahr il-wa:ji الشّهر الواجي

next year
is-sana il-ga:dima السّنة القادمة

next Friday
yawm il-jumaca il-ga:dim يوم الجمعة القادم

Substitution drill Ⓣ

Model sentence
aru:ḫ il-usbu:c il-ga:dim in sha:' alla:h اروح الاسبوع القادم ان شاء اللّٰه
I'm going next week.

Example substitution

cue	*huwa* —— *yawm il-ithnayn il-ga:dim* he —— next Monday	هو——يوم الاثنين القادم
response	*yiru:ẖ yawm il-ithnayn il-ga:dim in sha:' alla:h* He's going next Monday.	يروح يوم الاثنين القادم انشاء الله

Cues

1	*iẖna* —— *il-usbu:^{c} il-ga:dim*	احنا —— الاسبوع القادم
2	*hum* —— *il-usbu:^{c} il:ga:dim*	هم —— الاسبوع القادم
3	*ana* —— *is-sana il-ga:dima*	انا —— السّنة القادمة
4	*hiya* —— *ish-shahr il-ga:dim*	هي —— الشّهر القادم
5	*hum* —— *ish-shahr il-ga:dim*	هم —— الشّهر القادم
6	*iẖna* —— *yawm il-jum^{c}a il-ga:dim*	احنا —— يوم الجمعة القادم
7	*ana* —— *yawm il-khami:s il-ga:dim*	انا —— يوم الخميس القادم
8	*hum* —— *is-sana il-ga:dima*	هم —— السّنة القادمة
9	*hiya* —— *is-sana il-ga:dima*	هي —— السّنة القادمة
10	*huwa* —— *il-usbu:^{c} il-ga:dim*	هو —— الاسبوع القادم

4 Personal suffixes and verbs

Just as the personal suffixes can be added to prepositions, so can they be added to verbs to convey the equivalent of the English object pronoun. For example, 'I want to see *you*', 'He wants to see *her*'. The major feature for you to get used to is writing the personal suffixes as part of the verb they follow unless, of course, the last letter of the stem of the verb is a non-connector, in which case the suffixes will stand alone. Therefore, in reading and writing Arabic, you must get used to recognising that when a suffix is added to the last letter of the stem of a verb, the final form of that letter becomes a medial form.

Note that in all cases the personal suffixes are identical to those used with nouns and prepositions *except* 'me' which with verbs only is:

-ni ني

In the transliteration of the examples below, the personal suffixes are joined by a hyphen to the stem of the verb.

Here we show all the personal suffixes used with 'see'.

Ⓣ He wants to see me.
yibgha yishu:f-ni يبغى يشوفني

they (m) want to see you (ms)
yibghu:n yishu:fu:n-ak يبغون يشوفونك

I want to see you. (fs)
abgha ashu:f-ik ابغى اشوفك

We want to see him.
nibgha nishu:f-a نبغى نشوفه

He wants to see her.
yibgha yishu:f-ha يبغى يشوفها

They want to see us.
yibghu:n yishu:fu:n-na يبغون يشوفونّا

I want to see you. (mp)
abgha ashu:f-kum ابغى اشوفكم

He wants to see you. (fp)
yibgha yishu:f- kin يبغى يشوفكن

We want to see them. (m)
nibgha nishu:f-a نبغى نشوفهم

I want to see them. (f)
abgha ashu:f-hin ابغى اشوفهن

Points to note

a 'It' will be expressed by *a*, 'him', if referring to a masculine noun. For example:
I want to see it (referring to a house).

abgha ashu:f-a ابغى اشوفه

b 'It' will be expressed by *ha*, 'her', if referring to a feminine noun. For example:
I want to see it (referring to a car).

abgha ashu:f-ha ابغى أشوفها

Go back and look at all the verbs you have learned so far and try substituting other verbs for 'see'. You will discover that only a few verbs can be substituted and still make sensible sentences. The personal suffixes you will find most useful at the moment are 'him' and 'her' standing for 'it'. Try making up sentences using 'eat', 'drink', 'shut', 'finish', 'open' and 'close'.

5 Some new verbs

As before, we introduce these new verbs in the 'he' form to show you the helper vowel.

Vocabulary D Ⓣ

take *ya:khudh*	ياخذ	buy *yishtari*	يشتري
let, allow *yikhalli*	يخلّي	understand *yifham*	يفهم
give *ya^{c}ṯi*	يعطي	live *yiskun*	يسكن
write *yiktub*	يكتب	learn *yit^{c}allam*	يتعلّم
help *yisa:^{c}id*	يساعد	get, obtain *yiẖas̱s̱il*	يحصّل
work *yishtaghil*	يشتغل	study *yidrus*	يدرس
sit *yajlis*	يجلس		

In the early stages of learning to use these verbs you may find it convenient to keep a cumulative list of all the verbs you have learned so far written out in all the persons. It will provide you with a very handy form of reference. Practise using your widening range of verbs as much as you can and gain confidence in using and understanding the different persons. Think up things to say using these verbs and use them at every opportunity, say the same thing in as many different situations as possible. Volunteer information in Arabic before you are asked a question.

Supplementary section 14
Medical vocabulary

doctor	*ṭabi:b*	طَبيب
nurse	*mumarriḍ*	مُمَرِّض
hospital	*mustashfa*	مُسْتَشْفى
chemist, pharmacy, drug store	*ṣaydaliyya*	صَيْدَلِيَّة
ill, sick	*mari:ḍ*	مَريض
illness	*maraḍ*	مَرَض
pain	*waja*^{c}	وَجَع
feverish	*musakhkhan*	مُسَخَّن
medicine	*dawa*	دَواء
pill	*ḥabb (ḥubu:b)*	حَبّ (حُبوب)
clinic	^{c}*ayya:da*	عيّادَة
aspirin	*asbiru*	أَسْبِرو
temperature	*ḥara:ra*	حَرارَة
headache	*suda:*^{c}	صُداع

Pharmacy sign in Arabic

New vocabulary in Unit 14

to be able	*yigdir*	يِقْدِر
to know	*ya^crif*	يَعْرِف
to drive	*yisu:g*	يَسوق
to swim	*yisbah̲*	يِسْبَح
to forget	*yinsa*	يِنْسى
to worry, fear	*yakha:f*	يَخَاف
to return	*yirja^c*	يِرْجَع
next	*ga:dim*	قادِم
	wa:ji	واجي
to take	*ya:khudh*	ياخُذ
to let, allow	*yikhalli*	يِخَلّي
to give	*ya^ct̲i*	يَعْطي
to write	*yiktub*	يِكْتُب
to help	*yisa:^cid*	يِساعِد
to work	*yishtaghil*	يِشْتَغِل
to sit	*yajlis*	يَجْلِس
to buy	*yishtari*	يِشْتَري
to understand	*yifham*	يِفْهَم
to live	*yiskun*	يِسْكُن
to learn	*yit^callam*	يِتْعَلَّم
to get, obtain	*yih̲as̲s̲il*	يِحَصِّل

Unit 15

1 More about the future

Although there is no direct equivalent to 'am', 'is' or 'are' in Arabic, there is a verb to express 'I will be', 'you will be' etc. This verb is formed like any other verb in the present tense, but it is only used when talking about the future.

Vocabulary A Ⓣ

I will be *aku:n*	أَكون	she will be *taku:n*	تَكون
you (ms) will be *taku:n*	تَكون	we will be *naku:n*	نَكون
you (fs) will be *taku:ni:n*	تَكونين	you (mp) will be *taku:nu:n*	تَكونون
he will be *yaku:n*	يَكون	they (m) will be *yaku:nu:n*	يَكونون

The exclusively feminine plurals are:

you (fp) will be *taku:nin*	تكونن	they (f) will be *yaku:nin*	يكونن

Practice sentences Ⓣ

1 Will he be at home tomorrow?
yaku:n fil-bayt bukra?
يكون في البيت بكرة؟

2 We'll be busy tomorrow.
naku:n mashghu:li:n bukra
نكون مشغولين بكرة

3 I will be in London in a week's time.
aku:n fi lundun baᶜd usbu:ᶜ
اكون في لندن بعد اسبوع

4 She won't be there.
hiya ma taku:n mawju:da
هي ما تكون موجودة

5 Will you (ms) be there?
taku:n mawju:d?
تكون موجود؟

Use these sentences as models for making further sentences of your own using the different persons of the verb and the vocabulary you have learnt.

Not only does the 'he' form, *yaku:n*, function as a verb with future meaning, but it also functions as the future of *fi:* في 'there is', 'there are' and *ᶜand* عند 'have', 'have got'. When functioning in this way, *yaku:n* is invariable, it does not modify for either gender or number. The negative form is made with the addition of *ma* ما

Practice sentences Ⓣ

1 Will there be many people?
yaku:n fi: na:s kathi:r? يكون في ناس كثير؟

2 Will you have enough money?
yaku:n ᶜand-ak flu:s ka:fi? يكون عندك فلوس كافي ؟

3 I won't have time.
ma yaku:n and-i wagt ما يكون عندي وقت

4 There won't be any food.
ma yaku:n fi: ṯaᶜa:m ما يكون في طعام

5 Will there be time?
yaku:n fi: wagt? يكون في وقت؟

2 Tag questions

We often end a question or statement in English with a 'tag question', for example, 'It's hot today, isn't it?'. 'Isn't it?' is a tag question. There are many others, 'didn't he', 'did she', 'will you' etc. In Arabic, though, there is one phrase which is the equivalent to all English tag questions. This is:

mu kida مو كِدا

Your Arabic will sound more natural if you use this phrase. This is purely a spoken form, however, you will very rarely see it written.

Practice sentences Ⓣ

1 You speak Arabic, don't you?
titkallam ᶜarabi, mu kida? تتكلّم عربي مو كدا؟

2 He knows how to drive, doesn't he? يعرف يسوق مو كدا؟
ya^c^rif yasu:g, mu kida?

3 They can come with us, can't they? ممكن يجون معنا مو كدا؟
mumkin yiju:n ma^c^-na, mu kida?

4 You'd like to see her, wouldn't you? تحبّ تشوفها مو كدا؟
tahibb tashu:f-ha, mu kida?

5 She's from Abu Dhabi, isn't she? هي من ابو ظبي مو كدا؟
hiya min abu dabi, mu kida?

6 They're Americans, aren't they? هم امريكيين مو كدا؟
hum amri:kiyi:n, mu kida?

7 He'll be back in a week, won't he? يرجع بعد اسبوع مو كدا؟
yirja^c^ ba^c^d usbu:^c^, mu kida?

8 They've got two sons, haven't they? عندهم ولدين مو كدا؟
^c^and-hum walad-ayn, mu kida?

9 She's got a car with her, hasn't she? معها سيّارة مو كدا؟
ma^c^-ha sayya:ra, mu kida?

10 I'll see you there, shan't I? اشوفك هناك مو كدا؟
ashu:f-ak huna:k, mu kida?

Translation

Translate these sentences into Arabic. Take care over your spelling, and go back to check things you are unsure of. Compare your attempts with the key at the back of the book.

1 You don't speak English, do you?
2 He doesn't know how to swim, does he?
3 She can't come with us, can she?
4 You wouldn't like to go with him, would you?
5 He isn't married, is he?
6 They're not here, are they?
7 He won't come with her, will he?
8 They haven't got any children, have they?
9 He hasn't got an apartment, has he?
10 I shan't see you again, shall I?

Note that in certain areas you will hear variants for *mu kida* as follows:
In the Gulf and eastern Saudi Arabia:

mu chidi مو كِدي

and

mu:b chidi موب كِدي

In Yemen and amongst expatriate Egyptians:

mush kida مُش كِدا

and

mish kida مِش كِدا

3 Present perfect tense

There is a very straightforward way of saying 'I've been . . .', 'you've been . . .' etc in Arabic. It consists of the word:

s̱a:r صار

followed by the prefix:

l- ل

plus the relevant personal suffix to indicate who is being addressed or spoken about. Note the pronunciation of *l-* plus the personal suffixes:

(T) I've been . . .
s̱a:r l-i صار لي

you've (ms) been . . .
s̱a:r l-ak صار لك

you've (fs) been . . .
s̱a:r l-ik صار لك

he's been . . .
s̱a:r l-u صار له

she's been . . .
s̱a:r la-ha صار لها

we've been . . .
s̱a:r la-na صار لنا

you've (mp) been ... .
s̱a:r la-kum صار لكم

you've (fp) been ... .
s̱a:r la-kin صار لكن

they've (m) been ... .
s̱a:r la-hum صار لهم

they've (f) been ...
s̱a:r la-hin صار لهن

Remember that you will hear alternative pronunciations for some of the above depending upon where you are living. In the Gulf and eastern Saudi Arabia you will hear:

you've (fs) been ... .
s̲a:r l-ich صار لك

he has been . . .
s̲a:r l-a صار له

Practice sentences Ⓣ

I've been here for two months.
s̲a:r l-i shahr-ayn hina صار لي شهرين هنا

We've been in Bahrain for a year.
s̲a:r la-na sana fi l-bah̲rayn صار لنا سنة في البحرين

In some areas *s̲a:r* is omitted and the same idea is expressed simply by *l-* plus the personal suffixes.

I've been in Kuwait two years.
l-i sanat-ayn fi l-kuwayt لي سنتين في الكويت

She's been in London a fortnight.
la-ha usbu:ᶜ-ayn fi lundun لها اسبوع في لندن

To ask 'how long have you been?' begin the question with
kam? كم

How long have you been in Kuwait? (to a man)
kam s̲a:r l-ak fi l-kuwayt? كم صار لك في الكويت؟

How long have they been in London?
kam s̲a:r la-hum fi lundun? كم صار لهم في لندن؟

How long have you been in Yemen? (to a woman)
kam l-ik fi l-yaman? كم لك في اليمن؟

How long have we been here?
kam la-na hina? كم لنا هنا؟

Use whichever alternative you hear used most where you are living.

Substitution drill Ⓣ **Model question**

kam ṣa:r l-ak fi s-suᶜu:diyya? كم صار لك في السعودية؟

How long have you (ms) been in Saudi Arabia?

Example substitution

cue *huwa* —— *lundun* هو—لندن

he —— London

response *kam ṣa:r l-u fi lundun?* كم صار له في لندن؟

How long has he been in London?

Cues

1 *inti* —— *il-baḥrayn* انتِ —— البحرين

2 *hum* —— *jadda* هم —— جدّة

3 *huwa* —— *dubay* هو —— دبي

4 *hiya* —— *ṣanaᶜa* هي —— صنعاء

5 *iḥna* —— *hina* احنا —— هنا

6 *intum* —— *ir-riya:ḍ* انتم —— الرياض

7 *inta* —— *gaṭar* انت —— قطر

8 *hiya* —— *bayru:t* هي —— بيروت

9 *huwa* —— *amri:ka* هو —— امريكا

10 *inta* —— *hina:k* انت —— هناك

Substitution drill Ⓣ **Model sentence**

ṣa:r l-i shahr-ayn hina صار لي شهرين هنا

I've been here for two months.

Example substitution

cue *huwa* —— *usbu:ᶜ* هو—اسبوع

he —— a week

response *ṣa:r l-u usbu:ᶜ hina* صار له اسبوع هنا

He's been here a week.

Cues

1	*iẖna —— sanat-ayn*	احنا —— سنتين
2	*hum —— tagri:ban sittat ashhur*	هم —— تقريباً ستّة اشهر
3	*hiya —— usbu:^{c}-ayn*	هي —— اسبوعين
4	*ana —— tagri:ban shahr*	انا —— تقريبا شهر
5	*huwa —— shahr-ayn*	هو —— شهرين
6	*iẖna —— tagri:ban sana wa nus̱s̱*	احنا —— تقريبا سنة ونصّ
7	*hum —— yawm-ayn*	هم —— يومين
8	*ana —— usbu:^{c}*	انا —— اسبوع
9	*hiya —— tagri:ban sana*	هي —— تقريبا سنة
10	*huwa —— sanat-ayn wa nus̱s̱*	هو —— سنتين ونصّ

In combination with a present tense verb in the relevant person, the same phrase gives the Arabic for questions and statements on the following patterns: 'How long have you worked/been working in ———?' 'I've lived/been living in ——— for a month'. For example:

How long have you worked in Jedda?
kam s̱a:r l-ak tishtaghil fi jadda?

كم صارلك تشتغل في جدّة؟

I've been living in the Gulf for a year.
s̱a:r l-i sana askun fi l-khali:j

صار لي سنة اسكن في الخليج

Notice that in the English statement, the time phrase 'for a year' comes at the end of the sentence. In Arabic the time phrase immediately follows *s̱a:r l-i* and precedes the verb.

Questions and statements such as these are generally concerned with prolonged actions involving verbs like 'work', 'stay', 'live', 'learn', 'sit', etc.

In the following drills we are going to use these verbs which have already been introduced in Unit Fourteen.

Ⓣ work
yishtaghil
يشتغل

sit, stay
yajlis
يجلس

live
yiskun يسكن

study
yidrus يدرس

learn
yitᶜallam يتعلم

Read through the following sentences carefully. Use them for reading and writing practice, then listen to the tape and repeat after the models.

Practice sentences Ⓣ

1 How long have you (ms) been living in Jedda?
kam ṣa:r l-ak tiskun fi jadda? كم صار لك تسكن في جدّة؟

2 I've been studying Arabic for two months.
ṣa:r l-i shahr-ayn adrus ᶜarabi صار لي شهرين ادرس عربي

3 We've been working here for about six months.
ṣa:r la-na tagri:ban sittat ashhur nishtaghil hina صار لنا تقريبا ستّة اشهر نشتغل هنا

4 How long has she been learning Arabic?
kam ṣa:r la-ha titᶜallam ᶜarabi? كم صار لها تتعلّم عربي؟

5 He's been living in the Middle East for a year.
ṣa:r l-u sana yiskun fi sh-sharg il-awsaṯ صال له سنة يسكن في الشرق الاوسط

6 How long has he been staying with you?
kam ṣa:r l-u yajlis ᶜand-kum? كم صار له يجلس عندكم؟

7 How long have you (f) been studying English?
kam ṣa:r l-ik tidrusi:n ingli:zi? كم صار لك تدرسين انجليزي؟

8 They've been staying with us for a fortnight.
ṣa:r la-hum usbuᶜ-ayn yajlisu:n ᶜand-na صار لهم اسبوعين يجلسون عندنا

9 How long have they worked in Bahrain?
kam ṣa:r la-hum yishtaghilu:n fi l-baḥrayn? كم صار لهم يشتغلون في البحرين

10 She's been sitting here for ages.
ṣa:r la-ha mudda ṯawi:la tajlis hina صار لها مدّة طويلة تجلس هنا

Note the use of *ᶜand* عند 'near' in sentences 6 and 8 to mean 'with', in the sense of 'at the house of'. This is comparable with German 'bei' and French 'chez', but has no direct equivalent in English where we use the more general 'with'.

Substitution drill (T)

Model sentence

kam ṣa:r l-u yishtaghil ma^c sh-sharika? كم صار له يشتغل مع الشركة؟

How long has he been working with the company?

Example substitution

cue *hiya —— tiskun fi lundun* هي —— تسكن في لندن

she —— living in London

response *kam la-ha tiskun fi lundun?* كم لها تسكن في لندن؟

How long has she been living in London?

Cues

1 *hiya —— tit^callam ^carabi ?* هي —— تتعلّم عربي

2 *inta —— tiskun fi r-riya:ḏ ?* انتَ —— تسكن في الرياض

3 *inta —— tit^callam ingli:zi ?* انتِ —— تتعلّمين انجليزي

4 *intum — tajlisu:n ^cand-hum ?* انتم —— تجلسون عندهم

5 *hum —— yajlisu:n fi l-ḥadi:ga ?* هم —— يجلسون في الحديقة

6 *inta —— tishtaghil fi l-yaman?* انتَ —— تشتغل في اليمن

7 *hum —— yiskunu:n fi s-su^cu:diyya ?* هم —— يسكنون في السعودية

8 *inti —— tajlisi:n fi l-maktab?* انتِ —— تجلسين في المكتب

9 *huwa —— yishtaghil fi l-maktab ?* هو —— يشتغل في المكتب

10 *hiya —— tiskun fi ba:ri:s ?* هي —— تسكن في باريس

Translation

1 I've been studying Arabic for two months.
2 We've been living in the Middle East for a year.
3 He's been working in Manama for five months.
4 They've been living in Qatar for about a year and a half.
5 She's been staying with them for a fortnight.
6 I've been working with the bank for five years.
7 We've been living in Dammam for about six months.
8 He's been working with the company for a couple of years.
9 We've been sitting here for ages.
10 They've been staying in the hotel for a month.

Arabic graffiti in London

Supplementary section 15
Clothes

(T)

clothes			cotton		
	hudu:m	هُدوم		*guṯun*	قُطُن
	thiya:b	ثِياب	wool		
shirt				*s̱u:f*	صوف
	gami:s̱	قَميص	cloth, material		
trousers, pants				*guma:sh*	قُماش
	banṯalu:n	بَنْطَلون	silk		
laundry				*ẖari:r*	حَرير
	maghsala	مَغْسَلَة	tailor		
	du:bi	دوبي		*khayya:ṯ*	خَيّاط
jacket, vest			shoes		
	ja:kit	جاكِت		*gana:dir*	قَنادِر
pocket			sandals		
	jayb	جَيْب		*naʿa:l*	نَعال

Key to translation exercises

Page 73

1 *jadda fi s-suᶜu:diyya* جدة في السعودية

2 *wayn mat̲rah̲?* وين مطرح ؟

3 *min wayn ᶜazi:za?* من وين عزيزة ؟

4 *fa:t̲ima fi lundun?* فاطمة في لندن ؟

5 *inta min wayn?* انت من وين ؟

min wayn inta? من وين انت ؟

6 *muh̲ammad fi l-ga:hira?* محمد في القاهرة ؟

7 *ah̲mad fi wa:shint̲u:n* احمد في واشنطون

8 *kayf h̲a:l-ik?* كيف حالك ؟

9 *wayn ja:sim?* وين جاسم ؟

10 *aysh ism-ak?* ايش اسمك ؟

Page 76

1 *aysh ism-ha?* ايش اسمها ؟

2 *huwa min wayn?* هو من وين ؟

min wayn huwa? من وين هو ؟

3 *kayf h̲a:l-ak?* كيف حالك ؟

4 *ism-u ah̲mad wa huwa min il-kuwayt* اسمه احمد وهو في الكويت

5 *ana min dubay* انا من دبي

6 *inti min wayn?* انت من وين ؟

min wayn inti? من وين انت ؟

7 *aysh ism-u?* ايش اسمه ؟

8 *hiya min il-ᶜira:q* هي من العراق

9 *huwa min il-yaman?* هو في ايمن ؟

10 *hiya min wayn?* هي من وين ؟

min wayn hiya? من وين هي ؟

11 *huwa min gaṯar* هو من قطر

12 *ana min lundun* انا من لندن

13 *ism-ha ᶜazi:za wa hiya min abu ḏabi* اسمها عزيزة وهي من ابو ظبي

14 *wayn maṯraḫ?* وين مطرح ؟

15 *kayf ḫa:l-ik?* كيف حالك ؟

Page 114

1 *huwa muhandis* هو مهندس

2 *hiya ṯa-liba fi l-ja:miᶜa* هي طالبة في الجامعة

3 *huwa fi l-maktab* هو في المكتب

4 *fi: mutarjim fi l-maktab?* في مترجم في المكتب ؟

5 *huwa tabi:b fi l-mustashfa fi abu ḏhabi* هو طبيب في المستشفي في ابو ظبي

6 *ana sikriti:ra* انا سكرتيرة

7 *wayn il-mudi:r?* وين المدير؟

8 *fi: ṯabi:b fi l-bina:ya?* في طبيب في البناية ؟

9 *ana muwaḏḫḏhaf fi l-maṯar* انا موظف في المطار

10 *ana mudarris fi l-madrasa gari:b min hina* انا مدرس في المدرسة قريب من هنا

Page 147

1 *s̲adi:qat-i ᶜazi:za fi l-bayt* صديقتي عزيزة في البيت

2 *ᶜa:dil mu mawju:d huwa fi l-wiza:ra* عادل موجود. هو في الوزارة

3 *ah̲mad fi amri:ka maᶜ zawjat-u* احمد في امريكا مع زوجته

4 *wayn muh̲ammad? huwa fi l-maktab maᶜ hasan* وين محمد؟ هو في المكتب مع حسن

5 *inti mashghu:la?* انت مشغولة؟

6 *aysh shughl-ak?* ايش شغلك؟

7 *huwa t̲abi:b fi l-mustashfa l-jadi:d* هو طبيب في المستشفي الجديد

8 *hiya t̲a:liba fi l-ja:miᶜa* هي طالبة في الجامعة

9 *sami:ra mu fi l-bayt, hiya fi s-su:g̲ maᶜ shaykha* سميرة مو في البيت ، هي في السوق مع شيخة

10 *fi: mat̲aᶜam gari:b min hina?* في مطعم قريب من هنا؟

Page 155

1 *hiya mush taᶜba:na* هي مش تعبانة

2 *ih̲na mu jawᶜa:ni:n* احنا مو جوعانين

3 *hiya mustaᶜjila* هي مستعجلة

4 *hum mush muta'akkidi:n* هم مش متأكدين

5 *inta ᶜat̲sha:n?* انت عطشان؟

6 *inti muta'akkida?* انت متاكدة؟

7 *ih̲na mashku:ri:n* احنا مشكورين

8 *ana mu taᶜba:na* انا مو تعبانة

9 *huwa mari:d̲?* هو مريض؟

10 *hum mustaᶜjili:n* هم مستعجلين

11 *inta murta:h̲?* انت مرتاح؟

12 *ana muta^{c}assif* انا متاسف

Page 157

1 *il-mudarrisi:n mashghu:li:n* المدرسين مشغولين

2 *il-mudarrisa:t mashghu:la:t* المدرسات مشغولات

3 *il-at̲t̲ibba:' mas̲riyi:n* الاطباء مصريين

4 *il-muhandisi:n ingli:z* المهندسين انجليز

5 *il-mutarjima filast̲i:niyya* المترجمة فلسطينية

6 *it̲-t̲ulla:b bah̲rayniyi:n* الطلاب بحرينيين

7 *il-mudi:r amri:ki* المدير امريكي

8 *it̲-t̲abi:ba ^{c}iragiyya* الطبيبة عراقية

9 *it̲-t̲aliba:t yamaniyya:t* الطالبات يمنيات

10 *il-mudi:ra mush mawju:da* المديرة مش موجودة

11 *mudarrisat-na mitzawwija* مدرستنا متزوجة

12 *il-mudi:r mashghu:l* المدير مشغول

13 *it̲-t̲ulla:b ta^{c}ba:ni:n* الطلاب تعبانين

14 *is-sikriti:ra jaw^{c}a:na* السكرتيرة جوعانة

15 *il-kutta:b mashghu:li:n* الكتاب مشغولين

Page 186

1 *^{c}and-i sayyara jadi:da* عندي سيارة جديدة

2 *^{c}and-ha walad wa bint* عندها ولد وبنت

3 *^{c}and-na shigga fi jadda* عندنا شقة في جدة

4	*zawjat-i ^{c}and-ha shughl fi l-bank*	زوجتي عندها شغل في البنك
5	*ma ^{c}and-i wagt*	ما عندي وقت
6	*^{c}and-ik maw^{c}id*	عندك موعد؟
7	*^{c}and-ak sayya:ra?*	عندك سيارة ؟
8	*^{c}and-kum awla:d?*	عندكم اولاد؟
9	*^{c}and-i maw^{c}id ma^c t̲-t̲abi:b*	عندي موعد مع الطبيب
10	*^{c}anda-hum bayt fi lundun*	عندهم بيت في لندن

Page 214

1	*il-bina:ya ith-tha:litha*	البناية الثالثة
	or *tha:lith bina:ya*	ثالث بناية
2	*bayt tha:ni*	بيت ثاني
3	*is-sayya:ra il-u:la*	السيارة الاولى
	or *awwal sayya:ra*	أول سيارة
4	*ish-sha:ri^c ir-ra:bi^c*	الشارع الرابع
	or *ra:bi^c sha:ri^c*	رابع شارع
5	*wa:h̲id tha:ni*	واحد ثاني
6	*il-awwal*	الأول
7	*il-usbu:^{c} ith-tha:lith*	الاسبوع الثالث
8	*fikra tha:niya*	فكرة ثانية
9	*it̲-t̲a:lib ith-tha:ni*	الطالب الثاني
	or *tha:ni t̲a:lib*	ثاني طالب

10 *ish-shigga ith-tha:niya* الشقة الثانية

or *tha:ni shigga* ثاني شقة

11 *ith-tha:lith* الثالث

12 *il-maktab ir-ra:bi*^{c} المكتب الرابع

or *ra:bi*^{c} *maktab* رابع مكتب

13 *il-kita:b il-kha:mis* الكتاب الخامس

or *kha:mis kita:b* خامس كتاب

14 *il-bina:ya ith-tha:niya* البناية الثانية

or *tha:ni bina:ya* ثاني بناية

15 *sharika tha:niya* شركة ثانية

Page 233

1 *thala:thi:n t̲a:lib* ثلاثين طالب

2 *arba*^{c}*a kutub* أربعة كتب

3 *alf wa tis*^{c}*amiya wa khamsa wa sitti:n* ألف وتسعمية وخمسة وستين

4 *bina:yat-ayn* بنايتين

5 *miya wa khamsa muwad̲h̲d̲h̲afi:n* مية وخمسة موظفين

6 *thala:tha sayya:ra:t* ثلاثة سيارات

7 *alf wa tis*^{c}*amiya wa thama:niya wa sab*^{c}*i:n* ألف وتسعمية وثمانية وسبعين

8 ^{c}*ashra ayya:m* عشرة أيام

9 *saba*^{c}*a asa:bi:*^{c} سبعة أسابيع

10 *sitta sanawa:t* ستة سنوات

11 *thama:niya wa ᶜashri:n sana* ثمانية وعشرين سنة

12 *alf wa tisᶜamiya wa wa:ẖid wa khamsi:n* ألف وتسعمية وواحد وخمسين

13 *khamsa wa sabᶜi:n di:na:r* خمسة وسبعين دينار

14 *miya wa du:la:r-ayn* مية ودولارين

15 *thala:tha a:la:f wa tisᶜamiya wa khamsa wa* ثلاثة آلاف
وتسعمية وخمسة وسبعين

16 *thama:ntaᶜsh shahr* ثمانتعش شهر

17 *thama:niya ashhur* ثمانية أشهر

18 *ithnaᶜsh madi:na* إثنعش مدينة

19 *miyat-ayn wa khamsi:n ki:lu* ميتين وخمسين كيلو

20 *alf wa tisᶜamiya wa arbᶜa wa thama:ni:n* ألف وتسعمية وأربعة وثمانين

Page 243

1 *yibgha yiji?* يبغى يجي؟

2 *man tibgha tashu:f?* من تبغى تشوف

3 *meta tiji:n?* متي تجين؟

4 *abgha ashu:f it-tabi:b* ابغى اشوف الطبيب

5 *tibgha tiji:n?* تبغى تجين؟

6 *atkallam ᶜarabi shwayya* اتكلم عربي شوية

7 *wayn tibgha taru:ẖ?* وين تبغى تروح؟

8 *aysh tibgha taᶜmil?* ايش تبغى تعمل؟

9 *laysh tibgha taru:ẖ?* ليش تبغى تروح؟

10	*titkallami:n ʿarabi?*	تتكلمين عربي؟
11	*man tibgha tashu:f?*	من تبغى تشوف؟
12	*titkallam ingli:zi?*	تتكلم انجليزي؟
13	*mata tibgha taru:ḥ?*	متي تبغى تروح؟
14	*aysh yibgha yaʿmil?*	ايش يبغى يعمل؟
15	*titkallam ʿarabi shwayya*	تتكلم عربي شوية
16	*aysh taʿmil?*	ايش تعمل؟
17	*aysh taʿmili:n?*	ايش تعملين؟
18	*wayn yaru:ḥ?*	وين يروح؟
19	*laysh tiji?*	ليش تجي؟
20	*yiji maʿ-ha*	يجي معها

Page 265

1	*kam marra taru:ḥ ila jadda?*	كم مرة تروح الى جدة؟
2	*naru:ḥ ila lundun marrat-ayn fi s-sana*	نروح الى لندن مرتين في السنة
3	*yaru:ḥ ila s-su:g marrat-ayn fi l-yawm*	يروح الى السوق مرتين في اليوم
4	*kam marra taru:ḥ ila s-si:nama?*	كم مرة تروح الى السينما؟
5	*aru:ḥ ila s-si:nama marra aw marrat-ayn fi l-usbuʿ*	اروح الى السينما مرة او مرتين في الاسبوع
6	*yaru:hu:n ila l-baḥrayn marra fi sh-shahr*	يروحون الى البحرين مرة في الشهر
7	*kam marra taru:hu:n ila l-ja:miʿ?*	كم مرة تروحون الى الجامع؟
8	*naru:ḥ marrat-ayn fi l-usbu:ʿ*	نروح مرتين في الاسبوع
9	*taru:ḥ ila masgaṭ marra fi sh-shahr*	تروح الى مسقط مرة في الشهر

10 *aru:h̲ ila l-bank marra fi l-usbu:*^{c} اروح الى البنك مرة في الاسبوع

11 *yaru:h̲u:n ila l-maktab kull yawm* يروحون الى المكتب كل يوم

12 *taru:h̲ ila l-bah̲r marra aw marrat-ayn fi l-usbu:*^{c} تروح الى البحر مرة او مرتين في الاسبوع

13 *kam marra taru:h̲i:n ila s-su:g?* كم مرة تروحين الى السوق ؟

14 *yaru:h̲u:n ila amri:ka marra fi s-sana* يروحون الى امريكا مرة في السنة

15 *kam marra yaru:h̲ ila dubayy?* كم مرة يروح الى دبي ؟

Page 285

1 *ma titkallam ingli:zi, mu kida?* ما تتكلم انجليزي ، مو كدا؟

2 *ma ya*^{c}*rif yisbah̲, mu kida?* ما يعرف يسبح ، مو كدا؟

3 *mu mumkin tiji ma*^{c}*-na mu kida?* مو ممكن تجي ، معنا مو كدا؟

4 *ma tibgha taru:h̲ ma'-u, mu kida?* ما تحب تروح معه ، مو كدا؟

5 *huwa mu mutzawwij, mu kida?* هو ما متزوج ، مو كدا؟

6 *hum mu mawju:di:n, mu kida?* هم مو موجودين ، مو كدا؟

7 *ma yiji ma'-ha, mu kida?* ما يجي معها ، مو كدا؟

8 *ma* ^{c}*and-hum awla:d, mu kida?* ما عندهم اولاد ، مو كدا؟

9 *ma* ^{c}*and-u shigga, mu kida?* ما عنده شقة ، مو كدا؟

10 *ma ashu:f-ak marra tha:niya, mu kida?* ما اشوفك مرة ثانية ، مو كدا؟

Page 291

1	*ṣa:r l-i shahr-ayn adrus ʿarabi*	صار لي شهرين ادرس عربي
2	*ṣa:r la-na sana niskun fi sh-sharg il-awsaṭ*	صار لنا سنة نسكن في الشرق الاوسط
3	*ṣa:r l-u khamsat ashhur yishtaghil fi mana:ma*	صار له خمسة اشهر يشتغل في منامة
4	*ṣa:r la-hum tagri:ban sana wa nuṣṣ yiskunu:n fi gatar*	صار لهم تقريبا سنة ونص يسكنون في قطر
5	*ṣa:r la-ha usbu:ʿayn tajlis ʿand-hum*	صار لها اسبوعين تجلس عندهم
6	*ṣa:r l-i khamsa sini:n ashtaghil maʿ l-bank*	صار لي خمسة سنين اشتغل مع البنك
7	*ṣa:r la-na tagri:ban sittat ashhur niskun fi damma:m*	صار لنا تقريبا ستة اشهر نسكن في دمام
8	*ṣa:r l-u sanat-ayn yishtaghil maʿ sh-sharika*	صار له سنتين يشتغل مع الشركة
9	*ṣa:r la-na mudda ṭawi:la najlis hina*	صار لنا مدة طويلة نجلس هنا
10	*ṣa:r la-hum shahr yajlisu:n fi l-uti:l*	صا لهم شهر يجلسون في الاتيل

English-Arabic word list

The following word list contains all main and supplementary vocabulary in the book listed alphabetically, with a selection of additional useful items not introduced within the text.

Where there are alternatives for a given item, these are not generally included in the word list. Instead, the item is asterisked (*) and a reference given to the page where you can find additional information about it.

All useful broken plurals are indicated in brackets, as are the useful strong feminine plurals of non-person words. The plurals of person words (eg professions) are almost without exception on the strong masculine and strong feminine patterns and are not indicated. Broken plurals are given for those few person words which take them.

A

to be able
yigdir يقدر

Abu Dhabi
abu dhabi أبو ظبي

accountant
muha:sib محاسب

address
ʿanwa:n (ʿana:wi:n) عنوان (عناوين)

administration
ida:ra إدارة

Africa
ifri:qiya إفريقيا

after
baʿd بعد

afternoon *
baʿd dh-dhuhr بعد الظهر

afterwards
baʿdayn بعدين

again
marra tha:-niya مرة ثانية

agency
wika:la وكالة

air
hawa هواء

airport
mata:r مطار

Ajman
ʿajma:n عجمان

Algeria
il-jaza:'ir الجزائر

Algiers
il-jaza:'ir الجزائر

all
kull كل

also
aydan أيضا

always
da:'iman دائما

ambassador
safi:r (sufara:') سفير (سفراء)

America
amri:ka أمريكا

American
amri:ki أمريكي

Amman
^{c}amma:n عمان

among
bayn بين

and
wa, u: و

angry
za^{c}la:n زعلان

animal
hayawa:n حيوان

answer
jawa:b (ajwiba) جواب (اجوبة)

apartment
shigga (shigag) شقة (شقق)

apples
tuffa:h تفاح

appointment
maw^{c}id (mawa:^{c}id) موعد (مواعد)

apricots
mishmish مشمش

April *
abri:l أبريل

arm
dhira:^{c} ذراع

army
jaysh (juyu:sh) جيش (جيوش)

art
fann فن

ash tray
minfada منفضة

Asia
a:siya آسيا

to ask
yis'al يسأل

assistant
musa:^{c}id مساعد

at least
^{c}ala l-agall على الأقل

attaché
mulhag ملحق

August *
aghustus أغسطس

aunt (maternal)
kha:la خالة

aunt (paternal)
^{c}amma عمة

authority
maslaha مصلحة

autumn
il-khari:f الخريف

available
mawju:d موجود

B

bachelor
^{c}a:zib عازب

back
dhuhr ظهر

bag
shanta (shanat) شنطة (شنط)

Bahrain
il-bahrayn البحرين

baker
khabba:z خباز

ball
kura كرة

bananas
mawz موز

bank
bank (bunu:k) بنك (بنوك)

bar
ba:r بار

barber
halla:g حلاق

bathroom
hamma:m حمام

battery
battariyya بطرية

beans *
fa:su:liya فاصوليا

beard
lihya لحية

beautiful
jami:l جميل

because
li'an لأن

bed
takht تخت

bedroom
ghurfat in-nawm غرفة النوم

beef
lahm bagari لحم بقري

beer
bi:ra بيرة

behind *
wara وراء

Beirut
bayru:t بيروت

bell
jaras جرس

below
taht تحت

belt
hiza:m حزام

beside
bi-ja:nib بجانب

between
bayn بين

bird
ʿasfu:r (ʿasa:fi:r) طير(طيور)

bit
shwayya شوية

black
aswad أسود

blind
aʿma أعمى

blue
azrag أزرق

boat
markab (mara:kib) مركب (مراكب)

body
jism جسم

bone
ʿadhm عظم

box
sandu:g (sana:di:g) صندوق (صناديق)

boy
walad (awla:d) ولد (أولاد)

brain
mukh مخ

bread
khubz خبز

to break
yiksir يكسر

breakfast
futu:r فطور

bridge
jisr جسر

Britain
brita:niya برطانيا

British
brita:ni برطاني

broken
maksu:r مكسور

broom
maknasa مكنسة

brother
akh (ikhwa:n) أخ (إخوان)

brown *
bunni بني

building
bina:ya (-a:t) بناية (ـات)

biscuits
bisku:t بسكوت

bus
ba:ṣ باص

businessman
ta:jir (tujja:r) تاجر (تجار)

busy
mashghu:l مشغول

but
la:kin لكن

butter
zubda زبدة

to buy
yishtari يشتري

C

cabbage
malfu:f ملفوف

Cairo
il-qa:hira القاهرة

camera
ka:mira كامرا

can (able to)
mumkin ممكن

can, tin
giṣaᶜa قصعة

capital
ᶜa:ṣima عاصمة

car
sayya:ra سيارة

carpenter
najja:r نجار

carpet
sija:da سجادة

carrots
jazar جزر

to carry
yiḥmil يحمل

Casablanca
id-da:r il-bayḏa الدار البيضاء

cauliflower
garnabi:ṭ قرنبيط

ceiling
saṭḥ سطح

centre
markaz مركز

certain
muta'akkid متأكد

certainly
ṭabaᶜan طبعا

chair
kursi (kara:si) كرسي (كراسي)

chairman
ra'i:s il-ida:ra رئيس الإدارة

cheap
rakhi:ṣ رخيص

cheek
khad خد

cheese *
jubna جبنة

chest
ṣadr صدر

chicken
daja:j دجاج

child
walad (awla:d) ولد (أولاد)

chin
dhign ذقن

China
is-si:n الصين

Chinese
si:ni صيني

chocolate
shuku:la:ta شكولاطة

Christian
masi:hi مسيحي

Christmas
ᶜi:d il-mi:la:d عيد الميلاد

church
kani:sa (kana:'is) كنيسة (كنائس)

cigarette
sija:ra (saja:yir) سجارة (سجاير)

cinema
si:nama سينما

circular
mustadi:r مستدير

city
madi:na (mudun) مدينة (مدن)

class (school)
saff (sufu:f) صف (صفوف)

clean
nadhi:f (nidha:f) نظيف (نظاف)

to clean
yinadhdhif ينظف

clerk
ka:tib (kutta:b) كاتب (كتاب)

clinic
ᶜayya:da عيادة

to close
yibannid يبند

closed *
mubannad مبند

cloth
guma:sh قماش

clothes *
hudu:m هدوم

clouds
siha:b سحاب

club
na:di نادي

coal
fahm فحم

coffee
gahwa قهوة

coffee beans
bunn بن

commerce
tija:ra تجارة

commercial
tija:ri تجاري

cold
ba:rid بارد

colour
lawn (alwa:n) لون (ألوان)

to come
yiji يجي

company
sharika (-a:t) شركة (ـات)

consul
gunsul قنصل

consulate
gunsuliyya قنصلية

contract
ᶜagd (ᶜugu:d) عقد (عقود)

cook
tabba:kh طباخ

correct
s̱aẖi:ẖ صحيح

cotton
guṯun قطن

country
balad (bulda:n) بلد (بلدان)

courgettes
ku:sa كوسة

crime
jari:ma (jara:'im) جريمة

cucumber
khiya:r خيار

cup
finja:n (fana:ji:n) فنجان (فناجين)

curtain
sita:ra ستارة

customer
zabu:n (zubana:') زبون (زبناء)

customs
jama:rik جمارك

D

Damascus
ish-sha:m الشام

dance
ragṣ̱ رقص

to dance
yargus̱ يرقص

date
ta:ri:kh تاريخ

daughter
bint (bana:t) بنت (بنات)

dawn
fajr فجر

day
yawm (ayya:m) يوم (أيام)

death
mawt موت

December *
di:sambir ديسمبر

deep
^{c}ami:g عميق

delicious
ladhi:dh لذيذ

dentist
ṯabi:b il-asna:n طبيب الاسنان

to depart
yigu:m يقوم

department
gism قسم

desert
s̱aẖra صحراء

devil
shayṯa:n شيطان

dialect
laẖja لهجة

to die
yamu:t يموت

difference
farg فرق

difficult
s̱a^{c}b صعب

Dinar
di:na:r دينار

dinner
^{c}asha عشاء

diplomat
siya:si سياسي

director
mudi:r مدير

Dirham
dirham درهم

dirty
wasikh وسخ

distance
masa:fa مسافة

to do *
yisawwi يسوي

doctor *
tabi:b (atibba:') طبيب (أطباء)

dog
kalb (kila:b) كلب (كلاب)

Doha
du:ha دوحة

door
ba:b (abwa:b) باب (أبواب)

doubt
shakk شك

downstairs
taht تحت

dream
hilm (ahla:m) حلم (أحلام)

to drink
yishrab يشرب

E

ear
idhn إذن

east
sharg شرق

east(ern)
shargi شرقي

easy *
basi:t بسيط

to eat
ya:kul يا كل

education
ta^{c}li:m تعليم

egg plant
ba:dhinja:n باذنجان

eggs
bayd بيض

Egypt
masr مصر

Egyptian
masri مصري

eight
thama:niya ثمانية

eighteen
thama:nta^{c}sh ثمانتعش

eighth
tha:min ثامن

eighty
thama:ni:n ثمانين

eleven
hida^{c}sh حدعش

embassy
sifa:ra سفارة

employee
muwadhdhaf موظف

empty
fa:di فاضي

engineer
muhandis مهندس

England
ingiltarra إنجلتر

English
ingli:zi إنجليزي

to enter
yidkhul يدخل

especially
kha:satan خاصة

establishment
mu'assasa مؤسسة

Europe
u:rubba أوربا

European
u:rubbi أوربي

evening
masa مساء

every
kull كل

exactly
bi-ḍ-ḍabṭ بالضبط

examination
imtiḥa:n إمتحان

for example
mathalan مثلا

excellent
mumta:z ممتاز

expensive
gha:li غالي

expert
khabi:r (khubara:') خبير (خبراء)

'eye
^{c}ayn (^{c}uyu:n) عين (عيون)

F

face
wajh وجه

facilities
tashi:la:t تسهيلات

fact
ḥagi:ga (ḥaga:'ig) حقيقة (حقائق)

factory
maṣna^{c} (maṣa:ni^{c}) مصنع (مصانع)

family
^{c}a:'ila عائلة

famous
mashhu:r مشهور

far (from)
ba^{c}i:d (min) بعيد (من)

farm
mazra^{c} (maza:ri^{c}) مزرع (مزارع)

fast
ṣawm صوم

father
ab أب

feast, festival
^{c}i:d عيد

February*
fibra:yir فبراير

feverish
musakhkan مسخن

fifteen
khamsta^{c}sh خمستعش

fifth
kha:mis خامس

fifty
khamsi:n خمسين

figs
ti:n تين

film
film (afla:m) فلم (أفلام)

finger
iṣba^{c} (aṣa:bi^{c}) إصبع (أصابع)

finish
yikhalliṣ يخلص

fire
na:r نار

fish
samak سمك

five
khamsa خمسة

flat, apartment
shigga (shigag) شقة (شقق)

floor
arḍ أرض

flower
zahra زهرة

foot
gadam قدم

football
kurat il-gadam كرة القدم

to forget
yinsa ينسي

forehead
jabi:n جبين

foreign(er)
ajnabi (aja:nib) أجنبي (أجانب)

fork*
shawka (shawak) شوكة (شوك)

forty
arba^{c}i:n أربعين

four
arba ^{c}a أربعة

fourteen
arba^{c}ta^{c}sh أربعتعش

fourth
ra:bi^{c} رابع

France
faransa فرنسا

free
h̲urr حر

French
faransa:wi فرنساوي

fresh
t̲a:za طازة

Friday
yawm il-juma^{c}a يوم الجمعة

friend
s̲a:h̲ib (as̲h̲a:b) صاحب (أصحاب)
s̲adi:g (as̲diga;') صديق (أصدقاء)

from
min من

frontier
h̲udu:d حدود

full (sated)
shab^{c}a:n شبعان

full
malya:n مليان

furniture
sa:ma:n سامان

future
mustagbal مستقبل

G

garage
kara:j كراج

garden
h̲adi:ga حديقة
busta:n بستان

garlic
thu:m ثوم

gasolene
banzi:n بنزين

German
alma:ni ألماني

Germany
alma:niya ألمانيا

to get, obtain
yih̲as̲s̲il يحصل

to give
ya^{c}t̲i يعطي

glass (drinking)*
ka:s كاس

glass
zuja:j زجاج

God
alla:h اللّه

gold
dhahab ذهب

gold(en)
dhahabi ذهبي

good*
kwayyis كويس

good evening*
masa:' il-khayr مساء الخير

good evening (response)
masa:' in-nu:r مساء النور

good morning *
saba:h il-khayr صباح الخير

good morning (response)
s̱aba:ẖ in-nu:r صباح النور

goodbye *
ma^c^a s-sala:ma مع السلامة

government
ẖuku:ma حكومة

grandfather
jadd جد

grandmother
jadda جدة

grapes
^c^anab عنب

grateful
mashku:r مشكور

Greece
yu:na:n يونان

Greek
yu:na:ni يوناني

green
akhḏar أخضر

grey
rama:di رمادي

grocer
bagga:l بقال

guard
ẖa:ris حارس

guest
ḏayf (ḏuyu:f) ضيف (ضيوف)

the Gulf
il-khali:j الخليج

H

hair
sha^c^r شعر

hairdresser
ẖalla:g حلاق

half
nus̱s̱ نص

happy
farẖa:n فرحان

harbour
mi:na ميناء

he
huwa هو

he has
^c^and-u عنده

health
s̱iẖẖa صحة

to hear
*yisma^c^* يسمع

holiday
^c^uṯla عطلة

honey
^c^asal عسل

hospital
mustashfa مستشفى
(mustashfaya:t) (مستشفيات)

hot
ha:rr حار

hotel
fundug (fana:dig) فندق (فنادق)
u:til (—a:t) أوتيل (ـات)

house
bayt (buyu:t) بيت (بيوت)

how? *
kayf? كيف؟

how are you? *
kayf ha:l-ak? كيف حالك؟

(response)
il-hamdu li-lla:h الحمد لله

how many?
how much? *
kam? كم؟

hundred
miya مية

hungry
jawᶜa:n جوعان

hurry up!
yalla! يلا!

in a hurry
mustaᶜjil مستعجل

husband
zawj (azwa:j) زوج (أزواج)

I

I
ana أنا

idea
fikra ('afka:r) فكرة (أفكار)

if
idha إذا

ill
mari:d مريض

illness
marad مرض

important
muhimm مهم

impossible
mustahi:l مستحيل

in
fi في

India
il-hind الهند

Indian
hindi هندي

industry
sina:ᶜa صناعة

in front of
gudda:m قدام

inside
da:khil داخل

interpreter
mutarjim مترجم

interview
muga:bala مقابلة

to invite
yaᶜzim يعزم

Iraq
il-ᶜira:g عراق

Iraqi
ᶜira:gi عراقي

iron
hadi:d حديد

Islam
isla:m إسلام

Italian
talya:ni طلياني

Italy
ita:liya إطاليا

J

jacket
ja:kit جاكت

jam
murabba مربي

January *
yana:yir يناير

Jedda
jadda جدة

Jerusalem
il-quds القدس

job
shughl شغل

Jordan
il-urdun الأردن

Jordanian
urduni اردني

journalist
ṣaḥa:fi صحافي

journey
riḥla رحلة

judge
ga:ḍi (guda:) قاضي (قضاة)

juice
ᶜasi:r عسير

July *
yu:liyu يوليو

June *
yu:niyu يونيو

K

key
mifta:ḥ (mafa:ti:ḥ) مفتاح (مفاتيح)

Khartoum
kharṭu:m خرطوم

kidney
kila:wi كلاوي

to kill
yagtul يقتل

kilogramme, kilometre
ki:lu كيلو

kind, thoughtful
laṭi:f لطيف

king
malik (mulu:k) ملك (ملوك)

kitchen
maṭbakh مطبخ

knife
sikki:n
(saka:ki:n) سكين (سكاكين)

to know
yaᶜrif يعرف

Kuwait
il-kuwayt الكويت

Kuwaiti
kuwayti كويتي

L

lamb
laḥam ghanami لحم غنمي

lamp
lamba لمبة

land
arḍ (ara:ḍi) أرض (أراضي)

language
lugha (-a:t) لغة (ـات)

large
kabi:r (kiba:r) كبير (كبار)

last
a:khir آخر

late
muta'akhkhir متأخر

later
ba^{c}dayn بعدين

laundry
maghsal مغسل

du:bi دوبي

lawyer
muḥa:mi محامي

to learn
yita^{c}allam يتعلم

Lebanese
lubna:ni لبناني

Lebanon
lubna:n لبنان

left
yasa:r يسار

shima:l شمال

leg
rijl رجل

lemon
laymu:n ليمون

lentils
^{c}adas عدس

lesson
dars (duru:s) درس (دروس)

to let, allow
yismaḥ يسمح

letter
maktu:b (maka:ti:b) مكتوب (مكاتيب)

lettuce
khass خس

library
maktaba مكتبة

Libya
li:biya ليبيا

Libyan
li:bi ليبي

light (weight)
khafi:f خفيف

light (colour)
ḍaw ضوء

like
mithl مثل

zayy زي

to like
yaḥibb يحب

like this
kida كذا

lip
shifa شفة

to listen
yisma^{c} يسمع

literature
adab أدب

a little *
shwayya شوية

to live, dwell
yiskun يسكن

liver
kibda كبدة

local
maḥalli محلي

long
ṭawi:l طويل

look!
shu:f! شوف !

a lot
kathi:r كثير

love
ḥubb حب

to love
yahibb يحب

lunatic
majnu:n مجنون

lunch
ghada غداء

M

manager
mudi:r (mudara:') مدير (مدراء)

Manama
mana:ma منامة

March *
ma:rs مارس

market
su:g (aswa:g) سوق (أسواق)

married
mutzawwij متزوج

Masqat
masgat مسقط

May *
ma:yu مايو

meat
laham لحم

medicine
dawa دواء

meeting
ijtima:ᶜ (-a:t) إجتماع (ـات)

melon
batti:kh بطيخ

water melon *
batti:kh ahmar بطيخ أحمر

honeydew melon *
shamma:m شمام

middle
wasat وسط

The Middle East
ish-sharg il-awsat الشرق الأوسط

milk
hali:b حليب

minister
wazi:r (wuzara:') وزير (وزراء)

ministry
wiza:ra وزارة

mint
naᶜnaᶜ نعنع

minute
dagi:ga (daga:'ig) دقيقة (دقائق)

moment, just a moment!
lahdha لحظة

Monday
yawm il-ithnayn يوم الإثنين

money
flu:s فلوس

month
shahr (ashhur) شهر (أشهر)

moon
gamar قمر

more (than)
akthar (min) أكثر (من)

morning *
saba:h صباح

Morocco
il-maghrib المغرب

Moroccan
maghribi مغربي

Mosque
ja:miᶜ (-a:t) جامع (ـات)
masjid
(masa:jid) مسجد (مساجد)

mother
umm أم

mountain
jabal (jiba:l) جبل (جبال)

moustache
shawa:rib شوارب

mouth
fam فم

much
kathi:r كثير

museum
mathaf متحف

music
musi:qa موسيقى

muslim
muslim مسلم

must
la:zim لازم

mustard
khardal خردل

N

name
ism (asma:') اسم (أسماء)

narrow
dayyig ضيق

near (to)
gari:b (min) قريب (من)

neck
^{c}unug عنق

neighbour
ja:r (ji:ra:n) جار (جيران)

never
abadan أبدا

never mind
ma^{c}laysh معليش

new
jadi:d (judud) جديد (جدد)

news
akhba:r أخبار

newspaper
jari:da (jara:'id) جريدة (جرائد)

New Year
ra:s is:sana راس السنة

next *
ga:dim قادم

nice
tayyib طيب

night
layl ليل

nine
tis^{c}a تسعة

nineteen
tis^{c}ata^{c}sh تسعتعش

ninety
tis^{c}i:n تسعين

no
la لا

noon
dhuhr ظهر

North
shima:l شمال

north(ern)
shima:li شمالي

nose *
anf أنف

not *
mu مو

note
risa:la رسالة

notebook
daftar (dafa:tir) دفتر (دفاتر)

November *
nu:fimbir نوفمبر

now *
il-ḥi:n الحين

number
ragm (arga:m) رقم (أرقام)

nurse
mumarriḍ ممرض

O

October *
uktu:bir أكتوبر

of course
ṭabaᶜan طبعا

office
maktab (maka:tib) مكتب (مكاتب)

officer
ḍa:biṭ (ḍubba:ṭ) ضابط (ضباط)

official
rasmi رسمي

often
kathi:r كثير

oil (culinary)
zayt زيت

oil (petroleum)
nafṭ نفط

OK
tayyib طيب

okra
ba:miya بامية

old (people)
kabi:r (kiba:r) كبير (كبار)

old (things)
gadi:m قديم

olives
zaytu:n زيتون

Oman
ᶜuma:n عمان

Omani
ᶜuma:ni عماني

on (top of)
ᶜala على
fawg فوق

once
marra مرة

one
wa:ḥid واحد

onions
baṣal بصل

only
baṣ بص
fagaṭ فقط

open
mafku:k مفكوك
maftu:ḥ مفتوح

to open
yifukk يفك
yiftaḥ يفتح

opinion
ra:i راي

opposite
gudda:m قدام

or
aw أو
wa'illa وإلا

oranges
burtuga:l برتقال

ordinary
ᶜa:di عادي

organisation
hay'a هيئة

our
-na . . .ـنا

out of order
kharba:n خربان

outside
kha:rij خارج

owner
sa:hib (asha:b) صاحب

P

Palestine
filasti:n فلسطين

Palestinian
filasti:ni فلسطيني

party
hafla حفلة

peach
khawkh خوخ

peas
bizilla بزلة

pen
galam (agla:m) قلم (أقلام)

pencil
galam rasa:s قلم رصاص

bansil (bana:sil) بنسل

the Peninsula
jazi:rat il-ᶜarab جزيرة العرب

il jazi:ra il-ᶜarabiyya الجزيرة العربية

people
na:s ناس

pepper
filfil فلفل

per cent
bi-l-miya بالمية

petrol
banzi:n بنزين

pharmacy
saydaliyya صيدلية

pickles
tarshi طرشي

picture, photo
su:ra (suwar) صورة (صور)

pig
khanzi:r (khana:zi:r) خنزير (خنازير)

pilgrimage
hajj حج

pineapple
anana:s أنناس

place
mahall محل

plane
tayya:ra (tayra:n) طيارة (طيران)

plate
suhn (suhu:n) صحن (صحون)

to play
yilᶜab يلعب

please
min fadl-ak من فضلك

plum
bargu:g برقوق

pocket
jayb جيب

police
shurta شرطة

policeman
shurti شرطي

politician
siya:si سياسي

politics
siya:sa سياسة

poor
fagi:r (fugara:') فقير (فقراء)

pork
laham khanzi:r لحم خنزير

post office
maktab il-bari:d مكتب البريد

potatoes
baṭa:ṭa بطاطا

to pray
yiṣalli يصلي

prayer
ṣala: صلاة

to prefer
yifaḏḏil يفضل

present, available
mawju:d موجود

present, gift
hadiyya (hada:ya) هدية (هدايا)

president
ra'i:s رئيس

price
siʿr (asʿa:r) سعر (أسعار)

prime minister
ra'i:s il-wuzara:' رئيس الوزراء

prince
ami:r (umara:') أمير (أمراء)

private
khuṣu:ṣi خصوصي

programme
barna:mij برنامج

(bara:mij) (برامج)

project
mashru:ʿ مشروع

(mashari:ʿ) (مشاريع)

public
ʿumu:mi عمومي

Q

Qatar
gaṭar قطر

Qatari
gaṭari قطري

quarter
rubaʿ ربع

queen
malika ملكة

question
su'a:l (as'ila) سؤال (أسئلة)

quickly
bi-suraʿa بسرعة

quiet
ha:di هادي

R

Rabat
ir-raba:ṯ رباط

radio
ra:diyu راديو

rain
maṭar مطر

Ramadan
ramaḏa:n رمضان

to read
yigra يقرا

reading
gira:'a قراءة

the Red Sea
il-baḥr il-aḥmar البحر الأحمر

regular, ordinary
ʿa:di عادي

relax!
istari:h! استريح !

relaxed
murta:ẖ مرتاح

representative
mandu:b مندوب

responsible
mas'u:l مسؤول

rest, remainder
ba:gi باقي

restaurant
maṯ^c^am (maṯa:^c^im) مطعم (مطاعم)

to return
*yirja^c^* يرجع

rice
ruz رز

right
yami:n يمين

right, correct
maḏbu:ṯ مضبوط

ring
kha:tim (khawa:tim) خاتم (خواتم)

river
nahr (anhur) نهر (أنهر)

Riyal
riya:l ريال

road
ṯari:g (ṯurug) طريق (طرق)

roof
saṯẖ سطح

room
ghurfa (ghuraf) غرفة (غرف)

Russia
ru:siya روسيا

Russian
ru:si روسي

S

sad
ẖazi:n حزين

salt
milẖ ملح

Sana'a
ṣana^c^a:' صنعاء

sand
raml رمل

sandals
na^c^a:l نعال

Saturday
yawm is-sabt يوم السبت

Saudi Arabia
is-su^c^u:diyya السعودية

Saudi Arabian
su^c^u:di سعودي

to say
yagu:l يقول

school
madrasa مدرسة

science
^c^ilm (^c^ulu:m) علم (علوم)

sea
baẖr بحر

season
mawsim موسم

second
tha:ni ثاني

secretary
sikriti:r سكرتير

to see
yashu:f يشوف

to sell
*yabi:^c^* يبيع

to send
yirsil يرسل

September *
sibtambir سبتمبر

seven
saba^{c}a سبعة

seventeen
saba^{c}ta^{c}sh سبعتعش

seventh
sa:bi^{c} سابع

seventy
sab^{c}i:n سبعين

Sharja
sha:riga شارقة

she
hiya هي

sheet
sharshaf (shara:shif) شرشف (شراشف)

ship
safi:na (sufun) سفينة (سفن)

shirt
gami:s̠ (gums̠a:n) قميص (قمصان)

shoes
gana:dir قنادر

shop
dukka:n (daka:ki:n) دكان (دكاكين)

short
gas̠i:r (gis̠a:r) قصير (قصار)

should
la:zim لازم

shoulder
kitf كتف

showroom
ma^{c}riḏ معرض

sick, ill
mari:ḏ مريض

silver (metal)
fiḏḏa فضة

silver (colour)
fiḏḏi فضي

similar
musha:bih مشابه

sister
ukht (akhawa:t) أخت (أخوات)

to sit
yajlis يجلس

sitting room
majlis مجلس

six
sitta ستة

sixteen
sitta^{c}sh ستعش

sixth
sa:dis سادس

sixty
sitti:n ستين

skin
jild جلد

to sleep
yana:m ينام

small
s̠aghi:r (s̠igha:r) صغير (صغار)

soldier
jundi (junu:d) جندي (جنود)
^{c}askari (^{c}asa:kir) عسكري (عساكر)

some
ba^{c}ḏ بعض

something
shay' شيء
ẖa:ja حاجة

sometimes
aẖya:nan أحيانا

son
walad (awla:d) ولد (أولاد)
ibn (abna:') ابن (أبناء)

sorry
muta'assif متأسف

(I'm) sorry!
^{c}afwan! عفوا !

soup
shurba شربة

south
junu:b جنوب

south(ern)
junu:bi جنوبي

Spain
isba:nya إسبانيا

Spanish
isba:ni إسباني

to speak
yitkallam يتكلم

spoon *
mal^{c}aga ملعقة

sport
riya:ḍa رياضة

square (four sided)
murabba^{c} مربع

square (in a city)
mayda:n ميدان

to start
yibda يبدأ

state (nation)
dawla دولة

state (eg in the United States)
wila:ya ولاية

steel
fu:la:dh فولاذ

to stop
yu:gaf يوقف

straight on
si:da سيدة

strange
ghari:b غريب

street
sha:ri^{c} (shawa:ri^{c}) شارع (شوارع)

strong
gawi (agwiya:') قوي (أقوياء)

student
ṭa:lib (ṭulla:b) طالب (طلاب)

Sudan
is-su:da:n السودان

Sudanese
su:da:ni سوداني

sugar
sukkar سكر

suitcase
shanṭa (shanaṭ) شنطة (شنط)

sun
shams شمس

Sunday
yawm il-aḥad يوم الأحد

sunset
maghrib مغرب

sure
muta'akkid متأكد

sweet
ḥilu حلو

to swim
yisbaḥ يسبح

Switzerland
swisra سويسرا

T

table *
mi:z (amya:z) ميز (أمياز)

tailor
khayya:ṯ خياط

to take
ya:khudh ياخذ

tape recorder
musajjila مسجلة

tax
ḏari:ba (ḏara:'ib) ضريبة (ضرائب)

taxi
taksi تكسي

tea
sha:y شاي

to teach
yiᶜallim يعلم

teacher
muᶜallim معلم

mudarris مدرس

telephone
talifu:n تلفون

television
talifizyu:n تلفزيون

ten
ᶜashra عشرة

tenth
ᶜa:shir عاشر

thank you *
shukran شكرا

theatre
masraḥ مسرح

their (m)
-hum هم

their (f)
-hin هم

then
baᶜdayn بعدين

there
hina:k هناك

they (m)
hum هم

they (f)
hin هن

thick
thakhi:n ثخين

thin
ḏaᶜi:f ضعيف

third
tha:lith ثالث

a third
thulth ثلث

thirsty
ᶜaṯsha:n عطشان

thirteen
thalattaᶜsh ثلتعش

thirty
thala:thi:n ثلاثين

this (m)
ha:dha هذا

this (f)
ha:dhi هذه

thousand
alf ألف

three
thala:tha ثلاثة

throat
ḥalg حلق

Thursday
yawm il-khami:s يوم الخميس

ticket
tadhkira تذكرة
(tadha:kir) (تذاكر)

time *
wagt (awga:t) وقت (أوقات)

tired
ta[c]ba:n تعبان

to
ila إلى

today
il-yawm اليوم

together
sawa سوا

toilet
hamma:m حمام

tomatoes
tama:t طماط

tomorrow
bukra بكرة

tongue
lisa:n لسان

tooth
sinn (asna:n) سن (أسنان)

tourism
siya:ha سياحة

tourist
sa:'ih (suwwa:h) سائح (سواح)

towel
fu:ta (fuwat) فوطة (فوط)

transformer
muha:wila محولة

to translate
yitarjim يترجم

translation
tarjama ترجمة

translator
mutarjim مترجم

to travel
yisa:fir يسافر

tree
shajara (ashja:r) شجرة (أشجار)

triangular
muthallath مثلث

Tripoli
tara:blus طرابلس

trousers
bantalu:n بنطلون

Tuesday
yawm ith-thala:tha يوم الثلاثة

Tunis
tu:nis تونس العاصمة

Tunisia
tu:nis التونسي

Tunisian
tu:nisi تونسي

twelve
ithna[c]sh إثنعش

twenty
[c]ashri:n عشرين

twice
marrat-ayn مرتين

two
ithnayn إثنين

tyre
tayyar طير

U

ugly
gabi:h قبيح

Umm al-Qaywan
umm il-qaywa:n أم القيوان

uncle (maternal)
kha:l خال

uncle (paternal)
[c]amm عم

under
taht تحت

to understand
yifham يفهم

United Arab Emirates
il-ima:ra:t الإمارات العربية
il-ᶜarabiyya المتحدة
il-muttahida

university
ja:miᶜa جامعة

upstairs
fawg فوق

to use
yistaᶜmil يستعمل

usually
ᶜa:datan عادة

V

vacation
ᶜutla عطلة

vegetables
khadar خضر
khadarawa:t خضروات

very *
jiddan جدا

veterinarian
tabi:b baytari طبيب بيطري

view
mandhar منظر

village
garya (gura) قرية (قرى)

visa *
fi:sa فيزة

voice
sawt (aswa:t) صوت (أصوات)

W

wadi
wa:di وادي

to walk
yimshi يمشي

wall *
jida:r جدار

to want *
yibgha يبغى

war
harb حرب

warm
da:fi دافي

to wash
yighsil يغسل

we *
ihna إحنا

weak
daᶜi:f ضعيف

to wear
yilbas يلبس

weather
jaw جو

Wednesday
yawm il-arbaᶜa يوم الأربعة

week
usbu:ᶜ (asa:bi:ᶜ) أسبوع (أسابيع)

welcome *
ahlan wa sahlan أهلا وسهلا

well (noun)
bi:r بير

West
gharb غرب

west(ern)
gharbi غربي

what? *	*aysh?*	أيش ؟
when?	*mata?*	متى ؟
where? *	*wayn?*	وين ؟
white	*abyad*	أبيض
who?	*man?*	من ؟
whose? *	*hagg man?*	حق من ؟
why?	*laysh?*	ليش ؟
wide	*wa:siᶜ*	واسع
wife	*zawja*	زوجة
	mara	مرة
wind	*ri:h*	ريح
window	*shubba:k*	شباك
	ta:ga	طاقة
wine	*khamar*	خمر
winter	*ish-shita*	الشتاء
with	*maᶜ*	مع
wood	*khashab*	خشب
wool	*su:f*	صوف

word	*kalima*	كلمة
work	*shughl*	شغل
to work	*yishtaghil*	يشتغل
world	*ᶜa:lam*	عالم
to worry	*yakha:f*	يخاف
to write	*yiktub*	يكتب
writing	*kita:ba*	كتابة
wrong	*ghalta:n*	غلطان

Y

year	*sana (sini:n)*	سنة (سنين)
	(sanawa:t)	(سنوات)
yellow	*asfar*	أصفر
Yemen	*il-yaman*	اليمن
Yemeni	*yamani*	يمني
yesterday	*ams*	أمس
yoghourt	*laban*	لبن
you (ms)	*inta*	إنت
you (fs)	*inti*	إنتِ

you (mp)*
intum إنتم

you (fp)*
intin انتن

young
s̲aghi:r (s̲igha:r) صغير (صغار)

your (ms)
-ak ـك

your (fs)
-ik ـك

your (mp)
-kum ـكم

your (fp)
-kin ـكن

you're welcome *
ᶜafwan عفوا

Z

zero
s̲ifr صفر